The Impact of Organizational Ethical Climate on Organizational Commitment and Job Performance

AF846381

Keikoh Ryu

The Impact of Organizational Ethical Climate on Organizational Commitment and Job Performance

An Economic Ethics Analysis of Japanese-funded Manufacturing Enterprises in China

Science Press
Beijing

Springer

Keikoh Ryu
College of Business Administration
Ritsumeikan University
Osaka, Japan

ISBN 978-981-15-2815-6 ISBN 978-981-15-2813-2 (eBook)
https://doi.org/10.1007/978-981-15-2813-2

Jointly published with Science Press
The print edition is not for sale in China. Customers from China please order the print book from: Science Press.

© Science Press and Springer Nature Singapore Pte Ltd. 2020
This work is subject to copyright. All rights are reserved by the Publishers, whether the whole or part of the material is concerned, specifically the rights of translation, reprinting, reuse of illustrations, recitation, broadcasting, reproduction on microfilms or in any other physical way, and transmission or information storage and retrieval, electronic adaptation, computer software, or by similar or dissimilar methodology now known or hereafter developed.
The use of general descriptive names, registered names, trademarks, service marks, etc. in this publication does not imply, even in the absence of a specific statement, that such names are exempt from the relevant protective laws and regulations and therefore free for general use.
The publishers, the authors, and the editors are safe to assume that the advice and information in this book are believed to be true and accurate at the date of publication. Neither the publishers nor the authors or the editors give a warranty, express or implied, with respect to the material contained herein or for any errors or omissions that may have been made. The publishers remain neutral with regard to jurisdictional claims in published maps and institutional affiliations.

This Springer imprint is published by the registered company Springer Nature Singapore Pte Ltd.
The registered company address is: 152 Beach Road, #21-01/04 Gateway East, Singapore 189721, Singapore

Preface

This book analyzes the impact of organizational ethical climate on the organizational commitment and job performance of Japanese-funded manufacturing enterprises (JFMEs) in China based on a review of related research in economic ethics as well as a quantitative analysis of the various types of organizational ethical climates typically found in JFMEs operating in China. While previous studies have approached the subject from an ethical, psychological, philosophical, or sociological perspective, none have analyzed organizational ethical climate and its effect on organizational commitment and job performance under these circumstances. Nor has the relationship between organizational ethical climate, organizational commitment, and job performance been analyzed in the context of economic ethics. This book illustrates the feasibility of studying organizational ethics from an economic perspective, while laying out a theoretical basis for exploring the philosophy of economics from an ethical perspective. The abstract of this book is given below.

- **Related Research**
  Recent years have seen an increasing emphasis on organizational ethics in Chinese enterprises. As a specific type of organizational climate, organizational ethics can predict and motivate employee behavior in several respects, including ethics and morality, sense of identity and belonging, as well as job performance. A positive organizational ethical climate has the potential to promote cohesiveness among individual members, foster team productivity, reduce transaction costs, and increase operational efficiency while enhancing corporate image and branding. As a result, research into organizational ethical climate has drawn widespread interest, particularly in the fields of economic psychology and management, with both theoretical and empirical progress being made on several fronts.

  As summarized in Chap. 2, most studies on organizational ethical climate, organizational commitment, and job performance have approached the subject from a sociological or organizational behavioral perspective. These studies have found that organizational ethical climate can enhance job performance either directly, by improving employees' work behavior, or indirectly, by strengthening organizational commitment, and have primarily focused on: (1) the definition and structural measurement of organizational ethical climate and an empirical analysis of its various types; (2) the definition, structure, dimensions, and measurement of organizational commitment; (3) the definition, structure, and measurement of organizational or job performance; and (4) the theoretical basis and practical feasibility of organizational ethical climate. That said, relatively little research has been conducted on the role of economic ethics or, more broadly, the ways in which organizations engage in the types of non-economic behavior which have begun to play such an important role in measuring the performance of foreign enterprises in China.

- **Purpose of the Study**
  As the largest socialist country in the world, China has experienced profound social and economic reform that has affected economic trends and corporate behavior. But what are the ethical premises and behavioral rules of this reform? How do economic ethical values inform the behavior of economic entities in China? And what role do Japanese companies with Chinese operations and investments play from the perspective of economic ethics? These questions necessarily implicate the goals and incentives of individuals engaging in economic behavior as well as the cultivation of an organization's ethical climate. The aim of this study is, therefore, to analyze the ways in which the organizational ethical climate of JFMEs in China can inform effective human resource management (HRM) measures so as to maximize team productivity, with a particular focus on the impact of non-market strategies and behavior on the economic performance of these enterprises.
- **Research Design and Methodology**
  The impact of organizational ethical climate on organizational commitment and job performance is typically studied within the theoretical framework developed by Victor & Cullen (1998). Under this framework, organizational ethical climate involves making judgments about ethical conduct and responding to employees' ethical issues and consists of nine dimensions: self-interest (instrumental), corporate profit (instrumental), efficiency, friendship (caring), team interest (caring), social responsibility, personal morality (independence), rules and procedures (rules), and laws and professional codes (law and code). Each of these dimensions, in turn, includes several indexes, with Stata applied to distinguish latent variables. Victor has also drawn upon this framework to develop a questionnaire evaluating the effectiveness of organizational ethical climate based on a five-point scale which has now been used in more than 170 studies across various industries and cultures.

This book begins with a review of the literature to shed light on the definition, structure, and measurement of organizational ethical climate, organizational commitment, and job performance, along with the antecedent and outcome variables which affect them. This is followed by a quantitative analysis of data compiled from Victor's questionnaires. Principal factor analysis is combined with structural equation modeling (SEM) to determine relationships between observed variables reflecting the ways in which the impact of various organizational ethical climates on organizational commitment and job performance can differ in degree and scale. The results are then used to lay a foundation for the development of HRM measures conducive to the cultivation of more effective organizational ethical climates for JFMEs in China.

- **Implications**

  By analyzing organizational ethical climate in the context of supply and demand theory, dual labor market theory, and labor policy with an emphasis on the growing importance of ethics, this research has the potential to make a significant contribution to the field of economic ethics, which is concerned not only with the growth of wealth but also the distribution of this wealth and the effect of inequality on social harmony. As discussed above, little research has been done on organizational climate and economic ethics in countries like China where non-market factors tend to play an outsized role.

  The fact that organizational ethical climate continues to be viewed almost exclusively in terms of ethics, as opposed to economics, is also a major weakness of prior research. Insofar as economic ethics is concerned with the behavior of the "rational man" in the market, it has the potential to offer more convincing theoretical explanations for employee behavior and how such behavior is informed by an organization's ethical climate, and will undoubtedly play an increasingly important role in the study of organizational ethical climate.

  It is important to note, however, that the concepts of organizational ethical climate, organizational commitment, and job performance referenced in this book are themselves based on definitions derived from prior research. It may, therefore, be necessary at some point to redefine these ideas by developing new questionnaires, which could lead to very different results. Further studies based on rooting theory should be conducted to address this potential shortcoming.

  As far as China is concerned, the development of its economy has continued to attract foreign-funded enterprises eager to expand their business overseas. But as the country seeks a balance between economic and social development, the criteria for success is no longer limited to economic indexes and traditional market theory is no longer adequate to address the political and cultural ramifications of China's economic issues. Therefore, if JFMEs are to increase their market share in China, they must not only compete with other Chinese enterprises and multinational corporations, but also focus on corporate social responsibility and regional branding while making real and lasting contributions to society.

This book is published due to the support of the Ritsumeikan Inamori Philosophy Research Center and completed during my yearlong sabbatical research stay at Harvard University and Stanford University. This book is also a part of the result of Inamori's management philosophy research project sponsored by the Ritsumeikan Inamori Philosophy Research Center.

My profound gratitude goes out to Professor Amartya Sen at Harvard University, a Nobel Prize winner of economics research, for exposing me to the latest theoretical and methodological trends to my research and to Professor Takeo Hoshi at Stanford University, a well-known pioneer of economics research in the world, for offering much-needed guidance on the theoretical analysis of multinational corporations. Over the course of my research, I received much-needed advice from these two professors.

I cannot adequately express my gratitude to the many people in China, Japan, and the United States, without whose help this book would never have come to fruition. As for the executives from the Tokyo offices of the Japanese corporations I visited and their Japanese employees in China, all of whom offered thoughtful and exhaustive answers to my questions, I offer the results of my research as a testament to their enthusiastic cooperation and hard work.

Lastly, I would like to convey my deepest thanks to friends and family members who have given me their unwavering support over the years but whom I cannot thank individually due to space limitations.

Osaka, Japan
Dies Faustus, 2020

Keikoh Ryu

Contents

List of Figures

List of Tables

Chapter 1
Introduction

1.1 Research Background

China, the largest socialist country in the world, has experienced profound reforms that have led to a revolution of its economy as well as enormous changes in the behavior of its companies. But what are the stages of Chinese economic reform? What are its features? What are the ethical premises and behavioral rules? And what role does economic ethics play in the behavior of corporations and other economic entities? At the most fundamental level, all of these questions deal with the incentives behind economic decisions and finding answers to them are a prerequisite for the cultivation of an ethical climate. Finally, how can insights into these questions help Japanese companies establish effective operations in China, as Japan is an important geopolitical neighbor and major investor in China?

1.1.1 The Practice of China's Economic System Reform and Changes in Ethical Ideology

1. China's economic system reform practice

(1) The trial stage of economic system reform from 1978 to 1984

In 1978, the Third Plenary Session of the 11th Central Committee of the CPC[1] put forward the ideological path of "emancipating the mind and seeking truth from facts," under which the restoration and development of the economy became the primary focus. In April 1979, the Central Conference of the CPC established the

[1] In this paper CPC is the abbreviation of Communist Party of China. The Communist Party of China was established in July 1921. Since October 1949, it has been the only ruling party of the People's Republic of China, which represents the working class and leads the union of workers and peasants and the united front, and implements the people's democratic dictatorship in Mainland China.

© Science Press and Springer Nature Singapore Pte Ltd. 2020

K. Ryu, *The Impact of Organizational Ethical Climate on Organizational Commitment and Job Performance*, https://doi.org/10.1007/978-981-15-2813-2_1

guiding principle[2] that the national economy should be primarily regulated through government planning, while the supplemental effect of market regulation should also to be taken seriously. In September 1982 the 12th Congress of the CPC confirmed the centrality of this principle[3] in China's economic reform, after which the market began to play an increasingly important role with significant benefits for the economy. Basing China's economic reform on a combination of planning and market regulation led to an incremental decentralization of power under which public ownership was emphasized at the same time that individual, private and foreign-funded enterprises were allowed to develop. In addition, the scope of the state's mandatory planning was narrowed, while local governments were granted more autonomy. Yet the underlying insistence on a traditional planned economy remained.

(2) The development of systematic reform (1984–1992)

As China implemented its initial economic reforms, the central government was also in the process of refining its conception of a socialist economy, which began with the "socialist planned commodity economy" theory[4] put forward by the Third Plenary Session of the 12th CPC Central Committee on October 1984. The goal of this reform was to develop independent companies responsible for their own profits and losses, as well as a competitive market system. At the same time, the state's management of the economy became more indirect, with the scope and extent of the planning narrowed considerably.

Enterprises, prices, and macro-management were also reformed. Enterprise reform was focused on invigorating enterprises and developing a system, in which companies operated independently, assumed responsibility of their own profits and losses, and participated in market competition. The main goal of price reform was to gradually eliminate price controls, especially with respect consumer goods. Control of production materials was also gradually relieved, with the pricing of production materials based on a double-track system.[5] At the same time, macro-management

---

[2]Put forward the policy of "adjusting, reforming, rectifying and improving" the national economy. This means an important shift in the guiding ideology of China's economic construction.

[3]At the 12th Congress of the CPC, Deng Xiaoping put forward a new proposition of "building socialism and with Chinese characteristics." He also pointed out: "Our modernization must proceed from the reality of China". We must pay attention to learning and learning from foreign experience. However, it is never successful to copy other countries' experiences and other countries' models. We have had combine the universal truth of Marxism with the concrete reality of our country, take our own path, and build socialism and economic with Chinese characteristics.

[4]At the Third Plenary Session of the 12th Central Committee of CPC analyzed the current economic and political situation in China and summarized the positive and negative experiences of China's socialist construction, especially the experience of urban and rural economic system reform in recent years. It is necessary to combine the basic principles of Marxism with the realities of China, build the general requirements for socialism with Chinese characteristics, further implement the policy of invigorating the economy and open to the outside world, and accelerate the reform of the entire economic system with a focus on cities. The pace is to better create a new situation in socialist modernization.

[5]As the name implies, the two systems are in parallel. The double-track price system refers to the price management system in which the unified pricing and market-adjusted prices of the same

reforms were implemented to stabilize the macro-economy while leading state-owned enterprises—particularly large and mid-sized ones—to the market. The government relaxed the conditions for investment approval and sought to cancel the use of mandatory plans for loans. Central and local governments also began to permit plans for the companies' investments that accumulate their own capital. These measures effectively shifted the focus of economic reform from the country to the cities, broadening the role of market forces in the national economy.

In October 1987, based on the planned commodity economy, the 13th Congress of the CPC then developed a new theory of the so-called "socialist market economic system,[6]" which as its name suggests, was an attempt to integrate planned and market economy approaches at the most fundamental level. In the spring of 1992, a series of lectures[7] by Deng Xiaoping during his visit to southern China further clarified the significance of the reform and opening-up effort and set the basic principles for establishing the socialist market economy, which in turn paved the way for the third phase of China's economic reform.

(3) The establishment of a socialist market economy (1992–2002)

The promotion of Deng Xiaoping's lectures in the south led to further theoretical discussion concerning the relationship between planning and market forces. Those culminated in the official consensus that the market should, in fact, play a leading role in the national economy. In October 1992, the 14th Congress of the CPC, clarified that the objective of Chinese economic reform was to establish a socialist market economic system, under which the market should play a fundamental role in the allocation of resources in socialist countries. Under this system, economic activities were to follow to the law of value and adapt to changes in the relationship between supply and demand. In addition, the market was to allocate resources efficiently through price leverage and competition, thereby pressuring and incentivizing enterprises to operate according to the principle of survival of the fittest.[8] Generally speaking, while relying on the sensitivity of the market to promote the coordination of production and demand, the theory recognized that the market has its own weaknesses, which would require robust regulation.

With the establishment of socialist market economic system, China's economic development accelerated, and performance of its enterprises improved significantly.

---

commodity countries coexist. It is formed by the simultaneous implementation of two operational mechanisms: plan adjustment and market regulation.

[6]It also called "socialism with Chinese characteristics," is an economic from practiced in the People's Republic of China.

[7]From January 18 to February 21, 1992, Deng Xiaoping inspected Wuchang, Shenzhen, Zhuhai, Shanghai and other cities to give a series of lectures. It puts forward the requirement of "taking advantage of the favorable opportunity, accelerating the pace of reform and opening up, and striving for a better new national economy to a new level", laying the ideological foundation for China to embark on the road of socialist market economy with Chinese characteristics.

[8]The principle was describing the mechanism of natural selection, which originated from Darwinian evolutionary theory. Now we also refer to this point in various fields.

However as the reform progressed to the extent that many of the traditional institutions began to be replaced, increasing number of people became concerned that the pro-market reforms and the establishment of a market economy was irreconcilable with their Marxist notion of property ownership. They worried it would shake the foundation of the state-run economic system, thereby altering the nature of socialism itself.

(4) Deepening and improving the socialist market economic system (since 2002)

In December 2001 China had joined the World Trade Organization, marking its entry into the tide of economic globalization. This event greatly influenced Chinese politics, economics, and society. After joining the WTO, the Chinese government accelerated the pace of economic reform and limited the role of market regulation to curb local protectionism and promote an open domestic market with fair competition. The government strengthened supervision mechanisms, improved administrative efficiency, clarified its role as a public manager and owner of state-owned assets, and improved its management of these assets. The government also further improved the tax, finance and foreign exchange management systems,[9] intervening into market mainly through economic and legal means rather than administrative means.

The government further accelerated the establishment of a modern enterprise system by adapting WTO rules, thereby enabling enterprises to become legal entities, which operate independently and take responsibility for their own profits and losses. Also, corporate governance structures were improved with the establishment of multiple investment entities whose stakes are shared by various owners. The state-owned enterprise system[10] reform was the key initiative, speeding up the pace of the strategic adjustment of the state-owned economy.

2. Changes in Ethical Ideology in the Process of China's Economic System Reform

(1) Changes in the ideology of Chinese State-owned enterprises and private enterprises

In the process of China's economic reform, the ideology of Chinese State-owned enterprises and private enterprises have undergone significant changes. As a direct embodiment of China's economic policy, Chinese State-owned enterprises followed the shift ideology of Chinese enterprises, further accompanied by a major change in the cognitive reshaping and mission orientation of State-owned enterprises. From 1978 to 1992, State-owned enterprises adopted the policy of "decentralization and profit-sharing", allowing them to have more responsibility and management rights, implementing a contract responsibility system, and expanding the rights and benefits of State-owned enterprises, while at the same time focusing on the planned economy. From 1992 to 2003 the further expansion of enterprises' autonomy established the

[9]The national government authorizes the country's monetary and financial authorities to control foreign exchange receipts, payments, loans, transfers, and international settlements, foreign exchange rates.

[10]It also called "government-owned corporation" which is a legal organization that conducting commercial activities under the leadership and policy of the state.

modern enterprise system, also regarded as a socialist market economic system. At the same time, the Chinese government established policies according to the modern enterprise system, namely "clear property rights, clear powers and responsibilities, separate government and enterprise, and science management".

(2) The direction of enterprise reform

Since 2004, the reform of Chinese state-owned enterprises continues to deepen, lead by the reform of share trading of the listed companies, and state-owned enterprises have taken on additional social responsibilities.

Since the reform and opening-up, the non-public ownership economy has flourished, and the rise of a new social class represented by private entrepreneurs has arisen. The rise of Chinese private enterprises is a major practical issue in the transformation of Chinese society and a core ethical issue in China's ideological transformation. In 1978, after the wave of thoughts on "a big discussion on truth" in China, private enterprises were no longer the object of revolutionary opposition, but a part of socialist construction. Private enterprises were determined by social status rather than class. For a period of time, private enterprises released the burden of the previous ideas. A large number of private enterprises have been operating, and famous private enterprises such as Wantong and Changhong emerged.

After 1987, the Chinese central government affirmed the birth of "private enterprises". Private enterprises became a supplement to the predominant public ownership entities, thus reconfirmed the mainstream position of enterprises in China. Private enterprises have gradually grown and became an important part of society. After entering the 21st century, private enterprises continue to develop rapidly, and the Chinese Communist Party has begun to expand the political participation to private enterprises, and their status continues to improve. Private enterprises not only create benefits, but also undertake a larger extent of social responsibilities. At the same time, during the current stage, the Communist Party of China has continuously strengthened the management and guidance of the ideology of the private enterprise, complementary to the continuous improvement of the social status of the private enterprise.

(3) Changes in Chinese Individual Ideology

At the beginning of the 20th century, China had just ended a period of thousands of feudal monarchies and entered a stage of semi-colonial, semi-feudal society. The traditional concept of "thousands of years" is deeply rooted in people's thinking, and the impact of post-proletarian thinking on Chinese values and thoughts is enormous, especially for society's lower tiers. Before the reform and opening up of China in the mid-20th century, the "class struggle" occupied the major part of Chinese ideology.

After the reform and opening up, people gradually began to shift from the ideology of "class struggle" as the leading concept towards gradually emerging market factors and market systems, and to form the market value orientation. In particular, after state-owned enterprises carried out the "reform of production, rights, responsibility, and profit", a large number of Chinese workers were laid off, Many went to work in private enterprises, and even started their own businesses, becoming individual industrial and commercial households. In the process of China's economic system reform, the private sector has become the leading force to accommodate employment. In practice, it has gradually formed a distribution system with the main principle of distribution according to work. Especially after the establishment of the market economic system, the notion of material interests that is compatible with the development of the market economy has gradually gained people's respect and was adapted to economic development. In terms of ethics and morality, the concept of family and clan has also become blurred, and people have generally accepted the principle of maximizing utility. The market factor has become an important part of the social market economic system. Meanwhile, in the 21st century, the Chinese began to pursue a higher level of spirituality. They are no longer satisfied with material interests only, but also began to pursue fairness, the rule of law, equality, and obtain higher spiritual needs in terms of ideas, values, and their philosophy of life. Therefore, non-market factors have also been incorporated in the process of market economic system reform (Fig. 1.1).

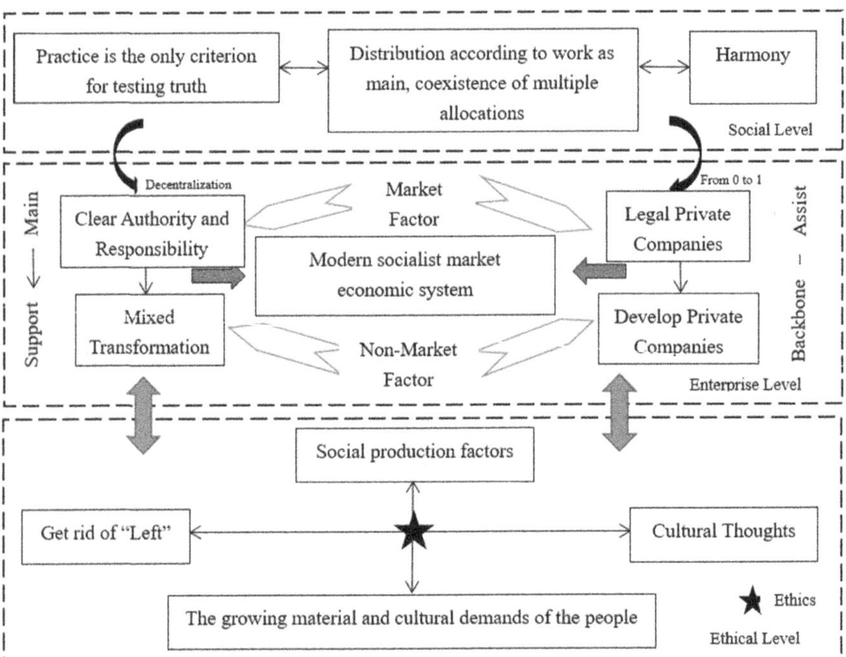

Fig. 1.1 The path of the changes in Chinese individual ideology

1.1.2 The Ethical Premise of Economic Behavior in the Reform of China's Economic System

Marx established a new economic system and created Marxist political economics. We generally refer to his economic system as the "classical political-economic system", and we refer to Marx's "classical political economy" as "traditional political economy". Traditional political economy emphasizes the analysis of the duality of labor and the creation of value, the transformation of the value-form of goods into money, and the conversion of money to capital, revealing the production law and capital of surplus-value. Based on the accumulation law of the production of commodity goods, the system's logic concludes that capitalist society and commodity economy are inevitably destroyed.

The idealistic ethics of traditional political economy occupied China's economic construction, recognized as the establishment of an all-encompassing, highly centralized planned economic management system and social management. Such system changes the production relationships and overcomes the contradiction between the socialization of labor and the privatization of means of production. This thinking is based on the political and economic theory of the former Soviet Union, calling on people to set off a massive socialist transformation to achieve communism. However, under the guidance of this idealistic ethical principle, the Chinese economy has experienced serious issues. To a certain extent, such system only pays attention to the production relationship, while neglecting the development of productive forces, it brings in imprisoning ideas and strengthens centralization. As the same time, non-market factors, such as the role of ethics in the market economy, are ignored.

Unlike previous economic activities performed under the guidance of idealistic ethical principles, after the Third Plenary Session of the 11th CPC Central Committee in 1978 the standards of economic operations in China became more practical. Such approach was fundamentally different from the traditional political and economic mindset, which attempted to encourage people to engage in economic activity by preaching ethics and promoting the idea of creating an ideal future. Given this gradual decline in the impact of traditional political economic ethics in China, this research is intended to establish an economic operation system more in line with China's current conditions by recognizing the practical implications of an ethical approach to economic activities.

1. *Economic activity is social activity through which economic actors achieve material benefits*

During the third Plenary Session of the 11th CPC Central Committee, the Communist Party explicitly promoted the slogan of "allowing local and industrial and agricultural enterprises to have more management autonomy under the guidance of national unification." As opposed to the traditional political economy, this new slogan was actually recognition that the principle of economic interest remains the basic starting point for people to engage in economic activities. Therefore, all economic theories (with the exception of traditional political economics[11]) regard human economic behavior as fundamentally rational, insofar as people who engage in economic activities are assumed to adjust their behavior in accordance with their own interests to achieve greater economic gain. In fact, it is the rational characteristics of this activity, which make economic theory possible.

2. *Independent economic agents are the key to economic behavior*

The basic premise of the traditional political-economic theory is that once production agency belongs to the public, people will naturally become the material interests of the producers and users, and everything can be adjusted and allocated by the "visible hand[12]" to achieve social fairness. Under this scenario, in the distribution process, only the national organization is related to the material benefit, the output and the allocation between units. Both individuals and enterprises are subordinated to this central plan, with any attempt to escape from its control being viewed as a betrayal and attack on the overall interests of society.

The first thing that was eliminated by the reform and opening-up policy was this belief in the ethical rationality of some central organization pursuing the interests of the people. Underlying this shift was the recognition that individuals and organizations are naturally incentivized to engage in economic activity once their ownership and management rights of assets are clear, and that larger and clearer profits tend to improve economic efficiency. At the same time, basic rights were also granted to the main economic actors, such as natural and legal persons, who were allowed to legally own property and increase their economic behavior. As individuals, they were given the right to choose their own jobs according to their own capabilities; as economic legal persons, they were given the right to decide what staff to employ as well as the means to determine products to produce and how to operate effectively in the market; and as natural individuals, they were afforded the right to choose their own consumption practices and lifestyles. Naturally, these basic rights were also viewed as ethical prerequisites and basic rules of conduct for engaging in economic behavior.

3. *A market economy provides the means for economic actors to realize their economic interests*

The market economy is a method to maximize the benefits of real economic activities, the most effective way to allocate resources, and the most equitable system of economic activities. On the one hand, under the market economy system, market price adjustments also result in relative independence and equality. When everyone is pursuing their own interests and competing in the market, they are able to adjust their entire social resource attribution in order to maximize their own interests. When the market reaches its maximum efficiency, consumers also get the largest benefit from

[11]The so-called traditional political economics is based on the "economic man" as a theoretical premise to study economic activities and economic relations in society.

[12]As the traditional policy economics, Formation and development of industrial clusters rely on the regulation of the government, which is a so-called 'visible hand'.

the competition. In addition, the market economy has an added benefit of minimizing the role of status, rank, and privilege in the traditional political economy, where the basic ideals of moral equality are not reflected in reality. On the other hand, because the Chinese market is full of non-market factors, such as the inequality caused by the role of status, class and rights leaded by thoughts of communism and the government which differ from the western world, thus the classical Western economics cannot be fully applied in China.

Take China's housing prices as an example: The pricing system is not entirely determined by the cost of the house itself. In different districts of the same area, housing prices may be affected by the occupational types of residents. For example, if the residents of a certain community are mostly intellectuals such as university professors, since intellectuals are highly regarded in Chinese social ethics, the housing prices in this community may be higher than those in neighboring communities in the same area. This shows the impact of China's non-market factors on the market. Another example is the public ethical incident in 2018 regarding the quality of China's biological vaccines, which prompted the introduction of vaccine regulations to regulate the medical market. Therefore, the market economic system in China can be explained as one of a limited allocation of resources under the influence of the nation's macro-control and non-market factors.

1.1.3 The Impact of Chinese Ethical Values on the Development of Economic Behavior

Almost 40 years after the implementation of the reform and opening-up policy, there can be no doubt that China's production forces have been greatly developed and its standard of living has improved considerably. At the same time, once the public realized it could pursue individual agendas, people also began to attempt to maximize their own interests. So while the environment in which people have been engaging in economic activities is constantly changing, rules and ethical norms restraining such behavior also have changed. Specifically, the idea that making money is always right has given way to the realization that social responsibility is also important and that, in fact, one can create wealth by undertaking greater social responsibility.

1. *Making money is always right*

One of the problems addressed by China's reform and opening-up was how to eliminate the debt incurred by state-owned enterprises. The intent was to divest the strategic burden of state-owned enterprises through gradual market-oriented reform and to cultivate their viability. At the same time, enterprises in townships and villages served as precursors to private enterprises established for making money. In 1987, Deng Xiaoping called the emergence of township enterprises as "the most unexpected harvest in rural reform." After a long period of reform, the responsibility of an enterprise is to make profit while ensuring political security and correctness. But from an economic perspective, the primary task of the enterprise is innovation and production. As the creator of social material wealth, the main purpose of enterprises is to provide material products and spiritual products for society. As the basic economic unit supporting the existence of human society, if the enterprise loses its production and innovation functions, then it loses the basic value of its existence. Therefore, the priority of any enterprise is to engage in efficient production while creating market benefits, and its failure to do so will prevent it from being competitive. Moreover, the pursuit of profits by enterprises also indirectly contributes to society by creating jobs and increasing revenues. In conclusion, whether Chinese enterprises should undertake social responsibility in addition to their economic responsibility depends on their stage of development and the specific practice of systematic reform. At least in the early stages of reform and opening-up, however, economic responsibility took priority.

2. *Shouldering social responsibility while making money*

In the 21st century, as Chinese enterprises became more deeply integrated into the global economic system, their focus on economic responsibility was viewed as increasingly problematic. They attempted to avoid taxes and social security contributions, ignored social employment issues, and engaged in the destruction and pollution of the environment. Many enterprises even went so far as to provide unqualified services and products as well as false information to deceive consumers. Others formed monopolies, which suppressed market competition. While these enterprises made profits for their owners at the expense of the welfare of their employees and society, it leads to an decline of credibility among the public. A widespread mistrust of state-owned enterprises arose from such fraudulent practices as filing bankruptcy to eliminate debt, as well as engaging in false advertising through the use of fake packaging. Finally, these practices resulted in increasing demands both by the government and the public that enterprises begin to fulfill their responsibilities to society. Enterprises themselves also gradually became aware that a stronger focus on social responsibility would enable them to improve their corporate image by fostering better relationship with consumers producing high-quality products, reducing pollution, eliminating discrimination, and giving back to the community.

3. *Creating opportunities to make money by taking on social responsibilities*

There are enormous business opportunities in China. Some entrepreneurs have used these opportunities to indirectly earn profits by establishing and operating public platforms and social networks. Alibaba[13] was the first to create such a fair market environment. Whether through Taobao, Tmall, Alipay, Ali cloud, Rookie Logistics or other similar services,[14] Alibaba embedded applications in various business fields, providing a basic internet device and market platform for enterprises across China. It claims that in future its services will become the fourth essential resource for

[13]Alibaba Group Holding Limited is established in China in 1999. It is a company whose main business is the online market (B2B) online market, and conduct own business in more than 240 countries and regions.

[14]Companies and affiliated entities of Alibaba Group.

enterprises, behind water, electricity, and land. Other opportunities have emerged in the form of a shared economy, a prime example of which is bike-sharing apps.[15] They are to address "the last three kilometers" dilemma in cities by letting people make short-distance trips conveniently and reducing traffic jams and pollution. Bike-sharing apps have achieved success by attracting customers through extremely low prices, which increases participation, and using advertising revenues to make a profit.

1.1.4 The Important Position and Business Development of Japanese-Funded Enterprises in China in the Reform of China's Economy

1. *The important economic status of Japanese-funded enterprises in China in the reform of China's economic system*

China is an important target country for Japan's foreign direct investment. As of 2015, cumulative investments of Japan in China was US $101.825 billion, accounting for 6.2% of China's total foreign investment. After Hong Kong and the British Virgin Islands, it is China's third-largest source of foreign investment. Since the 1980s, the industrial structure of Japanese investment in China has undergone significant changes. In the 1980s, Japan's direct investment in China was mainly concentrated in non-manufacturing industries, such as services and commerce, while manufacturing investment was rare, mainly in the electronic machinery industry. Since the 1990s, share of manufacturing has increased rapidly and today it dominates Japan's direct investments in China. According to the data of the Ministry of Commerce of the People's Republic of China, with 71.3% of the total volume, manufacturing is the most important industry for Japan's direct investment in China. With the development of Chinese manufacturing and consumption level, Japanese companies have begun to strengthen their activities in the Chinese market in order to provide quality goods, technology, and experience to Chinese consumers. Japanese companies have always played an important role in China's efforts to improve the quality and efficiency of economic development and to expand the scale of the economy. Moreover, Japan is an important trading partner for China. Japan ranked second among all export destinations in China in 2017, amounting to US $137.3 billion. Imports also ranked second with an amount of US $165.7 billion.

2. *The development of Japanese-funded enterprises in China in the reform of China's economic system*

The evolution of Japanese-funded enterprises (JFEs[16]) in China, starting from China's reform and opening-up policy, can be divided into four stages.

---

[15]Bike-sharing apps refer to bicycle sharing services provided by enterprises on campus, subway stations, bus stations, residential areas, commercial areas, and public service areas in 2017. It is a new type of environmentally friendly sharing economy with time-sharing, which is in line with the concept of low-carbon travel.

[16]In this paper, JFEs is the abbreviation of Japanese-funded Enterprises in China.

The first stage began with the enforcement of China's reform and opening-up policy in 1978 through 1995. Although China possessed a potentially large market, low national income, and market imperfections restricted Japanese investments. Investors mostly focused on establishing production centers in China because of preferential policies and cheap labor, and paid little attention to the Chinese market.

The second stage was from 1996 to 2001, when JFEs gradually shifted their focus from simple production to a combination of production and marketing in China. The initial establishment of market-oriented systems for production, promotion, pricing, and trading channels laid the foundation for the development of the Chinese market.

The third stage, namely the market development stage, lasted from 2002 to 2008. In this stage, JFEs continued to expand in the Chinese market. Factors such as product development for the Chinese market and nationwide logistics networks to transporting commodities gradually became the focus of Japanese investment in China, which in turn, formed an indispensable and large-scale market focused on the production of cars and electronic products.

In the fourth stage, starting in 2009, China's role as a production base began to decline mainly due to the financial crisis and higher labor costs. However, with the development of policy reforms in the areas of investment, resources, logistics, transportation, and environmental protection as well as trade and technological innovation, the overall market for JFEs in China has experienced sustained growth. In fact, according to data from Japan's Ministry of Economy, Trade, and Industry (METI), there were 5,878 JFEs operating in China in 2011, accounting for 30.5% of Japan's overseas enterprises. In 2013, this number grew to 7,700 (including Hong Kong and Macao), accounting for 33% of all overseas enterprises. According to the "External Import and Export Japanese-funded Enterprise Operation Survey 2017 Summary" published by the Japanese Ministry of Foreign Affairs, the total number of Japanese-funded enterprises (business outlets) in China reached 32,313.

Research on JFEs in China began to increase during the third stage of their development. However, these studies have mainly focused on strategy, technology, localization and diversification, and the most pressing problems have not been addressed with little to no attention paid to organizational ethical climate.

1.2 Proposal of Research Question and Significance of Research

1.2.1 Proposed Research Question

JFEs in China as Japanese companies that do business in China, not only should combine the Japanese management and Chinese culture, also need to strengthen Chinese management philosophy, build atmosphere which is suitable for the enterprise ethics with Chinese characteristics, They should make the Japanese enterprises in China not only obtain the identity of the Chinese government, but also get the support of the local Chinese employees. The organizational ethical climate is, therefore, the embodiment of an organization's ethical environment, which includes both common experiences and perceptions of its members. Instead of formal rules and norms, ethical climate is an informal system that guides employees' behavior as well as the direction of an organization's moral decision-making. In order to understand what JFEs must do to create a suitable organizational ethical climate in a Chinese cultural context and in light of Sino-Japanese relations,[17] we must first differentiate the ethical climate of JFEs in China with that of local Chinese enterprises to determine what makes JFEs unique.

Moreover, as numerous studies (Joseph and Deshpande 1997; Deshpande 1996; H. Moore and T. Moore 2014; Okpara and Wynn 2008) have shown, organizational ethical climate also affects the organizational commitment and job performance of employees. Yet JFEs in China have their own unique organizational ethical climate, which affects organizational commitment and job performance in a distinctive way. Therefore, to help them achieve sustainable development in China, they should be research on mentioned ethical climate issues in order to lay a solid theoretical foundation for business and human resource management practices. Therefore, this study mainly studies the following problems:

Question 1: What is the organizational ethical climate of Japanese-founded companies in China?

Question 2: How does the different type's organizational ethical climate affect the different type's organizational commitment in Japanese-funded companies in China?

Question 3: How do the different type's organizational commitments affect the relationship between organizational ethics and organizational performance in Japanese companies in China?

Although many studies have explained the impact of organizational climate on organizational commitment and on job performance, Japanese companies in China, as mentioned earlier, have a unique "blood relationship", which lacks in-depth studies. Because China and Japan have a "rule-free" relationship for historical reasons, not all researchers, especially Western ones, have the same sensitivity on the relationship mentioned above. At the same time because China and Japan are important economic partners, this field of investigation is extremely suitable for studying the impact of non-market factors on the corporate economy. Therefore, the problems explored in this study have both universal economic significance as well as special historical value.

---

[17] Sino-Japanese relations are best described as "near and far," geographically, culturally, and economically close, but far apart in politics, customs, and attitudes. For a more detailed description of Sino-Japanese relations, please refer to the author's paper, Strategic Localization for Japanese Corporations in China: The Nexus of harmonious Society and Public Value Creation[J]. Rikkyo Business Review. 2010, 3:53–59.

1.2.2 Significance of Research

The practical significance of this study is essentially threefold:

1. *Matching employees' ethical cognition with organizational ethical climate*

First, the cultural differences between China and Japan cannot be ignored. Although separated by a narrow strip of water, the two countries possess very different traditional cultures. Both JFEs in China and their Chinese employees need to fully understand and properly navigate these differences. Enterprises should provide employees with access to the original culture of the company, which will enhance employees' cultural sensitivity and adaptability. At the same time, enterprises also need to understand the preferred organizational ethical climate of Chinese employees through business and cultural training. Through mutual cultural understanding and recognition, employees' ethical cognition and preferences can be matched with organizational ethical climate, thereby enhancing the job satisfaction and organizational commitment of Chinese employees while reducing turnover.

2. *Encouraging Chinese employees*

Like China, Japan has a culture of collectivism, which has played an important role in the development and growth of Japanese enterprises. But there is a huge difference in the degree of collectivism between China and Japan. Japanese employees are deeply influenced by the idea of collectivism, which demands unconditional loyalty and dedication to the group. In traditional Chinese culture, however, work is merely a means of subsistence (Jin 2011). In this sense, Japanese enterprises are more compelling in terms of a caring ethical climate, and Japanese employees experience more care in their working organizations. But because the caring ethical climate is based on Japanese traditional culture, such encouragement is far beyond what is required for Chinese employees in JFEs. In a survey of 43 JFEs affiliated with the Japanese Chamber of Commerce in China, Xue Jun and Nishimura Haotai (2006) found that dissatisfaction with income and welfare was the main reason for the high turnover of Chinese employees (62.8%). JFEs in China should, therefore, adopt measures to reform motivation policies for Chinese employees using a combination of material and non-material incentives. These policies should be in line with employees' own interests so that they can feel the caring ethical climate and avoid instrumental behavior.

Japan's groupism culture is characterized by internal peace and harmony, external struggles, and market competition among groups; there are vertical social organization principles, layered social structures, and ubiquitous hierarchical concepts in social life; In terms of ethics, there is a lack of absolute standards of good and evil, and little control over the group's behavior. Compared with Chinese traditional culture, Japanese groupism culture emphasizes the individual's loyalty to the group. Japanese companies also pay more attention to the employee's spiritual incentives and pay attention to shaping an organizational ethics climate. Contrary, in China's traditional culture, work is a means of earning a living and is more focused on compensation and benefits. Therefore, Japanese-funded enterprises in China often face difficulties in achieving the same spiritual incentives as Japanese companies in Japan do. This also suggests that Japanese-funded enterprises in China need to implement different incentives for Chinese employees. To ensure that incentive measures achieve intended results, those should be according to the ethical underpinnings of organizations in both countries. In addition, there are other major differences between Chinese and Japanese companies: Japanese companies have slow evaluation and promotion systems, and their work is relatively stable (Xue Jun, Nishimura Haotai, 2006). The relationships between employees and enterprises are mostly lifelong, and employees have a strong sense of belonging to the company. In contrast, Chinese companies promote employees more frequently, conduct cross-professional promotion, and see frequent employee turnover. Employees' sense of belonging to the company is also comparably low.

3. *Instilling uniform ethical values*

At the strategic level, Yu (2009) argues that an independence ethical climate has a significant positive impact on the organizational commitment of employees. However, in the actual situation of JFEs in China, there is little room for promotion for Chinese employees, as management teams typically consist of Japanese managers. Yin (2006) has pointed out that the traditional Japanese culture of groupism leads to exclusion and mistrust of other cultures, and many studies have shown that Chinese employees' failure to advance can be at least partially attributed to the difficulty of gaining the trust of JFEs (Song 2006; Jin 2007; Niu 2008). Without equal rights and clear career paths, employees can neither experience the caring ethical climate nor easily form a strong commitment to the organization. Enterprises should, therefore, enhance the education and training of employees, develop training systems in line with China's national conditions and promote an organizational ethical climate more aligned with employees' perspectives.

In recent years, JFEs in China have also suffered from a series of ethics failures, including recalls of low quality products, employee strikes, excessive overtime, and unequal pay. For example, the Toyota safety problems in 2010 and the TOTO strike of 2014 were direct reflections of these problems. Liu Songbo (2013) has pointed out that moral leadership can inhibit employees' self-interest orientation in organizations and reduce non-moral behavior in employees. Therefore, in order to realize long-term development in China, JFEs should establish and instill organizational ethics that are conducive to social development and enhance their education and training of their employees.

1.3 Research Innovation

This research attempts to be innovative in the following ways:

1. By analyzing the type and impact of organizational ethical climate on organizational commitment and job performance in terms of economic ethics;
2. By providing an empirical study of the organizational ethical climate, organizational commitment and job performance of JFEs in China;
3. By systematically exploring the relationship between organizational ethical climate, organizational commitment, and job performance as well as the impact of different organizational ethical climates on organizational commitment and job performance;
4. By studying the impact of organizational ethical climate within the manufacturing industry in China in order to provide theoretical and practical guidance for the development of effective ethical climates in JFEs in China.

1.4 Research Content and Roadmap

1.4.1 Research Content

As discussed above, the goal of this research is to study human resource management and its specific activities from the perspectives of organizational ethical climate, organizational commitment, and job performance. First, this study reviews prior research results to lay a solid foundation for subsequent research. Second, it studies the types of organizational ethical climates of JFEs in China by using questionnaires to collect information on JFEs, Due to the large population and demographic dividend of China; many developed countries have placed parts of their production and processing. Japanese-owned enterprises such as electronic products, automobile manufacturing, textiles and garments, apparel industry, food manufacturing, etc. are also doing their production and processing in China. In addition, although being a traditional industry, Chinese manufacturing has a large proportion in the secondary industry. In Chinese manufacturing which predominantly consists of labor-intensive industries, the organization ethic climate is particularly important for the job performance, thus highlighting the research problem and value of this paper.

First, survey results are analyzed using the Principal Factor Analysis and Load Factor Matrix to identify variables that could effectively measure different organizational ethical climates. Then, combined with the Structural Equation Modeling (SEM),[18] relationship between the observed variables and different organizational ethical climates are studied. Third, the types of organizational commitments that exist

[18]Structural equation modeling is a special class that uses covariance to make covariance structure analysis, which can examine the relation among multiple constructs. And in this paper, SEM is the abbreviation of structural equation modeling. The SEM in this paper uses three indicators,

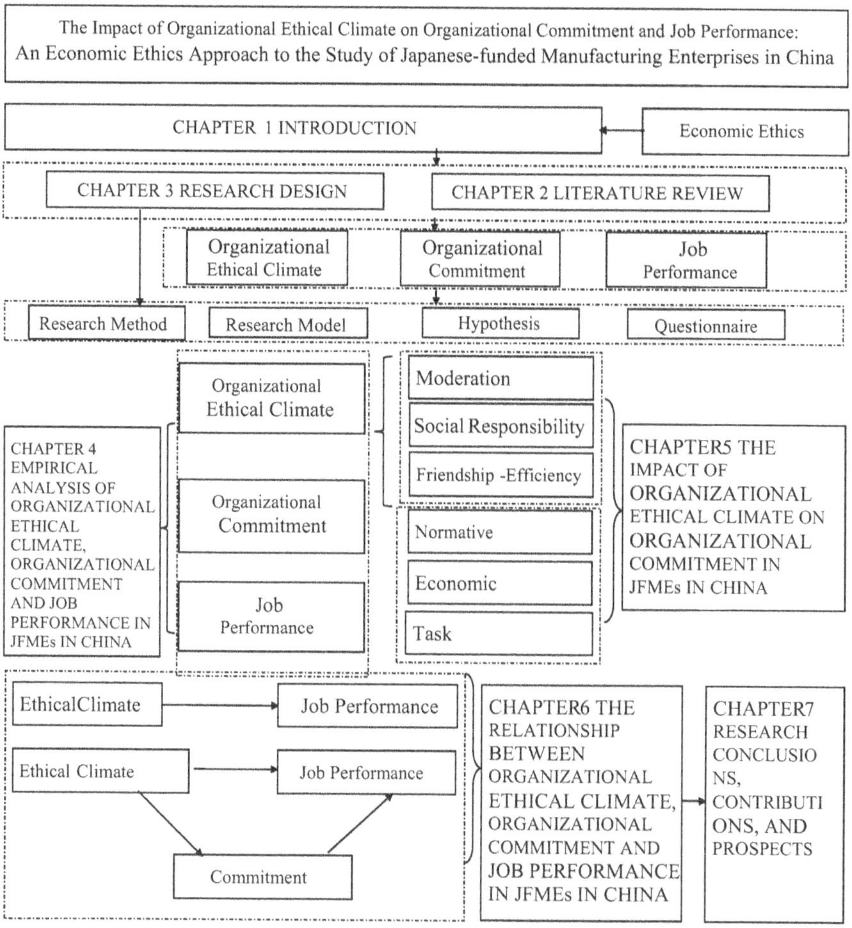

Fig. 1.2 Research content

in these JFEs are explored using questionnaires to collect information and applying Principal Factor Analysis, Load Factor Matrix and SEM to identify variables that could effectively measure different organizational commitments. Fourth, the same methodology is used to identify the types of job performances that exist in these JFEs. Fifth, the impact of organizational ethical climate on organizational commitment is studied. Sixth, the impact of different organizational ethical climates on organizational commitment and job performance is studied. Finally, the results and findings

the goodness-of-fit index GFI; the adjusted goodness-of-fit index GFI; the X2 goodness-of-fit test. Estimation results in all the SEM model in this paper, both the goodness-of-fit index GFI and the adjusted goodness-of-fit index GFI are greater than 0.9, and all passed the X2 goodness-of-fit test.

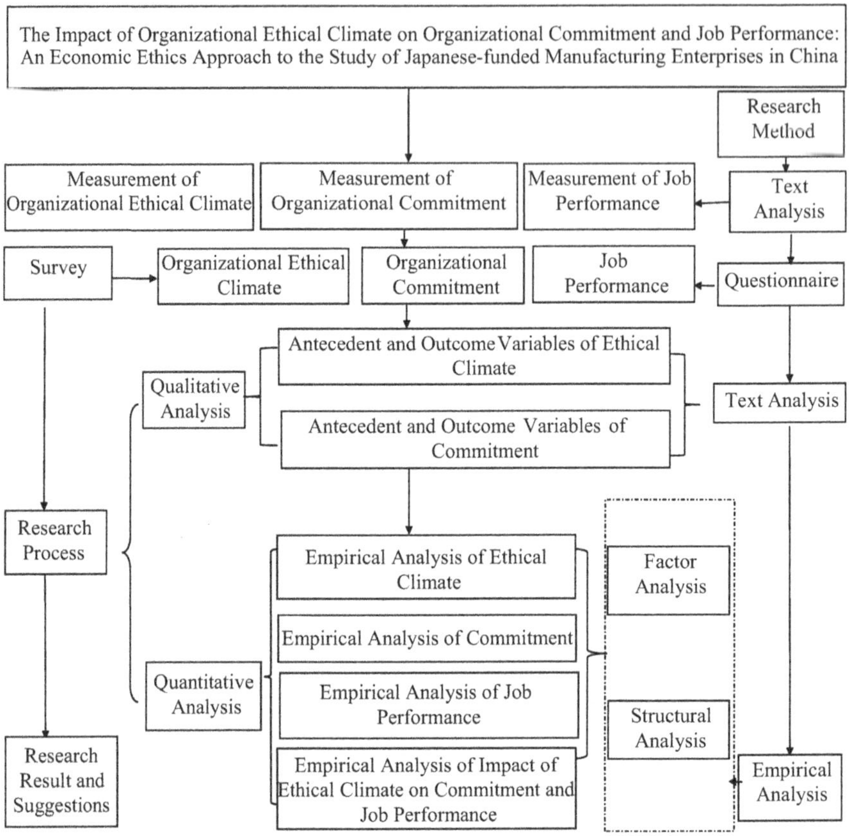

Fig. 1.3 Research roadmap

of this research are analyzed in order to propose corresponding measures for improving the organizational ethical climate of JFEs in China. A detailed summary of this research plan is given above (Fig. 1.2).

1.4.2 Research Roadmap

The review of prior research on organizational ethical climate, organizational commitment, and job performance indicates that the most common frameworks for analysis are sociological and behavioral. But this study mainly focuses on economic ethics, which is concerned with the perspective of the rational person. On the basis of the relevant studies, three questionnaires—"Organizational Ethical Climate, "Organizational Commitment" and "Job Performance"—were designed to evaluate the impact of organizational ethical climate on the organizational commitment and job performance of JFEs in China. Ultimately, specific measures are proposed for developing an effective organizational ethical climate, as set forth in more detail above (Fig. 1.3).

Chapter 2
Literature Review

As discussed above, prior research on this subject can be broken down into the following categories: (1) research on organizational ethical climate, including the definition of organizational ethical climate, the structural measurement of its scope and an empirical analysis of its types; (2) research on organizational commitment, including the definition of organizational commitment as well as its structure, dimensions and measurement techniques; (3) research on organizational performance, mainly referred to as "job performance" in China, including its definition, structure and measurement; and (4) research on the theoretical basis of organizational ethical climate from the perspective of economic ethics.

2.1 Research on Organizational Ethical Climate

2.1.1 Current Research on Organizational Ethical Climate

1. *Definition of organizational ethical climate*

In 1981, Murphy first proposed the concept of organizational ethical climate in his study of marketing ethics, which was subsequently developed in a breakthrough study by Victor and Cullen in 1987. According to this study, the organizational ethical climate is as a distinct category of organizational climate, insofar as it reflects both the characteristics of an organization in dealing with ethical issues as well as the shared understanding of its members with respect to what constitutes ethical behavior. Follow-up studies then elaborated on the notion of organizational ethical climate, as shown in Table 2.1.

Generally speaking, the organizational ethical climate is, therefore, the embodiment of an organization's ethical environment comprised of the common experiences and perceptions of its members. Instead of formal rules and norms, it is an informal system that guides employees' behavior as well as the direction of an organization's moral decision-making.

© Science Press and Springer Nature Singapore Pte Ltd. 2020

K. Ryu, *The Impact of Organizational Ethical Climate on Organizational Commitment and Job Performance*, https://doi.org/10.1007/978-981-15-2813-2_2

Table 2.1 Definitions of organizational ethical climate

Study	Definition
Murphy (1981)	An important factor influencing the ethical behavior of employees, whereby changes in the ethical climate of an organization necessarily leads to changes in the ethical behavior of its marketing employees
Victor and Cullen (1987)	Not only the characteristics of an organization in dealing with ethical issues but also the shared understanding of its members in what constitutes ethical behavior and how to deal with ethical issues
Wimbush and Shepard (1994)	The ways that employees perceive and solve ethical problems and dilemmas. It is not an emotion or attitude, but the common experience and cognition in making ethical decisions. In terms of morality, it belongs to the normative structure of ethical behavior
Falkenberg and Herremans (1995)	An informal system dealing with organizational and personal ethical issues, whose impact is often greater than that of formal ethical standards and normative systems
Cohen (1998)	The conceptual construction of ethical climate is based on "decision making with morality." The climate is the general perception of organizational signals with respect to morality
Babin (2000)	The dominant organizational practices and procedures, which impact an organization's view of right and wrong
Dickson (2001)	The perception, policies, and practices of organizational incentives and procedures
Malloy and Agarwal (2002)	The psychological perception structure of organizational ethical behavior, which makes employees understand the common values and goals of the organization, what is not allowed in this context of values and goals, how to deal with and solve ethical issues after they arise, and who should be responsible, etc.
Cullen and Victor (2003)	Organizational ethical climate not only has a regulatory effect on the internal level of the organization but also is an embodiment of the ethical behavior of dominant powers
Stawiski (2009)	As with culture, the ethical climate is composed of subjective factors such as the shared beliefs of the ethical position of the enterprise and plays an important role in enterprises lacking standards or implementation measures
Lemmergaard and Lauridsen (2008)	A working climate that represents the norms of how to solve moral problems, but also the perception of employees' morale practices

(continued)

Table 2.1 (continued)

Study	Definition
Arnaud (2010)	The integrated perception of values, norms, and behavior of members of a social system

2. *Types and measurement of organizational ethical climate*

Victor, Cullen and various others have theorized that while there may be a particular ethical climate that takes the dominant position in an organization or group, many other types of ethical climates can also coexist in regulating ethical behavior. In 1987, Victor and Cullen proposed nine types of organizational ethical climates, five of which were verified through an empirical study in 1988. In 1990, Victor then reexamined and refined his original system of classification into six distinct types, which have continued to form the theoretical framework for subsequent research.

While attempts have been made create alternative categorizations—Agarwal, for example, proposed five types in 1999, Schwepker developed a scale in 2001 and Arnaud developed his Ethical Climate Index in 2004—the original framework proposed by Victor and Cullen remains the standard adopted by more than 75% of all studies on organizational ethical climate over the past 20 years. In addition, the ethical climate questionnaire (ECQ) developed by Victor and Cullen also remains the most widely used (Fritzsche 2000), which is why it has been adopted for the purposes of the present study as well.

(1) Types of organizational ethical climate

Victor and Cullen stated that organizational ethical climates can be classified according to a locus of analysis and ethical standards. They took analytical orientations (individual, local, and cosmopolitan) as the horizontal axis, and ethical standards (egoism, benevolence, and principle) as the vertical axis, and then deduced nine potential types of organizational ethical climates. As shown in Table 2.2, while there may be a particular ethical climate that takes the dominant position in an organization or group, many other types of climates can coexist to regulate ethical behavior. As a result, the ethical decision-making of employees is the result of a combination of various organizational ethical climates.

Generally speaking, ethical standards refer to the methods or ideas used to judge morality. Using the theory of developmental psychology, Kohlberg (1981) proposed

Table 2.2 Nine types of organizational ethical climate

Ethical standards	Analytical orientations		
	Individual	Local	Cosmopolitan
Egoism	Self-interest	Organizational interest	Efficiency
Benevolence	Friendship	Team interest	Stakeholder orientation
Principle	Personal morality	Organizational rules	Laws and public interest

Source Victor and Cullen (1987)

three ethical standards: egoism, benevolence, and principle,[1] along with three ethical dimensions: egoism, utilitarianism, and deontology. In a climate of egoism, the self is the exclusive consideration in the identification and resolution of ethical issues; in utilitarianism, the main consideration is others' welfare; and in deontology, standards are based on the interpretation and application of rules, regulations, and laws. As the reference group in the decision-making process, which extends from individual to society as a whole, the three analytical orientations adopted by Victor and Cullen based on Kohlberg's research into individual moral cognition include individual, local and cosmopolitan. Moreover, studies have shown that individuals go through three stages in the ethical decision-making process: individual, organizational and societal.

(2) Measurement of organizational ethical climate

Based on the above results, Victor and Cullen (1988) developed the ECQ to understand organizations' conception of organizational ethical climate.[2] As set forth in Table 2.3, they conducted empirical research on 822 employees from a company and verified through factor analysis the existence of five types of organizational ethical climates: instrumental, caring, independence, rules, and law and order. Two years later, Victor and Cullen (1990) conducted further theoretical and empirical research on the relationship between organizational ethical climate and deviant behavior, as a

Table 2.3 Types of organizational ethical climate

Type	Perception of organization members
Instrumental	Tend to believe that the purpose of individual decision-making is primarily for personal gain, and do not generally consider the impact of their decisions on others. May sacrifice the interests of others, teams and the organization for their own benefit
Caring	Tend to think that they must not only care about the interests of the individual but also be concerned about stakeholders who are influenced by their decision-making. Often take full account of others, teams, and organizations, and attempt to pursue a balance of interests for all parties
Independence	Tend to argue that individual decisions should be primarily based on individual moral standards and values. Organizations have relatively little constraints, and they should advocate making decisions based on accepted ethical principles
Rules	Tend to think that "since the organization requires us to strictly abide by various rules and regulations, I should do so in accordance with the requirements of the organization." Individual decision-making must therefore be based on organizational principles, rules, and regulations
Law and code	Tend to believe that the laws, regulations, industry norms and ethical principles that are external to the organization are most important and that the regulations of the organization itself do not play a leading role

Source Victor and Cullen (1988)

[1]W., Liu.

[2]Victor, B., Cullen, J.B. The organizational bases of ethical work climates [J]. Administrative Science Quarterly, 1988, 33(1):101–125.

result of which they revised their original categorization of ethical climates into six types: professional, caring, rules, instrumental, efficiency and independence. Both the earlier and subsequent classifications are summarized in the analytical framework of organizational ethical climate by Victor and Cullen in 1987.[3]

As discussed above, the resulting ECQ developed by Victor and Cullen remains the most widely used measurement tool for organizational ethical climate due to its high level of stability in different countries, cultural contexts and sectors of organizations (Fritzsche 2000). So far, more than 170 studies have used it in their own research, either directly or indirectly.

3. *Studies on the effectiveness of organizational ethical climate*

(1) Impact of organizational ethical climate on employee satisfaction

Employee organizational commitment is the degree of pleasure that employees perceive by feeling that the job satisfies their values (Morrison 1994). Specifically, employee satisfaction is mainly comprised of six dimensions: the works itself, salary, promotion, work team, working conditions, and leadership. Employees' perception of these six dimensions has a direct impact on their satisfaction level, and their organizational commitment is influenced by their perception of how well the organizational ethical climate matches their own personal preferences (Sims and Kroech 1994). Martin and Cullen's (2006) analysis showed that employee satisfaction with work, promotion, co-workers, and supervisors were related to ethical climate. Tsai and Huang (2008) studied nurses in Taiwan and found a correlation between different types of organizational ethical climate and different dimensions of employees' sense of belonging or organizational commitment. For example, an instrumental climate was found to be negatively correlated with promotion satisfaction, a caring climate was positively correlated with satisfaction with wages as well as the work itself, and a rule climate was positively correlated with satisfaction with leaders and teams or co-workers. Importantly, nurses tended to work in law and professional code climate, which supports Deshpande (1996) conclusion that "professionalism" remains the dominant climate for nonprofit organizations.

(2) Impact of organizational ethical climate on individual and organizational performance

Valentine et al. (2002) studied 304 young organization members and found that the organizational ethical climate was positively correlated with many outcome variables (Donaldson 1991; Wimbush 1994). More recently, it was discovered that the construction and perfection of an organization's ethical atmosphere has a direct positive impact on its overall performance (Simha and Stanusch 2013). Therefore, organizations can improve their overall competitive advantage by implementing management practices that foster an organizational ethical climate conducive to organizational development.

(1) The mediating effect model

The mediating effect model holds that organizational ethical atmosphere is indirectly influenced by intermediate variables that affect individual, group and organizational

---

[3]W., Liu.

outcome variables. These variables can affect the ethical behavior of individuals by influencing their trust in leadership (Konovsky 1994). They can also impact performance by strengthening team cohesiveness and morale. Moreover, they affect members' behaviors, task performance, and contextual performance by informing the organization's sense of fairness (both procedural fairness and distributional) as well as ethical expectations (Dickson 2004). Finally, they can also make a difference in employees' organizational commitment, job satisfaction, and turnover by impacting the development of leaders' moral cognition.

Yet since the organizational ethical climate is closely related to variables of individual mind and behavior, its impact on employee performance is necessarily indirect and primarily accomplished through the promotion of organizational citizenship behavior (OCB) and a sense of organizational fairness. Based on the theory of social exchange, OCB has been found to play an important role in improving relationship performance. In terms of fairness, when employees perceive that an organization is fair, they will feel their expectations have been met and will therefore tend to believe that their efforts will pay off in the future, which will, in turn, encourage extra-role behaviors and enhance both contextual and artificial performance. As a form of extra-role behavior, OCB serves the purpose of altruistic orientation that promotes organizational development.

Studies have further found that caring and rule ethical climates can both boost OCB, either directly or indirectly. Liu (2010) investigated a Wenzhou family business and concluded that organizational ethical climate and OCB are related. Wang (2014) focused on the impact of a caring climate on the OCB of employees at different levels and found that it had a positive effect on behaviors oriented toward the individual, organization, and society. Such behaviors are also regulated by collectivism. In his study of organizational ethical climates, Zhang (2013) found that both caring and rule climates can be good predictors of OCB, but that instrumental climates are not. The reason, the author argued, was the mediation role based on social exchange theory and organizational fairness. The mediation role is also based on the influence of organizational ethical climate on job performance and the matching between individuals and organizations. Generally speaking, as a feature of every organization, the organizational ethical climate is a factor considered by both employers and employees whereby individuals tend to seek climates that are well-matched with their own level of moral development while organizations select members who share similar values.

(2) The moderating effect model

Some researchers attribute the impact of organizational ethical climate on outcome variables to the so-called moderating effect. Three stages precede the moral action of individuals: problem confirmation, ethical judgment and behavioral intention (Rest 1986). According to this model, as shown in Fig. 2.1, ethical climate does not directly impact the ethical behavior of individuals, but rather regulates relations between the four stages. Rule and professional code climates have a moderating effect on individual moral judgments and behavioral intentions. In addition, a positive ethical climate necessarily entails regulation between individuals and organizations, whereby

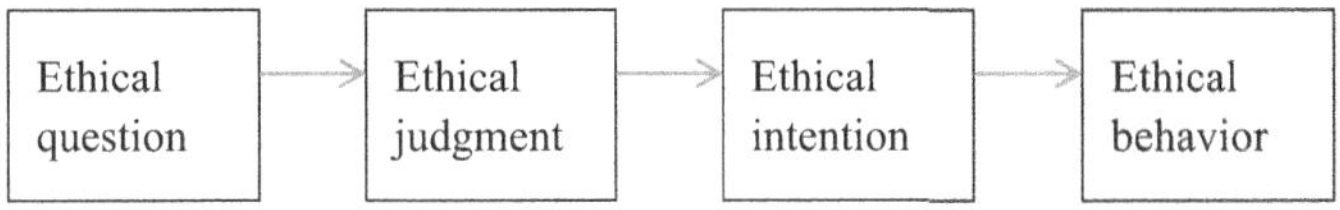

Fig. 2.1 The logic of ethics

positive interaction serves to strengthen members' perception of organizational ethical climate and thereby enhance their level of commitment. The identification of organizational ethical climate also enables a higher degree of coordination between members and organizations.

It is important to keep in mind that the above is a general classification only and that some effects cannot be clearly defined. For example, to explain the effect of organizational ethical climate on job performance, either the main effect model or the buffer effect model can be used. In either case, however, there seems to be a consensus that organizational ethical climate has a positive impact on job performance.

As mentioned above, organizational ethical climate also has an effect on both individuals and organizations and is itself a product of the social environment and leadership of the organization. This relationship is illustrated in Fig. 2.2.

(3) Impact of organizational ethical climate on member performance

Studies have shown that organizational ethical climate has a significant effect on employee behavior and extra-role behavior such as deviant and anti-productive behavior in particular. In fact, Wimbush et al. (1992) confirmed what Victor originally suggested was the relationship between organizational ethical climate and ethical behavior. In general, a caring or rule climate has positive effects on the ethical behavior of individuals and organizations, while self-interest ethical climate is likely to induce unethical behavior (Yanfei Wang). In 1997, Wimbush launched another study on the impact of ethical climate on unethical behavior, the results of which suggested that climates based on individuality, caring, and laws and professional codes were negatively correlated with crime, disobedience, and lying. A service climate was also negatively correlated with stealing and lying (Silong Zhang).

More recently, Vardi (2001) also examined the relationship between ethical climate and misconduct in the workplace but found only three kinds of ethical climate: laws and rules, caring and self-interest. Misconduct by managers and employees were negatively correlated with all three climates. In contrast, Peterson (2002) studied the relationship between ethical climate and immoral behavior and identified seven ethical climates, which were negatively correlated with misconduct—i.e. between a climate of rules and laws and misconduct in property, and between a caring climate and misconduct in politics and production. Peterson's study provides strong evidence of the impact of organizational ethical climates on misconduct.

The reason these studies tend to focus on employees' negative behavior is that such behavior tends to adversely affect job performance, and organizational ethical climate has been found to impact employees' negative extra-role behavior. Job performance can be divided into task performance and conduct performance, the latter of which

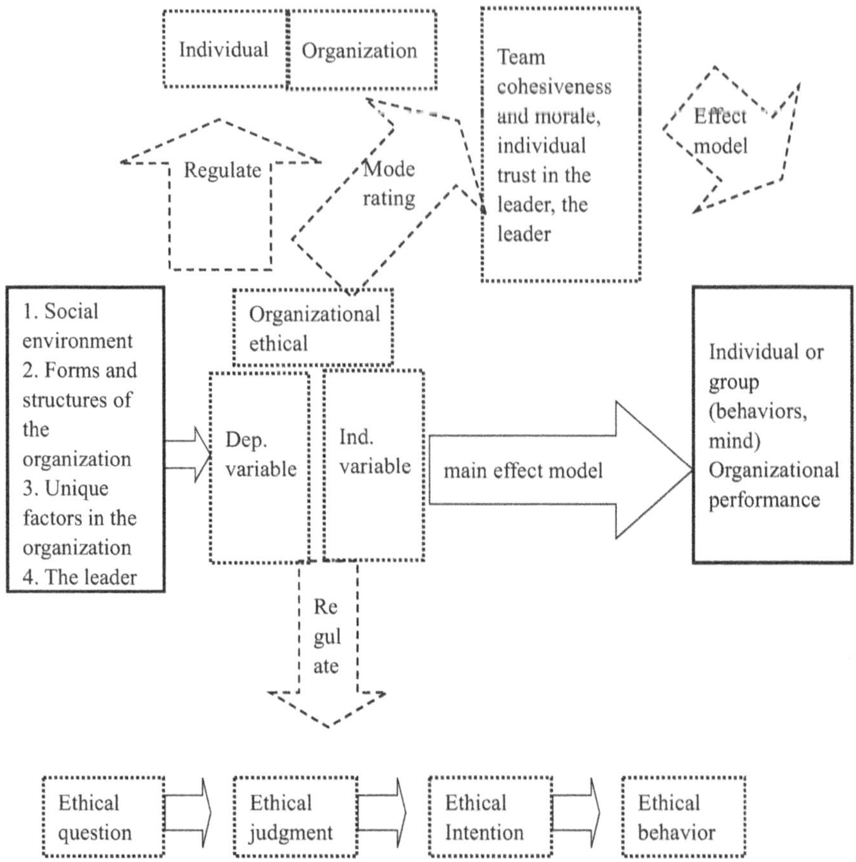

Fig. 2.2 The relationship between the antecedent and dependent variables in the organizational ethical climate

mainly involves behavioral factors that are related to work. In the workplace, conduct performance is primarily represented by spontaneous and extra-role behaviors, the latter of which can be further divided into positive behaviors (such as organizational citizenship behaviors) and negative behaviors.

Several studies of the factors that influence employees' negative extra-role behaviors on the individual and organizational levels have been conducted using various analytical models, which combine intervening and regulatory mechanisms. Specifically, negative extra-role behaviors have been attributed to certain necessities and contingencies. For example, a negative incident may grow out of the employees' control, and thus influence their emotions, causing them to take negative actions and harm the organization. At the same time, employees are also unconsciously affected by organizational ethical climate and culture. In addressing negative incidents, different corporate cultures react differently. Generally speaking, however, a positive reaction is better equipped to resolve conflicts and lower risks to a controllable level. Another factor that has received increasing attention is personality traits, which mostly appear as regulated variables, like agreeableness and conscientiousness. Such traits have been found to significantly regulate different types of organizational ethical climates and extra-role behaviors.

2.1.2 A Synopsis of Research on Organizational Ethical Climate

Though organizational ethical climate has been extensively studied, there is still no general consensus as to its classification, with some adhering to Victor and Cullen's five-factor structure and others to the six-factor structure. This lack of consensus if mainly due to the following reasons. First, organizational culture contains and determines organizational ethical climate, though the two concepts are conceptionally different. Organizational culture refers to the basic assumptions and values shared by members of the organization. These basic assumptions and values are gradually formed by these members in the process of solving external problems and dealing with internal contradictions. The organizational ethical climate is subordinate to organizational culture but is easier to measure because it reflects the specific approaches that members take in dealing with various problems (Liu 2010). Second, the concept of organizational ethical climate is not universally recognized, and some ethical behavior exhibited by members may not be consistent with the accepted ethical standards of society. Third, there are no consistent standards for the organizational ethical climate. The term "organizational ethical climate" could be misinterpreted to mean that there is a strong climate within the organization, where members have common standards and judgments concerning what constitutes ethical and non-ethical behavior. In fact, however, it may very well vary among different departments (Grojean 2004). Fourth, organizational ethical climate does not really measure an organization's sense of morality or ethics but is rather an assessment and description of the ethical mentality which dominates the organization and influences the attitudes, beliefs, motivations, and behaviors of its members with respect to ethical issues as a whole.

Finally, to some extent, an organization's ethical climate is partially dependent on the underlying culture of its individual members. Although they are both located in East Asia, for example, the management practices of Japanese and Chinese enterprises could not be more different, though Japanese-funded enterprises in China have tended to adopt a strategic a mixture of the two, which has led to a special type of organizational culture all its own. The aim of this study is to explore the organizational ethical climate of Japanese-funded enterprises in China in light of this unique organizational culture in an effort to provide a useful reference for both academics and practitioners alike.

2.2 Research on Organizational Commitment

2.2.1 Current Research on Organizational Commitment

1. *Structure and measurement of organizational commitment*

Scholars initially studied job satisfaction to explain various behaviors of employees in their daily work, such as employee performance, turnover, and absenteeism. But the results of this research were inconclusive, suggesting a disconnect between employee job satisfaction and daily behavior (Chan 1997). Scholars subsequently began to identify other factors with a stronger correlation to employee behavior, which is how the concept of organizational commitment was raised. Specifically, it was found that organizational commitment tends to be a better predictor of individual behavior in organizations than job satisfaction. Since that time, several studies have confirmed that organizational commitment plays an important role in strategic human resource management. In particular, a study by Huselid (1998) indicated a positive correlation between high-commitment human resource management and job performance, with the former shown to effectively improve organizational performance. Other studies have also shown organizational commitment to be an important intermediate variable between the individual and job performance (Meyer 1997; Mowday 1998).

Becker (1960) first defined the notion of organizational commitment as a psychological contract that maintains the employment of individuals in an enterprise. Buchanan (1974) then defined organizational commitment as the degree of recognition that individuals have for their organization, which measures the close relationship between employees and organization. According to Mowday (1974), it consists of three basic components: the recognition of organizational goals and values, a willingness to contribute, and clear expectations for the organization, while Wiener (1982) defines it as the internalization of corporate goals and values through management ideas, corporate culture, and ethical climate. Finally, O'Reilly and Chatman (1986) have approached organizational commitment as a type of psychological contract between employees and organizations which is reflected in compliance (behavior arising out of incentive mechanisms), identity (the recognition of organizational values) and internalization (the degree to which individual behavior is consistent with organizational values).

Different dimensions have also been used to measure organizational commitment. Becker (1960), Buchanan (1974) and Porter and Mowday (1979) all believe that organizational commitment essentially refers to employees' dependence on organizations, with Becker viewing such dependence as instrumental and Porter and Mowday viewing it as effective. Allen and Meyer (1990) have in turn classified organizational commitment based on the two dimensions developed by Becker, Porter and Mowday, namely affective and continuance commitment, with Wiener (1982) proposing a third dimension consisting of normative commitment. More recently, Allen and Meyer (1997) developed the Organizational Commitment Survey Questionnaire on the basis of Wiener's three-dimensional model, with Swailes (2002) subsequently proposing behavioral commitment and Blau and Gary (2001) proposing choice commitment as a fourth dimension. In China, Ling Wenquan asked respondents to list their reasons for staying or leaving an organization in his questionnaire, and using a quantitative research method concluded that organizational commitment includes affective, normative, and economic commitment as well as two other dimensions unique to China: ideal and opportunity commitment. According to Ling, various types of organizational commitment are reflected in a combination of factors.

2. *Antecedent and outcome variables of organizational commitment*

According to Porter and Steers (1979), the antecedent variables of organizational commitment include personal characteristics, organizational position, organizational structure, and work experience, among others. In turn, the organizational position includes work content, challenges, and conflicts; organizational structure refers to the size of the organization as well as its degree of control and system of management (centralized or decentralized), while work experience refers to individual's dependence on the organization and expectations of the organization. Studies by Wiener (1982), have shown a positive correlation between organizational commitment and job satisfaction, while studies by Allen and Meyer (1990), Sheldon (1971), and Steers (1977) have all found a positive correlation between organizational commitment and working age.

In their study of the relationship between employee perception and affective commitment, including their common antecedent and outcome variables, Stinglhamber and Vandenberghe (2003) used longitudinal research methods to test the relationships of internal and external working conditions, the perception of support from management or the organization, the affective commitment of management or the organization, and employment turnover across 283 samples. It was found that the affective commitment of management is a complete mediating variable of employment turnover as well as the perception of support from management. The perception of support from the organization was also determined to be a partial mediating variable of satisfaction with internal working conditions and the affective commitment of the organization and a complete mediating variable of satisfaction with external working conditions and the affective commitment of the organization. Finally, the perception of support from management was found to bea complete mediating variable of the internal working conditions and affective commitment of management.

Other scholars have concerned themselves with the relationship between organizational commitment and organizational citizenship. Johnson and Chang (2006), for example, examined the connection and differences among employees' self-image, self-regulatory mechanisms, and organizational commitment, concluding that there is a significant correlation between affective commitment and employees' self-image due to the internalization of goals and norms of the group. Since employees tend to maintain individual investment interests and avoid negative results, continuance commitment was also found to have a relationship with self-image, which is the buffer variable between organizational commitment and organizational citizenship. Generally speaking, when employees have a strong group self-image, affective commitment appears to be more closely related to organizational citizenship; and when they have a strong individual self-image, continuance commitment relates more closely to organizational citizenship.

As recent research has focused more on the process, organizational commitment has also been increasingly viewed as an important intermediate variable in various research modeling, including leadership, employment turnover, organizational support, organizational citizenship, and human resources. These research models have also accounted for the adjustment or buffer effect of situational factors.

2.2.2 Review of Research on Organizational Commitment

Research on organizational commitment has addressed both the structure of organizational commitment as well as the various underlying factors that may affect it. Different scholars have different understandings of the structure of organizational commitment, with some measuring it from a single dimension and others using two, three or even four dimensions. As discussed above, organizational commitment in China has been categorized into five dimensions, two of which are unique to China, thereby suggesting that it can also vary geographically and that the use of organizational commitment questionnaires in different countries may yield different results.

That said, little attention has been paid to organizational commitment in Japanese-funded enterprises in China, particularly in the manufacturing industry, nor have many studies focused on the impact of organizational ethical climate on organizational commitment in general, much less in the context of Japanese-funded enterprises in China. Understanding these dynamics is essential in order to help them foster an organizational ethical climate that promotes widespread organizational commitment among employees.

2.3 Research on Job Performance

2.3.1 Current Research on Job Performance

1. *Definition of job performance*

Research to date offers several different definitions and measurements of job performance. Based on both domestic and international studies, Brouthers (2010) defines job performance as the realization of organizational working objectives and the value of employees. Borman and Motowidlo (1997) contend that job performance can be assessed by the individual's ability and level of achievement towards organizational goals, while Yang Jie and others have defined it in terms of the result of the working process, i.e. the achieved output in a certain period of time by an individual or organization through a certain approach. Finally, Fu and others believe job performance should be expressed as a combination of factors, behaviors and qualities, a definition, which appears to be especially useful for the management of job performance. Generally speaking, job performance is comprised of two components: organizational performance and individual performance. Organizational performance is the ultimate goal of individual performance, and individual performance is an integral part of organizational performance.

2. *Structure and measurement of organizational performance*

Research on the structure of job performance forms the basis for its accurate measurement, the study of which has evolved over time from a two-dimensional to a four-dimensional model. Borman and Motowidlo (1997) have argued that job performance is independently informed by both task performance and relationship performance, with task performance referring to the condition of tasks completed directly or indirectly by employees, and relationship performance referring to individual contributions of emotions and values. While job performance does not directly involve employees' production or service activities, it can have a significant impact on the completion of tasks and entails such organizational, social and psychological behavior as dedication, coordination and interpersonal relationships. It also benefits organizational communication, reduces tension and promotes cooperation, so as to help individuals achieve personal goals and improve the organization's effectiveness.

According to Luo (2001) and others who have studied the structure of job performance in China, task performance and relationship performance have been found to contribute independently to overall organizational performance while supporting each other at the same time. Han and Liao (2006) have also concluded that the separation of task and relationship performance has a significant effect on job performance while helping to enhance incentives and improve the enthusiasm and performance of employees.

Yet with increased economic globalization, employees must also adapt to environmental and organizational changes, the intensification of market competition, and the evolution of working tasks. Allworth has therefore proposed a third dimension of job performance known as adaptive performance, to assess the adaptability of employees to new working environments, tasks and technical requirements. In their study of middle managers, Tan and Sun (2009) have also identified a third component in individual characteristics performance, which they argue is essential to the fair and reliable assessment of managers.

According to Wen (2005), however, the performance of middle managers should include four dimensions, namely task performance, relationship performance, adaptation performance, and effort performance. Han et al. (2007) have also proposed a four-dimensional model comprised of task performance, relationship performance, learning performance, and innovation performance. In this model, task performance and relationship performance are continuance performances, while learning performance and innovation performance is improvement performances focused on developing employees' potential. Subsequent research conducted by Zhang (2009) has since confirmed the accuracy of this model.

2.3.2 Review of Research on Job Performance

In fact, scholarly insight on job performance in China is relatively mature. Yet there is still no universally accepted measurement for job performance, and most studies have failed to adequately address its relationship with organizational ethical climate and organizational commitment. Another aim of this research is therefore to measure job performance in Japanese-funded manufacturing enterprises in China using the four-dimensional model discussed above, as referenced in Han Yi's job performance measurement questionnaire.

2.4 The Theoretical Basis for the Feasibility of Organizational Ethical Climate from the Perspective of Economic Ethics

2.4.1 The Notion of Economic Ethics

1. ***Ethical thinking in western economics***

Business ethics is the ethics of business management. Ethical issues are involved in all business related organizations, and there are ethical issues in all business organizations, including ethics of business activities such as technology, business, finance, accounting, security, and management within the organizations. There are inherent ethical issues between any organization and society in conducting business activities. Therefore, business ethics mainly analyzes the business activities of organizations from an ethical perspective.

Economic ethics studies the moral phenomena and ethical issues in the socio-economic field and economic behavior subjects. It is an interdisciplinary subject of ethics and economics. It is based on moral theory and more includes production ethics, distribution ethics, consumption ethics, etc. It is based on the premise of revealing the inherent relationship between economy and ethics, and its starting point is to explain the consistency of ethical issues and economic issues from an economic perspective.

Therefore, business ethics can basically be attributed to the category of ethics, sometimes directly referred as corporate ethics. However, economic ethics belongs to the category of economics. It mainly studies ethical issues in the economic field and reveals the inherent consistency between economics and ethics.

This study attempts to study the impact of organizational ethical climate from the perspective of economic ethics. Although business and economic fields have a high degree of overlap, and business ethics and economic ethics have strong similarities, this research still advocates the use of economic ethics to study the issue of organizational ethics, to explain the consistency of organizational ethical issues in economic activities from a broader economic perspective, and to explain organizational ethical issues from the economic perspective, rather than confined to studying ethics in the economic field, which is also the difference between this study and other studies of economic ethics and business ethics studies.

Western ethical thinking, which evolved with western rational knowledge, extends from 'the natural law' of Aristotle to the 'the moral resources' of Fukuyama. And there is always an emphasis on a process from a target and result of scientific rational market competition to form 'freedom, equality, justice and fairness' in the end.

(1) Aristotle: human intent (the natural perspectives of the human)

Aristotle takes the obtaining and practice of all virtues as a way to reach a goal. Since Aristotle put forward the concept of human intent and the natural law, for a comparatively long period of time, all the developments of moral philosophy have centered on 'the natural law', and many philosophers are stamped deeply with the brand of 'the natural law'. Whether from the form of ethics or the behavior in practice, 'the natural law' bears great value to structure ethical economics in the development of moral philosophy.

(2) Adam Smith: The egoistic and altruistic behavior of humans (the perspectives of humanity)

Adam Smith believes that humanity involves both egoism and altruism. Instead of being unrestricted, egoism in humanity is restricted by ethical and moral factors. Therefore, a single egoism has significant negative externality and needs to be restricted by altruism. In his book *The Theory of Moral Sentiments*, based on the assumption that human nature is good, Smith proposes that things derive from human sympathy and altruistic sentiment as the general base and motivation of human ethical behavior. But in his book *The Wealth of Nations*, Smith views human nature as being evil as an assumption in political economics and believes that a basic motivation in human economic activities is a kind of pursuit of the interest of individual egoism. In his theories, the idea that the altruism of human nature is good is interwoven with the idea that the egoism of human nature is evil. Humans are seen as the product of social, economic life and moral life, and egoism coexists with altruism (Smith 1759, 1768).

(3) Marx: The alienation of labor and human alienation (the perspectives of institutions)

In Marx's book Capital, by means of depicting economies, he finds the alienation of labor, which leads to the phenomenon of human alienation, exposes the flaws in capitalist society and the exploitative features of capitalism, points to the exposed and oppressed social status of the proletariat, promotes the unification of the proletariat to rise up and overturn the rule of capitalism, and launches institutional revolution to develop economics and humans harmoniously. Marx thinks that the capitalist system cannot structure ethical economics and that only under the communist society system, could human all-round development be realized and realize the organic integration of ethics and economics (Marx 1867).

(4) McIntyre: Human internal interests and external interests (individual and social perspectives).

McIntyre thinks that as a species existing in society, human has the requirements of internal interests and external interests. In his book *After Virtue*, he thinks that internal interests come from efforts in humans. In other words, this is about how to use a brand new way to lead people to achieve their goal. In his opinion, a kind of practice includes various excellent standards, and compliance with rules and obtaining profit drives these internal interests.

The external interests that McIntyre proposes have a character, which is a kind of property of an individual, just like power, reputation, and money. In his view, external interest, from the point of characteristics, refers to a competitive object. And certainly, both winners and losers exist in a competition. External interest is entirely the consequence of competition. However, to obtain external interest is beneficial to the whole community in which people participate in practice (McIntyre 2003).

(5) Amartya Sen: human rights (the perspective of moral regression)

Amartya Sen believes that in the contemporary world, we need to focus on economic development, which is taken as an overwhelming issue. Sen discovers the ethnical tendencies of economic development and how it results in economic bottlenecks. Therefore, in his book Economics, he emphasizes the role ethics plays in economic development, and he appeals for ethics to return to economics. Sen focuses on human rights and takes it as the start of the research, trying to put ethical factors into an economic framework to strengthen and make more realistic the explanatory power of modern economics (Sen 2003).

(6) *Francis Fukuyama: ethical resource is a special transformable social capital (the perspective of competitiveness of the times requirement)*

In Francis Fukuyama's book *The Social Virtues And The Creation of Prosperity*, he empirically inspects and analyses the differences of social trust among Europe, Japan, and Southeast Asia nations. He reveals different impacts and effects which "social virtue", just like integrity and so on, bring to modernized economic life in those nations and districts. Although ethical factors cannot be proved inaccurate calculations to contribute to economics, it can be proved that things such as transaction cost and extra transaction cost can be reduced under the influence of ethical factors. Actually, it is a kind of benefit of economic growth.

2. ***The theoretical definition of Economic ethics***

Lee (1992) argues that economic ethics is the moral idea formed in real social-economic activities by people who criticize and impose restrictions on it. In fact, this moral idea refers to two things: the moral idea directly formed by people in their economic life and behavior, as well as people's perception and evaluation of such ideas. According to Simha (1972), economic ethics is the value system for moral ideas, evaluations, principles, and norms that specifically directs the economic life and behaviors of economic entities (enterprises or individuals). It coordinates economic interest relations between economic activities and entities in order to make economic activities harmonious and beneficial to the development of social-economic productive forces and to promote the material and spiritual development of economic entities. According to Wang (1997), however, economic ethics is the study of the basic rules of how people perfect their lives and coordinate their interests, including what constitutes value orientation and misconduct.

More recently, Weeks (2006) has suggested that economic ethics is both the ethical spirit or temperament of economic activities, or the fundamental moral view of such activities, as well as the theorization of such spirit, temperament and view, or the theorized moral understanding, evaluation and norm of economic activities. Shafer (2009) views economic ethics as values, norms and moral spirits formed in social-economic activities by people who restrict and regulate their economic interest relations with it. As such, it is not only a kind of behavioral norm for regulating economic interest relations between people but also a kind of practical spirit of how economic entities grasp their social-economic lives. The everyday ethics of enterprises, corporations, businesses, consumers and business management all belong to the category of economic ethics, which is comprised of three levels—micro (individuals), mid-level (business organizations such as enterprises) and macro (economic system, macroeconomic development strategy, and economic policy)—and four aspects (production, exchanges, distribution and consumption).

Although many Japanese companies in China are more concerned with local laws than organizational ethics, it is important to mention that these two aspects are not at the same level. The law is the minimum requirement for local Japanese companies, but ethics constitute a higher-level requirement that adheres to the law but goes beyond it. Steven (2004) emphasizes the role of "moral constraints" in the study of internal control of corporate governance. He pointed out that "the effectiveness of internal controls cannot be separated from the integrity and ethical values of those who establish, implement and monitor them. Integrity and ethical values are the primary factors controlling the environment, and they influence the design, implementation, and monitoring of other components of internal control."

Xiao (2004) believes that economic ethics generally refers to the ethical principles and ethics that the commercial industry and its practitioners should follow in market exchange activities. Another broad understanding includes all market entities in commodity circulation and exchange activities. The code of ethics and the code of conduct are a kind of exchange morality. It includes both: market competition ethics that the operators should abide by, as well as consumer ethics.

Liu (2013) believes that the external side effects of organizational activities are beyond the control of current laws and regulations and that they therefore need to be complementary to the behavior of economic ethics. Although the internal control of the organization is a form of behavior that stipulates various internal economic relations, it is essentially based on certain economic ethics.

3. ***The relationship between economics and ethics***

Scholars generally believe that there is a kind of isomorphism, or intrinsic unity of logic, between economics and ethics, just as there is between an "economic man" and a "moral man," and it is widely acknowledged that ethics continues to play a vital role in the development of the socialist market economy as well as the promotion of economic growth. Lee (1992) argues that morality does not necessarily restrict the self-interest of members of society, but rather remodels such interest within the causal system of historical development. Economic laws in and of themselves are the result of people's activities, but the understanding of such laws are also affected by people's values, and history shows that trying to analyze people's moral principles while ignoring their economic incentives will almost always fail. According to Simha (1972), the concept of economic ethics thereby functions as the coordinator of interest relations in economic life as well as interpersonal relationships in economic activities, so that economic life will benefit the orderly development of human society.

Theoretically, the relationship between economic activities and moral behaviors is a relationship of economic and non-economic factors, or in a more abstract sense, the relationship between material and spiritual production. In a certain way, economics is value-free, yet when judged in terms of its relationship with ethics as a reflection of economic conditions, the two are essentially the same. Weeks (2006) suggest that the birth of ethics does not naturally entail the elimination of material desires, nor does it mean the replacement of material relations. Rather, it offers a way to deal with these relations in a more reasonable manner that is more conducive to the acquisition of material goods, so as to maximize both individual and group interest.

Economics is the law of practical uses, and ethics is the law of people. The latter contains attributes of the former, and the two necessarily overlap: economics has ethical significance and ethics has economic functions. The development of an economy, society, and people all call for the driving force of humanism, of which ethics is the vital source. The unification of economic determinism and the theory of humanism-drive is a revelation of the relations between economics and ethics. According to Shafer (2009), mature economics and ethics give rise to each other insofar as ethics can be a driving force of production, and economics a moral field in which ethics is an intangible asset that can often take precedence over tangible ones. To an enterprise, brand products are both material and ethical entities. And when it comes to sustainable development, the realization of economic purposes must necessarily satisfy the ethical requirements of society. Intuitively, economics and ethics are therefore to some extent one and the same.

2.4.2 The Lack of Research on Organizational Ethical Climate from the Perspective of Economic Ethics

Most studies have approached organizational ethical climate and organizational commitment from the perspective of management, philosophy or ethics in the belief that the fields of ethics and economics are mutually exclusive, and that organizational ethical climate necessarily belongs to the former. But this is mistaken. After all, the study of organizational ethical climate is concerned with employees' behavior in an organization, and economics is also the study of human behavior. Thus, studies of organizational ethical climate and economics share the same foundation. Moreover, as more employees begin to work for foreign-owned enterprises and adapt to their corresponding organizational ethical climates, the field of economic ethics should be able to provide a more reasonable and persuasive theoretical basis for their behavior (Fig. 2.3).

In the research of organizational ethical issues, a simple economic perspective is inappropriate insofar as economics assumes that human behavior is cold, simple and rational. In fact, however, the individuals with whom economic ethics is concerned are complex and often unreasonable. Therefore, the study of ethical issues should be approached from both an ethical and economic perspective in order to achieve more authentic, persuasive and practical insights. Another advantage of studying organizational ethical climate in terms of economic ethics is its ability to approach organizational ethical problems from multiple perspectives. For example, economic ethics pays more attention to the localization of organizational ethical climates, which is more practical than the use of simple economic or ethical theories and is another reason for the adoption of economic ethics in this research (Fig. 2.4).

Moreover, the theory of economic ethics is also the most appropriate research paradigm. While the study of organizational ethics necessarily belongs to the category of ethics, research on organizational ethical climate also involves issues of human capital insofar as effective climates can promote productivity. The formation and manifestation of human capital in turn involves two aspects: employees' incentives for earning income and employers' purpose in developing the enterprise. In other words, the aim of employees' human capital investment is to meet their individual needs, while employers tend to treat human capital as an input or tool to support the development of enterprises. But because human capital also includes the bodies of employees, employers must also assume certain obligations in the development of enterprises. This is the basis for the bifurcation of related research into the study of

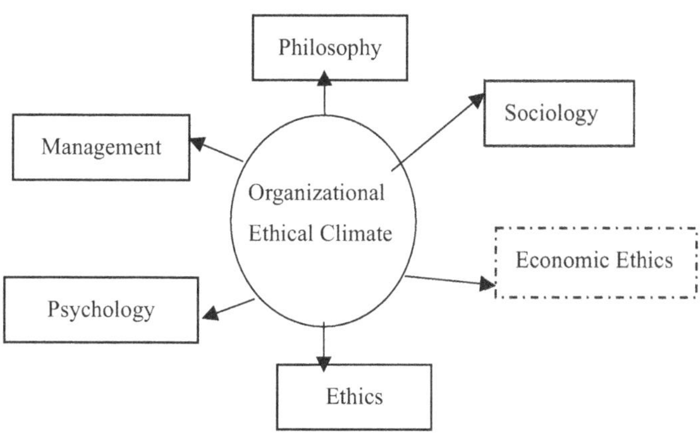

Fig. 2.3 Theoretical approaches to organizational ethical climate

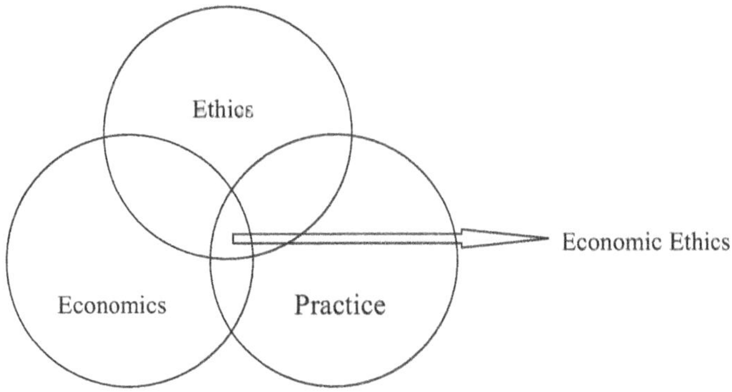

Fig. 2.4 Economic ethics

labor economics and human resources management. That said, while organizational ethics shares characteristics with human capital, its scope is necessarily broader in that it approaches the concept of human capital under the assumption that morality is also a force of productivity. Economic ethics was therefore developed in order to integrate organizational ethics and avoid the tendency of corporations to neglect aspects of human capital over the course of the development process (see Fig. 2.5).

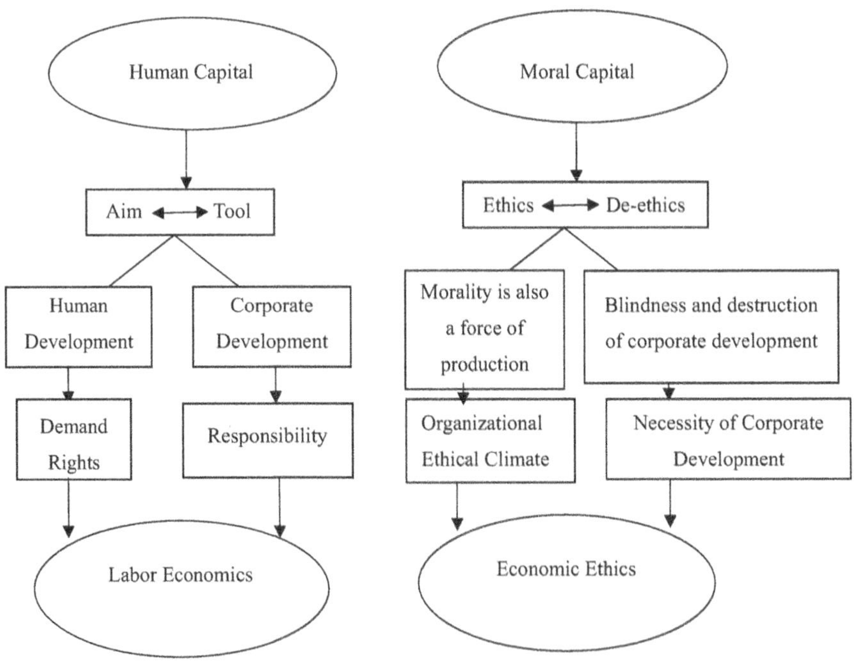

Fig. 2.5 Labor economics and economic ethics

2.4.3 The Feasibility of Research on Organizational Ethical Climate from the Perspective of Economic Ethics

The theoretical basis for studying the feasibility of organizational ethical climate from the perspective of economic ethics is as follows:

1. *The economic endogenous theory*

Wimbush (1992) holds that the economy is comprised of relationships and that any individual economic behavior is always based on and reflects these relationships among people who engage in economic activities. Thus, ethics and management are often in conflict and need to be coordinated.

Romer (1986) believes that the economy can promote sustainable growth without relying on external forces. The endogenous progress is the decisive factor for maintaining sustained economic growth internally, through the accumulation of human capital, technological progress, market conditions, political stability, etc.

2. *The essential consensus theory*

Ethics helps people rationally and effectively deal with material desire, which in turn maximizes individual and group interests. Economic tools can have ethical significance, while ethical practices also hold economic power, meaning the two methodologies can be combined. Economic, social and human development all relies on humanitarian development, of which ethics is a key part. Economic and ethical determinism together explain the relationship between economics and ethics. Other scholars believe that a rational economy is a perfect economy and that economics and ethics are mutually reinforcing. According to Xiaoxi (1997), for example, economics and ethics are the mutual conditions for co-existence in a mature economic and ethical system, and that as discussed above, morality represents an intangible force for production that can often be more important than tangible assets.

3. *The mutual penetration theory*

Trevino (1986) divides the social organism into three levels: the external material level, the mid-level management system, and the inner conceptual level which includes ethics. He also considers these three levels of the social organism to be subject to moral adjustment, which illustrates mutual penetration. Thus, economics and ethics are interactive with coordinated development. Yet another view (Zhang 1999) holds that the interaction of economics and ethics are necessarily conflicting in nature. It takes practice as the objective basis, ethical thoughts and their development as the subjective premise, and the interaction among different practice methods in the same social time and space for the achievement of the mechanism. Thus, economics and ethics are consistent in the overall historical development process, but there are conflicts in specific historical periods as well. The conflict between economics and ethics is the conflict of practice under their interacted relationships.

Romer (1986) believe that the economy can promote sustainable growth without relying on external forces. The endogenous progress is the decisive factor for maintaining sustained economic growth internally, through the accumulation of human capital, technological progress, market conditions, political stability, etc.

2.4.4 The Theoretical Foundation for Organizational Ethical Climate in Terms of Labor Economics

In terms of labor economics, there are three theoretical foundations for organizational ethical climate based on the theories of transaction cost, long-term contracts, and team production.

1. *Transaction cost theory*

The existence of external transaction costs ultimately drives enterprises to attempt to reduce these costs. But enterprises also have internal problems related to their division of labor and management costs, which include operational and internal transaction costs. As enterprises expand, their external transaction costs can be significantly reduced, while the cost of their internal transactions tends to increase. A high degree of consistency in behavior is therefore necessary to effectively minimize management and other operational costs.

According to Lynn Sharp Paine, "a generally accepted goal and a complete set of value systems are central to organizational power and the root of organizational personality (logo), which could bring organizational satisfaction and benefit long-term development and prosperity. In adversity, a reasonable set of value systems is a buffer against short-term temptations that avoid long-term benefits."[4] In this sense, a favorable ethical climate can therefore function as a flexible means of controlling employees while lowering supervisory costs. Generally speaking, the operation of organizations, therefore, requires an effective control system consisting of rules, regulations and supervisory schemes to control the behavior of employees. Although themselves non-productive, these systems tend to require significant human, material and financial resources as well as sufficient time to develop and maintain. And even after investing in such resources, organizations may still not be able to completely prevent unjust or immoral behaviors. Thus, compared with organizational control and supervisory systems, organizational ethical values tend to cost less and perform better.

2. *Long-term contract theory*

According to Victor (1988), organizational ethical climates have the potential to enhance employees' sense of identity and belonging towards the organization, while forming a common code of conduct, stabilizing the workforce and reducing turnover,

[4]Lynn S. Paine. Cases in Leadership, Ethics, and Organizational Integrity (Shenyang: Northeast University of Finance Press, 1999) 1999.

which is ultimately conducive to the improvement of corporate economic performance. In terms of economic ethics, the long-term stability of the workforce has a positive impact on organizational performance to the extent that a strong mutual understanding between employees and enterprises tend to form long-term implicit contracts that enhance the safety and satisfaction of work.

Second, because organizational ethics establish a common code of conduct, employees are able to work in harmony, and the more detailed the division of labor is, the higher the labor efficiency will be. At the same time, however, such increased division of labor also exacerbates the difficulty of coordination, thereby increasing management costs. Yet because the existence of a common code of conduct promotes mutual respect, tolerance, humility, and equality, it also tends to lower operational costs and increase overall organizational performance.

Finally, a good organizational ethical climate helps form a relatively stable relationship among employees, enabling enterprises to invest in human capital and employee training in order to improve the organizational commitment of employees while encouraging greater working efficiency.

3. *Team production theory*

According to the team production theory proposed by Armen Alchian and Harold Demsetz in *Production, Information Costs, and Economic Organization* (1972), team production is a cooperative production activity that uses several types of resources, though the products are not the sum of each resource. Supervision is also necessary to coordinate and manage team production, or else the losses from so-called free-riders will offset the achievements of the team. Teams also inevitably encounter the problem of individual salary measurement. For if members' salaries are based on the output of the entire team rather than individual contributions, some members may begin to shirk their responsibilities, eventually leading to lower output for the entire team. An important way to address this inefficiency is to establish an organizational ethical climate and common code of conduct designed to increase the team's efficiency while reducing the costs arising out of free-riders.

2.5 Summary

Previous studies have mainly focused on the fields of management and philosophy in their analysis of organizational ethical climate, organizational commitment, and job performance, while relatively few have approached the topic from the perspective of economic ethics. Yet members of organizations exhibit behavior, organizational commitment and job performance under a certain organizational ethical climate to maximize their individual preferences. Here, the term "preference" is used because members control certain behavior, including working hours, short-term or long-term goals, and various psychological perceptions based on their personal preferences. It is therefore a broader and much more inclusive approach than the concept of income maximization. In addition, employee preference also encompasses various types of balances, including work-life balance and work-personal perception balance, and generally exhibits strong stability, which could ultimately support an analysis of employee behavior under certain organizational ethical climates.

The reasons of why there aye only few literature studies on organizational ethical climate from the perspective of economic ethics, are as follows:

First, economic ethics includes three levels: the macro policy, the meso organization, and the micro individual. At the macro level, it mainly studies the ethical issues of the socio-economic system environment in which companies must operate. At the meso level, it mainly studies the relations between companies, manufacturers, various trade unions, consumer organizations, and industry associations. It also studies the rights and obligations of organizations and society, the state, and moral issues in their internal management. The micro level research focuses on issues related to personal interests and moral values. In essence, at the meso and micro levels, the issues of economic ethics research are related respectively to the business and economic fields, and there is a large overlap in the business and economic fields at the meso and micro levels, so from the literature in terms of types, they all fall into the category of ethics.

Second, ethical issues are cross-disciplinary issues. From the perspective of research approaches, most scholars have a background in sociology, philosophy, and education. With the expansion of the economic empire, economics began to penetrate into the study of ethical issues, mainly studying ethical issues in the economic field. However, according to the current literature review, few economists specialize in ethical issues, because the corresponding theories cannot be confirmed in ethical issues due to the immeasurability of ethics.

Third, in essence, although there are ethical problems in the economic field, it is a kind of existence outside the market, and cannot be adjusted by the market. Therefore, few economists are able to establish market theory to explain the problems existing outside the market, which is also an important reason why there are few corresponding ethical theories in economics at present.

Moreover, organizations not only engage in economic activities but also non-economic ones, which can be expressed, as non-market behavior. With the continuing development of its economy, China attracts a large number of foreign companies. Yet over the course of its social and economic development, the standard of success for enterprises is no longer limited to simple economic efficiency indicators, but also includes enterprises' contributions to society. In an effort to examine the non-market behavior of enterprises from the perspective of economic ethics, this study therefore focuses on the formulation of non-market strategies as well as their impact on economic performance. The following chapters explain how this research was carried out.

Chapter 3
Research Design

This study employs documentary and empirical analysis, as well as case studies, to explore how the ethical atmosphere of organizations affects organizational commitment and job performance.

3.1 Research Methods

As pointed out in the preceding section in reality, not only ethical system of the organization but also its ethical climate may affect the unethical behavior of employees. However, these concepts come from different research fields. Prior studies have looked at the impact of the ethical climate of the organization and ethical system of the organization on the unethical behavior of employees. At the same time, the impact of organizational fairness and its behavior on employees' behavior was studied in organizational behavior theory and social psychology.

However, there are few studies dealing with the concept of organizational ethical climate in economic ethics research. Also, in the research on organizational ethical climate, concepts of the economic ethics framework have rarely been used until recent.

It is surprising, because both research fields treat negative behavior, such as employees' unethical behavior and retaliatory actions that are disadvantageous to organizations, as a common research theme. Probably, the cause is the difference between the academic homes of researchers in both research fields. Until now only some forward-thinking economic ethics researchers and trainers from organizations focused on the synthesis of both fields and discussed only their involvement. It is obvious that further interdisciplinary research is required in the future, combining both fields.

In organizational ethical climate research, discussions related to corporate ethics research have been on rise in recent years. This is a serious trend that could become the first step in a new research integrating and merging the two fields that so far have been developed separately. Further development of organizational fairness research

© Science Press and Springer Nature Singapore Pte Ltd. 2020

K. Ryu, *The Impact of Organizational Ethical Climate on Organizational Commitment and Job Performance*, https://doi.org/10.1007/978-981-15-2813-2_3

is expected in the future. On the other hand, if we were to link both research fields by incorporating the discussion about organizational fairness into corporate ethics research, it would be possible to obtain new knowledge by extending the existing theory. By using that concept and methodology, it is possible that empirical studies will be expanded into corporate ethics research, which before was mainly based on normative methods. Even in practical terms, we can only estimate the effect from qualitative perspective, because it provides possibilities for quantitatively measuring the effect of the organizational ethical systems and measures. Accumulating this type of empirical research will lead to the development of measures and, as a practical matter, more effective institutions.

This research tackles the problem described above and examines from the empirical viewpoint ethical systems of organizations, ethical climate of organizations, and mechanisms that influence unethical behavior of employees. Specifically, we synthesize research on the organizational ethical system that has been discussed in corporate ethics research in the past with research on the organizational ethical climate that has emerged in research discussions in recent years as an organization's ethical environment, and we reexamine their impact on unethical behavior. In addition, we advance discussions of prior research on organizational ethical climate by clarifying mechanisms of impact of organizational fairness on unethical behavior of employees, and we link both research fields of economic ethics and organizational ethical climate. Furthermore, we also used these concepts to develop a quantitative survey and interviews for Japanese companies, therefore contributing to theory development in both research fields. Quantitative and qualitative results of the study are used to derive practical implications.

3.1.1 Literature Review Method

The review of the literature sheds light on the definition, structure, and measurements of organizational ethical climate, along with the antecedent variables and outcome variables that affect it, as well as the definition, classification, and measurements for organizational commitment and job performance. This helps to establish a solid foundation for both the research itself and empirical studies that follow.

Trevino and Weaver (2003) show a difference between normative research and empirical research in ethics by comparing five dimensions of research (Table 3.1). The first difference is that the scholarly background of normative research is in philosophy, theology, and liberal arts. In contrast, that of empirical research is in business administration and social sciences. Further, normative research evaluates phenomena from the ideal and include value judgments what is supposed to be ethical in the behavior of an individual and organization. In contrast, empirical research intends to describe, explain, and predict phenomena by keeping a distance from value judgments of right or wrong.

The second difference is the language used. For example, when thinking about the sense of the word "ethical behavior", normative research interprets it as "the correct

Table 3.1 Comparison of normative research and empirical research

	Normative research	Empirical research
Academic home	Philosophy, theology, liberal arts	Business administration, social science
Language (a definition of ethical behavior)	Evaluation (correct, impartial and fair behavior)	Description (ethical choice and decision-making, regardless of right or wrong and good or bad)
Underlying assumptions regarding human moral agency	Determinant, responsibility	Relationship than autonomy
Theory: purpose, scope, and application	Prescribed, abstract analysis and criticism	Explanation and prediction possible to measure concretely influence on behavior

behavior in terms of ethics and morality". In contrast, the interpretation of empirical research is "the behavior which includes ethical judgment", regardless of right or wrong in terms of ethics.

The third difference is in the underlying assumptions regarding human moral agency. In normative research, a human is an autonomous being and describe their own behavior and responsibility in terms of ethical and moral judgments. In empirical research, however, a human is in a relative existence and consists of various causal relationships inside and outside of the individual.

The fourth difference is in purpose, scope, and application of the theory. Normative research intends to analyze end evaluate the phenomenon by referring to an ideal. In contrast, empirical research describes, explain and predict the real phenomenon.

3.1.2 Empirical Research Methods

This study involves a quantitative analysis of data collected from questionnaires focusing on organizational ethical climate, organizational commitment, and job performance. According to the Annual Report of Statistics on Japanese Nationals Overseas of the Ministry of Foreign Affairs, as of October 2016, the number of Japanese-funded enterprises in Japan was 33,390, accounting for 46.94% of the total number of Japanese-funded enterprises in the world, which is the most. The number of Japanese-funded enterprises in China with an unclear industry distinction is 30,288, while the number of Japanese-funded manufacturing enterprises in China is 1,810, accounting for 58.35% of the Japanese-funded enterprises in China with clear industry distinction. Moreover, established, long-time Japanese-funded enterprises in China are in manufacturing, namely electric appliance manufacturing industry, to name Hitachi,

Panasonic, Toshiba, Sony, Mitsubishi, or Toyo among others. Therefore, this study mainly selects Japanese enterprises in the manufacturing industry as research objects.

In order to ensure the representativeness of the study, the data on the Japanese Enterprises in China (2016–2017 edition, Japanese Enterprises in China) were used. Initially, the manufacturing enterprises with a registered capital of more than US$100 million in China were selected, 71 companies in total (see details in Appendix 11). From these 71 companies, 22 were qualified as "Japanese enterprises in China", meeting the screening condition of a Japanese investment ratio of 100%, and investment in China for more than 10 years (as in the Table 3.2).

Because the company's management will integrate the cultural concepts of the home-country's management into the local corporate culture, it is expected that the Japanese leader of Japanese-funded enterprises in China will integrate Japanese business culture concepts into their Chinese companies. If a company is managed based

Table 3.2 The establish time and capital of qualified Japanese manufacturing enterprises in China

Name of enterprise in China	Established in	Registered capital (US$)
Nissan (China) Investment Co., Ltd.	2003.05	1 billion 15 million
Sony (China) Ltd.	1996.10	1 billion 6.935 million
Panasonic Corporation of China	1994.08	986.18 million
YKK (China) Investment Co., Ltd.	2002.12	375 million
Minebea Electronics & HI-Tech Components (Shanghai) Ltd.	1994.09	239.06 million
Denso (China) Investment Co., Limited	2003.02	221.4569 million
Fujifilm (China) Investment Co., Ltd.	2001.04	213.397 million
Eagle Industry (Wuxi) Co., Ltd.	2002.09	211 million
Hitachi Air-Conditioning Technology (Suzhou) Co., Ltd.	2004.10	200 million
Hitachi China Ltd.	1994.10	193 million
Suntory (China) Holding Co., Ltd.	1999.07	180 million
Tokuyama Chemicals (Zhejiang) Co., Ltd.	2005.05	177 million
SMC (China) Co., Ltd. China	1994.09	153.27 million
Kirin (China) Investment Co., Ltd.	2004.12	150 million
Honda Auto Parts Manufacturing Co., Ltd.	2005.10	150 million
THK (China) Co., Ltd.	2005.09	142.3 million
Shanghai Kyocera Electronics Co., Ltd.	1995.12	128.46 million
Toyota Motor (China) Investment Co., Ltd.	2001.07	118 million
Honda Motor (China) Investment Co., Ltd.	2004.01	115.94 million
NEC (China) Co., Ltd.	1996.12	106.774 million
Ajinomoto (China) Co., Ltd.	1996.12	102.83 million
Omron (China) Co., Ltd.	1994.05	100.6 million

on a several culture (among two or more countries), inevitably it will have a mixed-culture concept of different countries, which affects the overall atmosphere of an organization. In such cases it will be difficult to distinguish which organizational ethic climate has which impact on the final work performance. To ensure the maximum comparability of organizational ethics between the companies being investigated, we avoid the influence of multiple cultures on the corporate climate. For the research, companies with a 100% share of Japanese investment were chosen to confirm the interdependence of Japanese companies. We further set the screening conditions for "investment in China for more than ten years" to ensure that the business operations are relatively stable, the enterprise data are relatively complete, and the research can produce representative and correct results.

Further, from the list of 22 companies, enterprises for surveying were selected according to following three principles: (1) the largest number of manufacturing employees, (2) the widest distribution area, (3) the survey sample should cover 31 provinces, autonomous regions and municipalities in China. As a result, 13 companies were identified as research objects of this study. With participation of human resources departments of the selected 13 enterprises, and according to a certain proportion of the number of employees in the region, employees of the Japanese-funded manufacturing enterprises in China were randomly sampled. Human resource departments helped to distribute the questionnaires to these employees. Altogether, 20,000 questionnaires were distributed, and 11,083 valid responses collected at a high response rate of 51%.

Statistical methods were employed to research survey responses. Data were analyzed by the principal component analysis (PCA) method, and Structural Equation Modeling (SEM) used as a follow-up approach to determine relationships between observed variables and the bases, namely, how the effect of various types of organizational ethical climate on organizational commitment and job performance differs in degree and scope. The results should help establish a foundation for identifying effective human resource management measures.

In the research, both the "organizational ethical climate" and the "type of organizational commitment" are latent variables. Therefore, the observable variables were used to analyze the organizational ethical climate and the type of organizational commitment. The PCA is mainly used to divide complex multidimensional factors into several dimensions with independent relationships to measure the concept of relative comprehensiveness. Just as the organizational ethical climate generally has a relatively independent structural dimension, these are the main components of measuring the organizational ethical climate. Thus, the paper uses the PCA payload to measure the organizational ethical climate and the type of organizational commitment of the manufacturing industry of JFEs in China.

The results of the PCA were combined with the SEM analysis to study relationships between observed variables and organizational ethical climate, and relationships between observed variables and organizational commitment. Then relationships between organizational ethical climate and job performance, as well as relationships between organizational commitment and job performance were studied. The reason for choosing the SEM analysis is that by using this method latent variables can be measured by observable variables, and also relationships between latent variables and the adjustment between latent variables can be explored. Thus, SEM is the most appropriate method for this study. We also use SEM for empirical analysis in other parts of this research.

The SEM analysis is a typical method for dealing with latent variables. It is impossible to measure directly organizational ethics, organizational commitment, and job performance because all of them need to be measured in many dimensions. Therefore, these three variables are latent variables, which need to be measured in several dimensions to cover comprehensively all aspects of the organizational ethical climate, organizational commitment, and job performance. Other methods can't match SEM in this respect.

To verify the hypotheses set up of the previous chapter, this study surveys Japanese companies that are listed with the Tokyo Stock Exchange. Questionnaire surveys were conducted on employees of the companies, and statistical analysis of the data was carried out. The companies were selected from machinery and food product industries. Two companies have formal systems on ethics and compliance such as employee behavioral standards and codes of conduct.

We requested cooperation in the survey and signed confidentiality agreements with each of the selected company. The agreements limits use of results this research for purposes of academic research, publication of the research results should not include specific company names, advance agreement should be obtained from the companies before disclosing content of the research. Therefore, both companies were asked to review the content, and descriptions in the study were changed from specific ones to general and abstract, it that was asked by the reviewing company.

The following procedure was employed: first, questionnaires in envelopes were sent to all employees who are involved with this survey. Next, employees answered questionnaires by the designated date and each of them sent back these sealed envelopes to staff as in-house mail. Employees filled out the survey form anonymously, put it in a sealed envelope, and, before deadline, submitted it to the person responsible in each office. Then, responsible individuals in each company collected responses and delivered them to the researcher directly.

3.2 Empirical Research Design

3.2.1 Reasons for using PCA and SEM models

First, the PCA mainly is used to divide complex multi-dimensional measures into several dimensions with independent relationships that measure relatively comprehensive concepts. Just as that the organizational ethical climate and organizational commitment generally have relatively independent multiple structural dimensions, this method measures the main components of the organizational ethical climate based on real data. Using the PCA can we effectively study interactions between different types of the ethical climate of organizations and different types of organizational commitments, and their impact on job performance. This method can more clearly analyze the nature of the problem. Therefore, in this research we choose to use the PCA.

Second, the SEM analysis is a typical method for dealing with latent variables. It is not possible to measure organizational ethical climate, organizational commitment, and job performance directly because they all need to be measured from many dimensions. These three variables are latent variables and need to be measured through several dimensions to cover comprehensively the organizational ethical climate, organizational commitment, and work performance. Therefore, in this research, the SEM analysis provides advantage over other methods.

3.2.2 Definition and Measurement Model for the Variables

1. *Demographic variables*

The first part of the questionnaire is comprised of nine demographic variables, including gender, age, education, work experience, and job level of the employee and others.

2. *Definition and measurement model for organizational ethical climate*

According to the literature review in Chap. 2, many scholars have done extensive research on the types and measurement of Organizational Ethical Climate. Agarwal (1999) constructed the five types of Organizational Ethical Climate; Schwepker (2001) developed the Organizational Ethical Climate measurement scale; Further, Arnaud (2004) used it to construct The Ethical Climate index. However, the Organizational Ethical Climate theory and measurement scale proposed by Victor and Cullen (1988) occupy a dominant position both theoretically and empirically. It has become the main tool for Chinese scholars to study the Organizational Ethical Climate.

Many scholars have studied Organizational Ethical Climate. However, through synthesizing the literature, it can be found that the Organizational Ethical Climate studied by different scholars is not the same. Some scholars believe that there are six types of Organizational Ethical Climate, but others believe that there are five, and so on. It means that different scholars formed different understanding of Organizational Ethical Climate because of different research countries (cultures) and different research objects. Also, there are significant differences in the definition of the scope of Organizational Ethics. Different organizational cultures largely determine different understandings of organizational ethics. Although Japan and China are both Eastern countries and their cultures share many similarities, there are great differences in business administration. Especially for JFEs in China, many of them are managed by a combination of Japanese and local cultures, which forms a special corporate culture. Under this special corporate culture, what kind of Japanese-owned Organizational Ethical Climate do JFEs in China have? This is a problem that needs to be studied, and it is the goal of this research. Therefore, this study mainly analyzes the Organizational Ethical Climate of JFEs in China and specifically measures the organizational ethics formed by JFEs in China under the combination of Japanese and Chinese organization cultures. We also analyze differences between organizational ethics found in JFEs in China and research conclusions of other scholars.

This study explores Japanese-funded manufacturing enterprises in China based on Victor's influential definition of organizational ethical climates the principle of judging ethical conduct and responding to ethical issues among employees of an organization. Under this theoretical framework set forth in Fig. 3.1 below, organizational ethical climate consists of nine dimensions: self-interest (instrumental), company profit (instrumental), efficiency, friendship (caring), team interest (caring), social responsibility, personal morality (independence), rules and procedures (rules), and laws and professional codes (law and code). Each dimension includes several indexes, and Stata is used to construct latent variables and conduct confirmatory analysis.

The questionnaire developed by Victor, which consists of the nine dimensions mentioned above. It is also used to evaluate organizational ethical climate based on the five-point Likert scale with values: "1-doesn't fit", "2-unfit partially", "3-not sure", "4-fit partially", "5-fit completely". As shown in the Attached List 1, this questionnaire has been proven in more than 170 studies to be highly credible and efficient, exhibiting stability among a wide range of cultures, industries, and organizations (Martin and Cullen 2006). Using the survey response data, credibility and validity of the questionnaire were tested. The credibility analysis of the questionnaire showed that a total alpha coefficient was 0.82 and a re-retested credibility coefficient was 0.88, indicating that the questionnaire has strong intrinsic credibility and re-retested credibility (see Fig. 3.1).

3. *Definition and measurement model for organizational commitment*

According to the literature review in Chap. 2, many scholars have conducted in-depth research on the types and measurements of organizational commitments. Allen and Meyer (1990) have studied and classified organizational commitments based on the theory of "two kinds of organization commitments" proposed by Becker (1960) and Porter and Mowday (1979). They believed that organizational commitments are divided into two types, emotional commitment, and continued commitment. Later, on these original two dimensions, Wiener (1982) proposed that organizational commitment should include three dimensions, named emotional commitment, continued commitment, and normative commitment. In addition, Meyer and Allen (1997) built the Organizational Commitment Measurement Questionnaire based on the three dimensions of organizational commitment that were proposed by Wiener (1982). Swailes (2002) divides organizational commitment into four types of behavioral commitments: emotional commitment, ongoing commitment, normative commitment, and behavioral commitment. Besides this, Blau and Gary (2001) combines

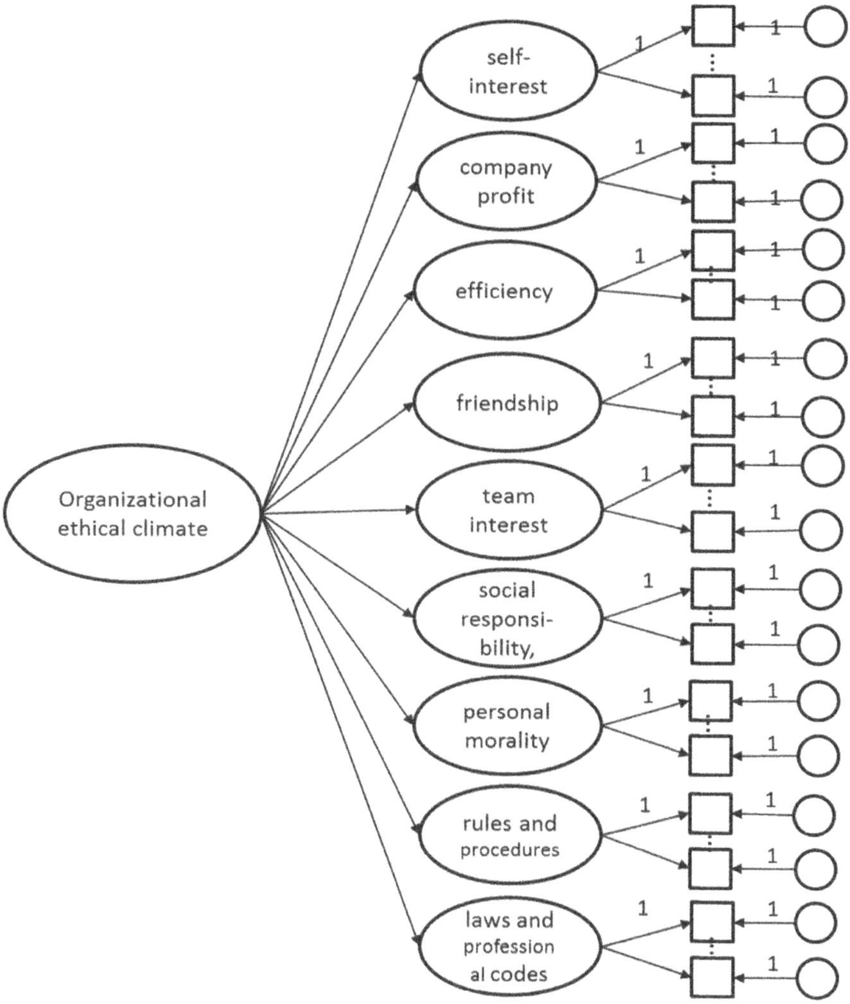

Fig. 3.1 Measurement model for organizational ethical climate

organizational commitment into four dimensions: emotional commitment, normative commitment, cost commitment, and choice commitment.

Ling Wenzhao used the method of semi-open questionnaires, which asked respondents to list the reasons why they were willing and unwilling to stay in a certain unit. His results allowed to establish through quantitative research the psychological structure of the organizational commitment of Chinese enterprise workers. According to Ling, the commitment of Chinese employees has five factors: emotional, normative, ideals, economic, and opportunity commitment. It includes the same parts as found in foreign research (emotional, normative, economic commitment), and also adds two unique types of commitment (ideals and opportunity). Ling believes that to some extent the resulting combination of factors also reflects the different manifestations of the organizational commitment. Regarding components and measurement dimensions of the organizational commitment, scholars have disparate views. Overseas studies propose using two, three, or even four dimensions of research organizational commitment, while Chinese scholars on organizational commitments propose five dimensions. Again, some of them are the same, some reflect the particularity of Chinese organizational commitments. Therefore, organizational commitment is also a variable that varies depending on geography (culture). Therefore, also questionnaires used to the study organizational commitment are not the same when researching different subjects or different management cultures.

Since this research mainly studies JFEs in China, the definition of organizational commitment is based on the findings of Ling Wenquan, Zhang Zhican and Fang Liluo, who have developed an "organizational climate questionnaire" for Chinese workers on the basis of interviews, pilot tests and scientific examination (see Attached Appendix 7 for questionnaire content). The results of this study suggest existence of five basic types of organizational commitment: normative, ideal, economic, effective, and choice commitment, each one comprised of several indexes.

The questionnaire used for the purposes of the this study (as shown in Attached Appendix 7) also reflects the existence of five basic types of commitment in Chinese employees: regulation, ideal, economic, emotional and opportunity commitment. Each of them includes several indexes measured on the five-point Likert scale described above. Using the survey data, reliability and validity of the questionnaire were tested. Credibility analysis gives the total alpha coefficient of 0.67 and a re-tested credibility coefficient of 0.87, indicating that the questionnaire has strong intrinsic and re-tested credibility. Efficiency analysis further indicates a variance interpretation of 66.1%, suggesting high structural efficiency (Fig. 3.2).

4. *Definition and measurement model for job performance*

According to research literature, the studies of job performance has developed from a two-dimensional structure to a three-dimensional, currently, has developed into a four-dimensional structure. At the beginning, Borman and Motowidlo used the questionnaire of military engineers to conclude that job performance consists of two dimensions: task performance and relationship performance. Both dimensions have independent contributions to job performance. Luo Zhengxue and other scholars studied the structure of job performance in China and further separated task performance and relationship performance from job performance. Both of them contribute to overall performance independently, and, at the same time, they are mutually reinforcing. Through empirical research Han Yi and Liao Jianqiao confirmed the separation of performance into task performance and relationship performance over again. It also concluded that performance dimension has a great influence on job performance. Performance dimension is conducive to targeted incentives, accordingly improving employee enthusiasm, and then promoting improvement of individual performance. By using knowledge workers as the research subjects, and constructing research from the definition and characteristics of knowledge workers, Zhang Jing verified the opinion proposed by Han Yi, and proved the scientific nature of the

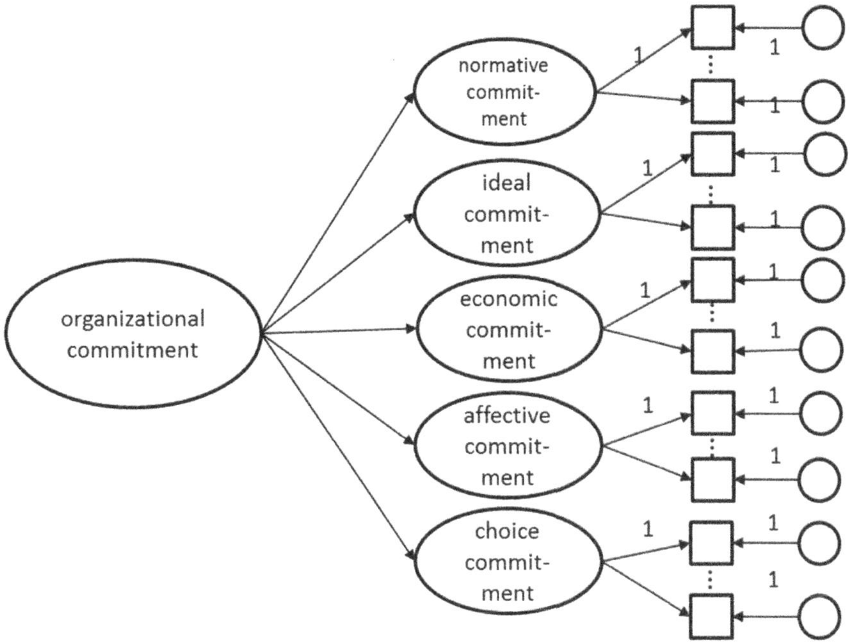

Fig. 3.2 Measurement model for organizational commitment

four-dimensional structure for the evaluation of knowledge workers, consisting of task, relationships, learning, and innovation. Our research mainly studies the manufacturing industry of JFEs in China. In terms of job performance measurement, it uses China's job performance dimensions and Han Yi's job performance measurement questionnaire to study job performance.

Since the paper mainly studies JFEs in China, the model developed by Han Yi, Zhang Jing and others,[1] which is used for the purposes of this study. According to it job performance is defined as the effective output realized by the working process of an organization or individual in order to achieve business objectives. It consists of four dimensions: task, contextual, learning and innovation performance. As shown in the questionnaire in Attached List 3, this four-dimensional scale is measured on the basis of 12 questions and includes four indexes for each dimension, each measured on the five-point Likert scale described above. Using the survey data, reliability and validity of the questionnaire were analyzed. Credibility analysis reveals the total alpha coefficient of 0.844 and re-tested credibility coefficient of 0.816, suggesting strong intrinsic and re-tested credibility. Efficiency analysis also indicates variance interpretation of 61.6%, suggesting high structural efficiency (Fig. 3.3).

[1]This paper adopts the definition of work performance definition and structure by Han Yi and Zhang Jing.

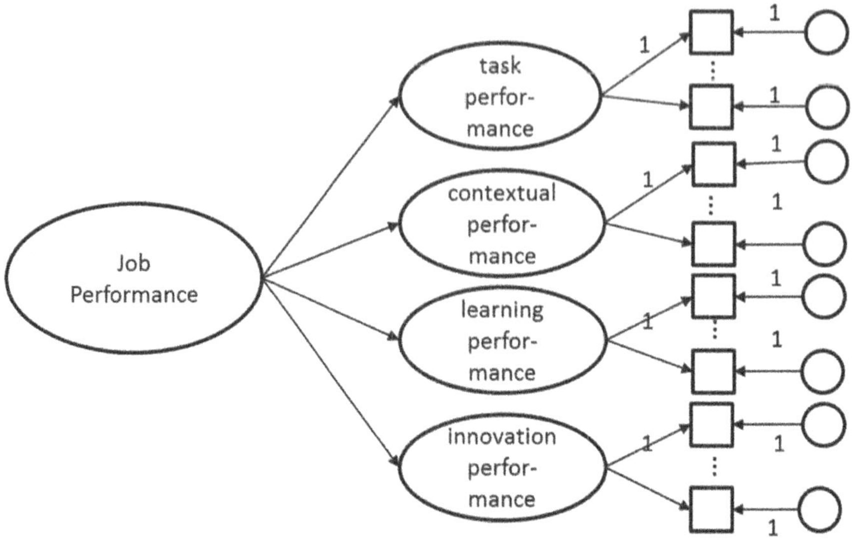

Fig. 3.3 Measurement model for job performance

3.2.3 The Design and Distribution of Organizational Ethical Climate Questionnaires for JFMEs

Research of the corporate ethical climate of JFEs in China tends to focus on the manufacturing industry for two reasons. First, China's manufacturing industry, though traditional, accounts for a major portion of secondary industries. Second, JFEs in China tend to be in manufacturing sectors. Therefore, the topic of the survey in this study is Japanese-funded manufacturing enterprises or JFMEs.

The questionnaire used to study ethical climate (shown in Attached List 1) is divided into four parts: basic employee information, the ethical atmosphere of organization, organizational commitment, and job performance. We will take the methods of division of ethical atmosphere by Victor and Cullen (1987) in the evaluation of the ethical atmosphere. We categorize ethical atmosphere through two dimensions, the ethical standard, and direction of analysis. Finally, there are nine types of ethical atmospheres: self-interest (self-interest), cooperation profits (self-interest), efficiency, friendship (care), team interest (care), social responsibility, personal morality (independence), rules of the company (rules), and industry laws and regulations (laws), with each dimension including several quotas measured on the five-point scale discussed above.

Organizational commitment questionnaire (shown in Attached Appendix 7) is similarly developed using the questionnaire by Ling Wenquan, Zhang Zhican and Fangliluo, whose study of organizational commitment in Chinese employees was based on interviews, preliminary experiments and scientific examination. It identified five basic types of commitment: regulation commitment, ideal commitment, economic commitment, emotional commitment and opportunity commitment. Under this model, organizational commitment is comprised of five dimensions, each of which includes several indexes, measured on the five-point Likert scale.

Finally, as discussed above, the questionnaire used to evaluate job performance (shown in Attached List 3) is based on Han Yi's four-dimensional scale, and includes 12 questions with four indexes for each of the four dimensions: task performance, relationship performance, learning performance and innovation performance, all of them measured on the five-point Likert scale.

All of the data in this study was collected anonymously via questionnaires distributed to the employees of JFMEs by the Human Resource Management (HRM) departments from January 2016 to August 2016. Full explanation of HRM-department-related questions, together with explanatory notes and frequently asked questions, were provided as part of the questionnaire to ensure the accuracy of the data. Of the 20,000 questionnaires handed out, 11,084 were retrieved with validity (51% recovery ratio) and used to provide the data for this research. The questionnaires, which form the basis of this dataset, were distributed as shown in Table 3.3 below. We collected less effective samples from companies D and E, mainly because these two did not allow us to conduct questionnaire surveys within their factories. However, it did not affect the validity of the overall sample, because companies D, E and F are very similar in the production of products and business processes.

As shown in Table 3.4, below, 4,204 (or 37.93%) of the samples investigated were male and 6,879 (or 62.07%) were female.

Among the samples, there was also quite a large range in terms of years of service: 664 were taken from employees with less than one year of service (5.99%), 1,767 were taken from employees with 1–3 years (15.94%), 1,055 were from employees

Table 3.3 Distribution of survey samples from JFMEs in China

	Freq.	Percent	Cum.
Company A	321	2.900	2.900
Company B	1,652	14.91	17.80
Company C	244	2.200	20
Company D	3	0.0300	20.03
Company E	64	0.580	20.61
Company F	5,490	49.54	70.14
Company G	1,175	10.60	80.75.
Company H	508	4.580	85.33
Company I	434	3.920	89.24
Company J	532	4.800	94.04
Company K	213	1.920	95.97
Company L	316	2.850	98.82
Company M	131	1.180	100
Total	11,083	100	

Table 3.4 Gender distribution of survey samples from JFMEs in China

Var2	Freq.	Percent	Cum.
Male	4,204	37.93	37.93
Female	6,879	62.07	100
Total	11,083	100	

Table 3.5 Distribution of years of service of employees in JFMEs in China

Var1	Freq.	Percent	Cum.
10–20 years of service	2,441	22.03	22.03
Less than 1 year of service	664	5.990	28.02
1–3 years of service	1,767	15.94	43.96
Over 20 years of service	3,015	27.20	71.17
3–5 years of service	1,055	9.520	80.68
5–10 years of service	2,141	19.32	100
Total	11,083	100	

Table 3.6 Distribution of staff positions of JFMEs in China

Var5	Freq.	Percent	Cum.
Officiated managerial staff	1,530	13.80	13.80
Operational managerial staff	250	2.260	16.06
General service staff	9,303	83.94	100
Total	11,803	100	

with 3–5 years (9.52%), 2,141 were from employees with 5–10 years (19.2%) and 2,442 were from employees with 10–20 years (22.03%) (Table 3.5).

Finally, samples were taken from three different positions of employees: 1,530 from officiated managerial staff (13.08%), 250 from operational managerial staff (2.26%) and 9,304 from general service staff (83.94%) (Table 3.6).

3.2.4 Empirical Research Hypotheses

There are differences between the types of Organizational Ethical Climate, and they have significantly different effects on job performance. Cai Tingting (2012) believes that job performance does not need to be subdivided, it can be measured directly as a whole. Cai considered that the Organizational Ethical Climate of care-orientation is significantly positive correlated to employees' performance, and the Organizational Ethical Climate of rule-orientation positively affects employee performance, while the Organizational Ethical Climate of profit-orientation has no significant impact on performance. However, some scholars believe that there are different dimensions of job performance. For example, based on the questionnaire of military engineers, Borman and Motowidlo proposed that job performance included task performance and relationship performance, and both of them contributed to job performance independently. Luo Zhengxue and other scholars studied the structure of job performance in China and separated task performance and relationship performance from job performance. Both of them contribute to overall performance independently, at the same time, they are mutually reinforcing. Through empirical research Han Yi and Liao Jianqiao further confirmed the separation of performance into task performance and relationship performance. They also concluded that performance separation has a great influence on job performance. Performance dimension is conducive to targeted incentives, accordingly improving employee enthusiasm, and then promoting the improvement of individual performance. By using knowledge workers as the research subject, and studying from the definition and characteristics of knowledge workers, Zhang Jing verified the opinion which was proposed by Han Yi, and proved the scientific nature of the four-dimensional structure for the evaluation of knowledge workers, consisting of task, relationships, learning, and innovation. Based on the prior research, relationships between the Organizational Ethical Climate and job performance is assumed to be following:

H1: Organizational ethical climate is positively correlated with job performance.

- H1.1 The ethical climate of self-interest (instrumental) is positively correlated with all four dimensions of job performance.
- H1.2 The ethical climate of company profit (instrumental) is positively correlated with all dimensions of job performance.
- H1.3 The ethical climate of efficiency is positively correlated with all four dimensions of job performance.
- H1.4 The ethical climate of friendship (caring) is positively correlated with all four dimensions of job performance.
- H1.5 The ethical climate of caring is positively correlated with all four dimensions of job performance.
- H1.6 The ethical climate of social responsibility is positively correlated with all dimensions of job performance.
- H1.7 The ethical climate of personal morality (independence) is positively correlated with all four dimensions of job performance.
- H1.8 The ethical climate of rules and procedures (rules) is positively correlated with all four dimensions of job performance.
- H1.9 The ethical climate of laws and professional codes (law and code) is positively correlated with all four dimensions of job performance.

In general, the hypothesis H1 can be shown in the Fig. 3.4.

Relatively little literature on organizational ethical climate and organizational commitment, and there are few studies on the impacts of different types of ethical climate on organizational commitment. Schwepker believes that if employees feel that the organizational value they feel in the enterprise contradicts their life value,

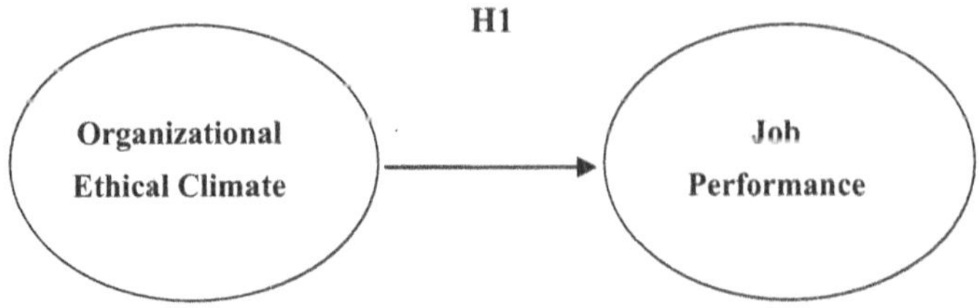

Fig. 3.4 The measurement model of organizational ethical climate and job performance

the organizational commitment of employees is relatively small.[2] Wech et al. believe that a caring organizational ethical climate enables employees to have a high organizational commitment, an instrumental organizational ethical climate reduces the organizational commitment of employees, and a team organizational ethical climate has a positive impact on organizational commitment.[3] When Schwepker studied the relationship between the concept of ethical climate and the organizational commitment of the level of enforcement in ethical norms and rules, it was found that the intensity of the implementation of ethical norms and rules was positively related to organizational commitment, and pointed out that future research trends will study the impacts of different types of ethical climate on organizational commitment.[4] Based on the above research and the study on organizational commitment dimensions, the relationship between organizational ethical climate and organizational commitment is assumed as:

H2: Organizational ethical climate is positively correlated with organizational commitment.

- H2.1 The ethical climate of self-interest (instrumental) is positively correlated with all five types of organizational commitment.
- H2.2 The ethical climate of company profit (instrumental) is positively correlated with all five types of organizational commitment.
- H2.3 The ethical climate of efficiency is positively correlated with all five types of organizational commitment.
- H2.4 The ethical climate of friendship (caring) is positively correlated with all five types of organizational commitment.
- H2.5 The ethical climate of caring is positively correlated with all five types of organizational commitment.
- H2.6 The ethical climate of social responsibility is positively correlated with all five types of organizational commitment.

---

[2]Jr C H S. Understanding Salespeople's Intention to Behave Unethically: The Effects of Perceived Competitive Intensity, Cognitive Moral Development and Moral Judgment [J]. Journal of Business Ethics, 1999, 21(4):303–316.

[3]Wech BA, Mossholder KW, Steel RP, et al. Does work group cohesiveness affect individuals' performance and organizational commitment? A cross-level examination [J]. Small Group Research, 1998, 29(4):472–494.

[4]Schneider B. Organizational Climate: An Essay [J]. Personnel Psychology, 2010, 28(4):447–479.

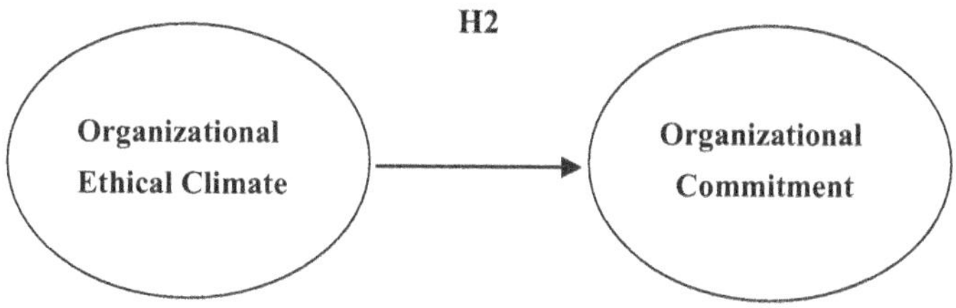

Fig. 3.5 The measurement model of organizational ethical climate and organizational commitment

H2.7 The ethical climate of personal morality (independence) is positively correlated with all five types of organizational commitment.
H2.8 The ethical climate of rules and procedures (rules) is positively correlated with all five types of organizational commitment.
H2.9 The ethical climate of laws and professional codes (law and code) is positively correlated with all five types of organizational commitment.

In general, the hypothesis H2 can be shown in the Fig. 3.5.

Some scholars have studied the relationship between organizational commitment and job performance. Meyer et al. (1997) found that lower-level managers' job performance is positively related to emotional commitment, but negatively related to continued commitment. The meta-analysis of Mathieu and Zajac (1990) found that the relationship between emotional commitment and employee's job performance is rather weak, far less significant than the relationship between separation and absence. Becker et al. (1996) found that organizational commitment has nothing to do with employee's job performance, but the commitment to superiors affects employee's job performance, as evidenced by Chen et al. (2002). Based on the above research and the research of organizational commitment dimension, combined with the Chinese background of Japanese-funded enterprises in China, the relationship between organizational commitment and job performance is assumed as:

H3: Organizational commitment is positively correlated with job performance.

H3.1 Normative commitment is positively correlated with all four dimensions of job performance.
H3.2 The ideal commitment is positively correlated with all four dimensions of job performance.
H3.3 The economic commitment is positively correlated with all four dimensions of job performance.
H3.4 The affective commitment is positively correlated with all four dimensions of job performance.
H3.5 The choice commitment is positively correlated with all four dimensions of job performance.

In general, the hypothesis H3 can be shown in the Fig. 3.6:

Some researchers believe that the influence of organizational ethical climate on the outcome variables is achieved through mediation and regulation. There are three prior

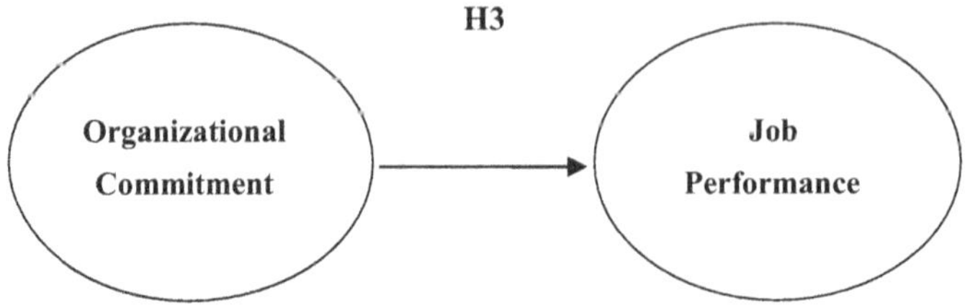

Fig. 3.6 The measurement model of organizational commitment and job performance

stages before individuals do ethical behaviors: confirming ethical issues, conducting ethical judgments and forming behavioral intentions (Rest 1986). Researchers believe that the ethical climate does not directly affect the ultimate ethical behavior of humans, but only regulates the relationship of four stages. For example, the ethical climate that emphasizes social responsibility based on norms and professional ethics has a regulatory effect on individual moral judgments and behavioral intentions (Tim 2000). Prior studies have shown several other routes of influence, e.g.: the organizational ethical climate can influence individual ethical behavior by influencing individual trust in leadership (Konovsky 1994); organizational ethics climate can influence job performance by strengthening organizational cohesion and team morale (Wickham 1996); organizational ethical climate affects individual organizational citizenship behavior, task performance, and relationship performance by influencing employees' sense of justice (procedural justice and distributional justice) and ethical expectations (Dickson 2000); organizational ethical climate has impacts on employee's organizational commitment, job satisfaction, and demission intentions by influencing leaders' moral cognition development and application levels because of the close relationship between organizational ethic climate and many individual psychological and behavioral variables.

At present, Chinese scholars have relatively mature research on job performance, such as Yu Chengju and Sun Jianmin, Wen Zhiyi, Han Yi, Zhang Jingran, etc.[5] However, there are still many shortcomings, especially regarding the impact of organizational ethics climate and organizational commitment on job performance. To synthesize, job performance may be influenced by organizational ethics climate and organizational commitment directly, and by organizational ethic climate indirectly through organizational commitment. Hence, based on the literature reviewed above, the impact of organizational commitment on job performance and the role of organizational commitment in the impact of organizational ethics climate on job performance is assumed to be following:

H4: Organizational ethics climate has positive impacts on job performance, Organizational commitment positively affects job performance, and organizational ethical climate plays a mediator role in affecting job performance.

[5]Refer to "Chap. 2. Literature Review": the section. "2 Antecedent and Outcome variables of organizational commitment" in "2.2.1 Current Research on Organizational Commitment" of "2.2 Research on Organizational Commitment".

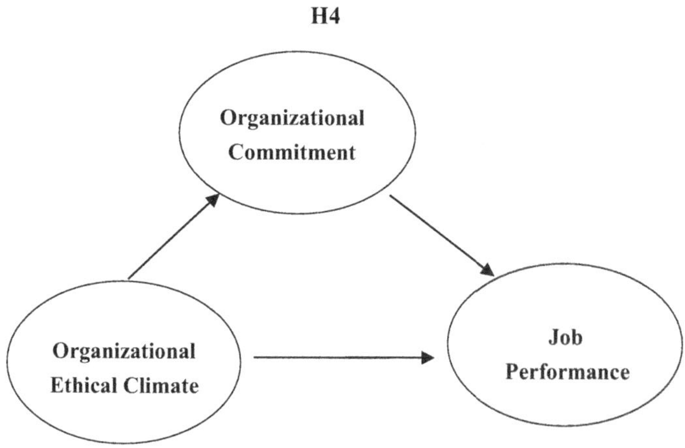

Fig. 3.7 The full measurement model of organizational ethical climate, organizational commitment and job performance

The hypothesis model of this study is drawn from H1, H2, and H3, as shown in Fig. 3.7 below. In general, the hypothesis H4 can be shown in the figure below:

The prior research on the impact of job performance mainly involves the direct influence of organizational ethics on job performance and the direct impact of organizational commitment on job performance, and there are few studies looking at the impact of both organizational ethics and organizational commitment simultaneously. Therefore, after verifying H4, it will become clear which factors actually affect the work performance. Is it influenced by the organizational ethical climate? Or do we actually see the impact of organizational commitment? Or does the organizational ethic climate affect job performance through organizational commitment? Finally, what is the effect of each factor? By clarifying the above issues, it is possible to advance the research on factors impacting job performance.

Chapter 4
Empirical Analysis of Organizational Ethical Climate, Organizational Commitment and Job Performance in JFMEs in China

Recent years have seen an increasing emphasis on organizational ethics among Chinese enterprises. As a type of organizational climate, organizational ethics can predict and motivate employee behavior in such areas as ethics and morality, a sense of identity and belonging, behavior and manner, and job performance. It also has the potential to enhance efficiency in organizational operation and management, and improve corporate image and brand. This is why research on organizational ethical climate has attracted so much attention in the fields of economic psychology and management, where significant progress has been made.

A positive organizational ethical climate promotes cohesiveness among individual members, and acts as a synergetic force that brings about team productivity, reduces organizational and transaction costs, and enhances efficiency. In this sense, the organizational ethical climate is the key to empirical studies on the most effective ways for HRM staff to motivate employees. In an effort to highlight its role in HRM among JFEs in China, this study explores how various existing ethical frameworks inform HRM measures so as to enhance team productivity.

4.1 An Empirical Analysis of Organizational Ethical Climate in JFMEs

Just as social norms differ among countries and societies, ethical decision-making differs in organizations with different cultures. For instance, the climate of Russian organizations tends to be characterized by strong rules and regulations and very little independence, while Japanese and American organizational climates tend to promote self-interest, though US employees tend to have a stronger sense of friendship, teamwork, and law than their Japanese counterparts. From a micro-perspective, the sense of community of an organization also has a significant effect on its ethical climate, in so far as the ethical decision-making of both the organization and its members are

© Science Press and Springer Nature Singapore Pte Ltd. 2020

K. Ryu, *The Impact of Organizational Ethical Climate on Organizational Commitment and Job Performance*, https://doi.org/10.1007/978-981-15-2813-2_4

Table 4.1 PCA for organizational ethical climate in JFMEs in China

Principal component	Characteristic root	Characteristic root difference	Variance contribution rate	Aggregate variance contribution rate
1	9.940	7.918	0.473	0.473
2	2.022	0.922	0.0963	0.570
3	1.100	0.119	0.0524	0.622
Observed value	10,688			

informed by a microculture nurtured by the community environment. The organizational ethical climate is also to some extent determined by its ethical values and regulations, while the history of an organization can also play a role by perpetuating certain cultures and experiences over others (Cullen etc. 1988). It should be noted, however, that these factors are specific to each organization, requiring unique solutions to issues concerning its survival and development.

In terms of organizational ethical policy, the key seems to lie in HRM systems and related practices through which employees familiarize themselves with ethical policies and norms, which in turn inform the judgments and behavioral preferences determining individual ethical behaviors. Organizational ethical climate can therefore be cultivated by such effective HRM strategies as the establishment of corporate moral standards and ethics training. In fact, to some extent, the development of a positive organizational ethical climate is often the direct or indirect aim of certain HRM practices.[1]

This paper adopts the PCA method to investigate various samples of organizational ethical climates of JFMEs in China. As shown in Table 4.1, only three characteristic roots are higher than 1, which suggests that these JFMEs exhibit three principal types of organizational ethical climates, accounting for 62.2% of the information across all metrics.

Moreover, as shown in Table 4.2, since the results for almost all observed questions presented in this study are higher than 0.9 (average value of 0.954), the data passes the KMO validity test and the PCA results have high credibility.

As shown in Table 4.3, an analysis of the loading factor matrix of the three principal components yields the following feature vectors. Principal component 1 has larger coefficients for the observed indexes EC4, EI1, EI3, BI4, EL1, BL3, BL2 and PI1, of which "E"represents corporate self-interest, "B" altruism, "I" individuals, "L" organizations, "C" society and "P" obligations.

Generally speaking, principal component 1 reflects an organizational ethical climate built on altruism (friendship), self-interest (instrumental), individuals (company profit) and organizations (team interest), which are often referred to as the "Golden Mean" insofar as it is comprised of both caring and instrumental orientations.

[1] Yanfei Wang, Yu Zhu. Research Progress and Forecast of Organizational Innovative Climate [J]. Advances in Psychological Science, 2006, 14(3): 443–449.

Table 4.2 Validity test for the organizational ethical climate in JFMEs in China

Variable	Kmo
EI1	0.961
EI2	0.975
EI3	0.927
EI4	0.973
EL1	0.973
EL2	0.956
EC1	0.929
EC2	0.967
EC3	0.945
EC4	0.968
BI1	0.970
BI2	0.948
BI3	0.949
BI4	0.977
BL3	0.973
BL2	0.956
BL4	0.946
BC3	0.921
PI1	0.974
PI3	0.896
PC1	0.897
PC2	0.908
PL1	0.897
PL2	0.900
BC1	0.901
BC5	0.968
Overall	0.954

Note The questionnaire for observed variables of organizational ethical climate is available in the appendix

Golden Mean is the orientation of our relationship between cognitive environment and self-environment. It contains both global and dialectical cognition as well as the value orientation of "He" (Yang Zhongfang 2009). First of all, the Golden Mean" value orientation shows a complex, dynamic, and global cognition. This comprehensive cognition can motivate people to perceive changes in the environment effectively (Chen Jianxun et al. 2010). In the specific thinking and judgment, the value orientation of the mean is reflected in the value orientation of "Zhe-Zhong", moderation and "He". Yang Zhongfang (2009) believes that "Golden Mean" is insisting on the Taoism

Table 4.3 The loading factor matrix of principal components for the organizational ethical climate in JFMEs in China

Observed variables	Principal component 1	Principal component 2	Principal component 3
BC3	0.162	0.758	0.569
BC5	0.176	0.513	-0.213
EC1	0.182	0.677	0.18
BI2	0.185	0.789	0.548
PI3	0.196	0.144	0.0585
EI2	0.197	0.252	0.0779
PC2	0.21	0.177	-0.0447
BI3	0.213	0.15	0.541
EC2	0.217	-0.0461	0.789
EI4	0.219	-0.152	0.106
BI1	0.225	-0.212	0.687
EC3	0.225	0.191	0.737
BL4	0.226	0.646	0.135
EC4	0.628	0.0177	-0.35
EI1	0.729	-0.123	0.17
EI3	0.835	-0.313	0.137
BI4	0.74	-0.107	-0.0898
EL1	0.643	0.0541	-0.00904
BL3	0.647	-0.129	-0.317
BL2	0.725	-0.236	0.023
PI1	0.643	-0.18	-0.071
PL1	0.342	0.241	-0.104
PL2	0.247	-0.134	-0.117
EL2	0.325	-0.146	0.043
PC1	0.143	-0.190	-0.061
BC1	0.243	0.0341	-0.0901

from time to time, however, keep changing to avoid being one if necessary, according to different situations. The moderation advocates "Du", which requires people to adhere to the principle of appropriateness when dealing with various things. The ultimate goal of the mean is "He". Zhao Zhiyu (2000) pointed out that "the goal of the mean is to achieve a harmonious realm", Wu Jiahui and Lin Yizheng (2005) think that "in the middle of the golden system, the inner and outer sections of the heart and the final result of the neutralization are the most central concept." In general, the Golden Mean value orientation can be expressed as a global-based, dialectical cognitive environment, by using the "He". Among them, the understanding of the external environment from the overall perspective and the overall concept is the basis of the Golden Mean value orientation. "Zhe-Zhong", "Shi-du" and "He" are the ultimate goals of the Zhong-yong value orientation (Du sheng, 2014). The doctrine of

Table 4.4 The Golden Mean style of organizational ethical climate in JFMEs in China

Ethical Standards	Analytic Approach		
	Individual	**Organization**	**World**
Self-interest	Self-interest (instrumental)	Company profit (instrumental)	Efficiency
Compassion	Friendship (caring)	Team interest (caring)	Social responsibility
Principles	Personal morality (independence)	Rules and procedures (rules)	Laws and professional codes (law and code)

the mean is not a simple vulgar compromise, but a temporary and partial adjustment under the premise of adhering to the principle (Sun Lili 2015).

There are two reasons why such a climate exists in Chinese culture as well as the management philosophy of Japanese enterprises.

First, it is closely related to the notion of the Golden Mean in traditional Chinese philosophy, with its emphasis on moderation, and is manifest in organizational ethical climates with a focus on self-interest and corporate profit as well as friendship and teamwork in equal measure. In fact, once foreign enterprises enter the Chinese market, their organizational ethical climate and leadership style tends to gradually evolve from one focused exclusively on self-interest and profit to the Golden Mean model. As this shift takes place, altruism and compassion come into play and a climate of friendship develops.

Second, while both China and Japan emphasize community spirit, Japanese enterprises tend to take better care of their employees through an altruistic ethical climate based on friendship and teamwork. At the same time, however, the primary reason Japanese enterprises have sought to enter the Chinese market is to reduce labor costs, thereby suggesting a management philosophy more aligned with the U.S. model based on self-interest. To some extent, it is these competing tendencies among JFMEs that have led to the development of the Golden Mean style of organizational ethical climate summarized in Table 4.4.

In order to explore the effect of the primary measuring loading factors of principal component 1, including EC4, EI1, EI3, BI4, EL1, BL3, BL2 and PI1, The descriptive statistics of the principal component 1 payload factors are as follows:

Variable	Obs	Mean	Std. dev.	Min	Max
EC4	11016	3.662	0.988	1	5
EI1	11007	4.173	0.894	1	5
EI3	11030	3.659	1.081	1	5
BI4	11035	3.847	0.955	1	5

(continued)

(continued)

Variable	Obs	Mean	Std. dev.	Min	Max
EL1	11015	4.125	0.821	1	5
BL3	11028	3.591	1.066	1	5
BL2	11029	3.638	1.022	1	5
PI1	11031	3.798	1.012	1	5

Because the moderate organizational ethics climate is a latent variable, it cannot be directly observed in the enterprise. Its performance is based on the measurable variables EC4, EI1, EI3, BI4, EL1, BL3, BL2, and PI1. And so on the Golden Mean style of organizational ethical climate, SEM has been used to link these observed indexes to organizational ethical climate. This paper chooses this method because the SEM structural equation can not only measure the latent variables and the contribution of observable variables to latent variables through observable variables, but also study the relationship among latent variables, as well as the adjustment and mediation relationship among latent variables. And other parts also use the SEM equation to make an empirical analysis.

As shown in Figs. 4.1 and 4.2, the results indicate that they are highly consistent with the coefficients in the loading matrix, suggesting that they contribute to the Golden Mean style of organizational ethical climate with a high degree of reliability.

As for principal component 2, the main loading factors include BC3, BC5, EC1, BI2 and BL4, in which "E" represents corporate self-interest, "B" altruism, "C" society, "I" the individual and "L" the organization. Comprised of self-interest,

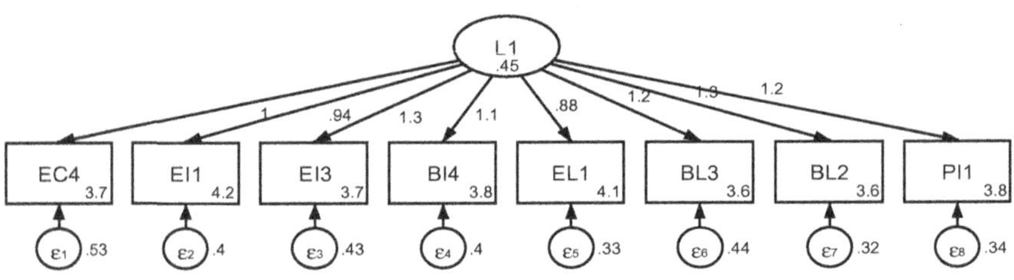

Fig. 4.1 Non-standardized loading factors of principal component 1 for ethical climate

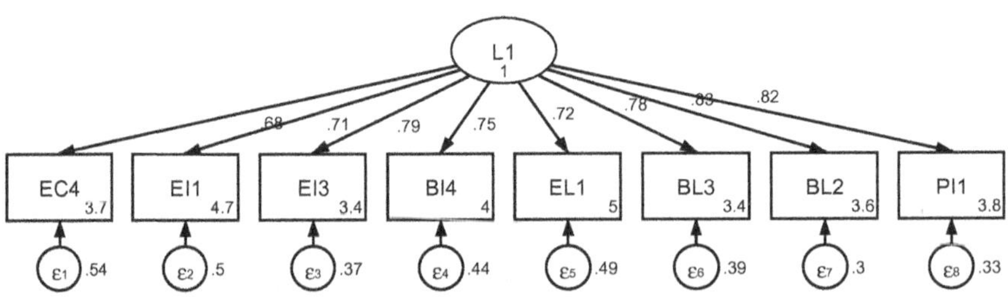

Fig. 4.2 Standardized loading factors of principal component 1 for ethical climate

altruism, society, individual and organization, principal component 2 is concerned primarily with other people and society and therefore embodies a social responsibility style of organizational climate. The descriptive statistics of the principal component 2 payload factors are as follows:

Variable	Obs	Mean	Std. dev.	Min	Max
BC3	11050	4.519	0.616	1	5
BC5	11027	3.951	0.939	1	5
EC1	11046	4.163	0.795	1	5
BI2	11044	4.237	0.777	1	5
BL4	11029	3.595	1.096	1	5

Again, there are two reasons why such a climate exists in China. First, as the country's economy has developed, its focus has shifted from economic growth to social welfare, thereby placing greater emphasis on corporate social responsibility (CSR) with respect to the reduction of pollution, the development of healthy products and the offering of social assistance. Enterprises are required to strictly adhere to government policies, which in turn influences their operations and philosophies. Although recent proposals have been made to extricate enterprise management from direct government control through the passage of macro-economic regulations, the socialist foundation of China's economic reform ensures that government intervention in the economy remains strong.

Second, due to the long-standing animosity between China and Japan as well as the resulting opposition to Japanese products in the Chinese market, JFEs have been forced to incorporate greater social responsibility into their organizational ethical climate in an effort to reduce such opposition and enhance their corporate image. This is especially true in the manufacturing industry, as shown in Table 4.5.

In sum, principal component 2 represents a social responsibility style of organizational ethical climate, whose primary measuring loading factors include BC3,

Table 4.5 The social responsibility style of organizational ethical climate in JFMEs in China

Ethical Standards	**Analytic Approach**		
	Individual	**Organization**	**World**
Self-interest	Self-interest (instrumental)	Company profit (instrumental)	Efficiency
Compassion	Friendship (caring)	Team interest (caring)	Social responsibility
Principles	Personal morality (independence)	Rules and procedures (rules)	Laws and professional codes (law and code)

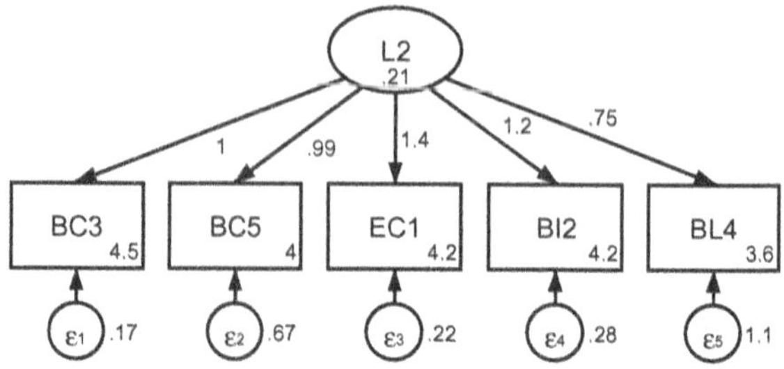

Fig. 4.3 Non-standardized loading factors of principal component 2 for ethical climate

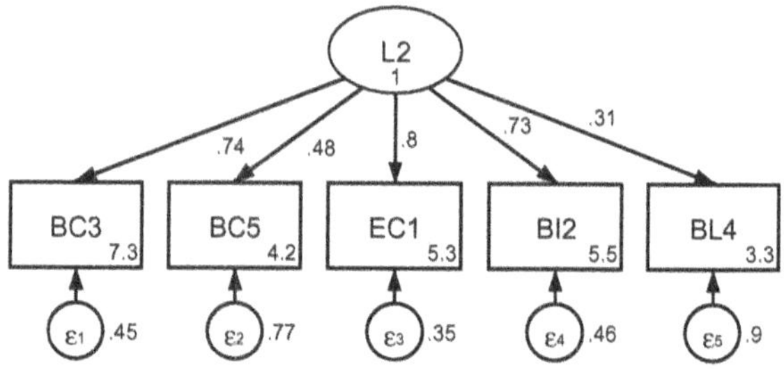

Fig. 4.4 Standardized loading factors of principal component 2 for ethical climate

BC5, EC1, BI2, and BL4. Moreover, as with the Golden Mean style of organizational ethical climate discussed above, the related observed indexes have all been shown by SEM to be highly consistent with the coefficients in the loading matrix, and can therefore be said to contribute to the social responsibility style of organizational ethical climate with a high degree of reliability (Figs. 4.3 and 4.4).

Principal component 3 has larger coefficients for the observed indexes BC3, BI2, BI3, EC2, EI4, BI1 and EC3, of which "E" represents corporate self-interest, "B" altruism, "I" individuals, and "C" society. As reflected in the friendship type indexes of BI2, BI3 and BI1 and the efficiency type indexes of EC2 and EC3, the organizational ethical climate reflected by this principal component is characterized by both caring and efficiency. As for the reason behind the prevalence of this type of ethical climate in JFMEs in China, these enterprises tend to act as multinational corporations (MNCs) in terms of their focus on localization as a means of achieving increased efficiency. Moreover, most executive and managerial positions of Japanese enterprises, regardless of the country in which they operate, are filled by Japanese, who tend to promote a traditional employee-oriented culture which in turn plays a pivotal role in determining organizational ethical climate. Research has shown that the development of an organizations' ethical standards are significantly affected by the psychological and behavioral features of their leaders, including but not necessarily limited to their approach to problems, the ethical values and standards reflected in their managerial practices, as well as the ways in which they reward and punish the ethical conduct of individual members. As Grojean's findings reveal, leaders can influence and shape employees' ethical values and behaviors in seven ways, while Sim and Brinkman (2004) have also described how leaders are uniquely positioned to shape and strengthen an organization's ethical climate. Therefore, in the case of

Table 4.6 The caring-efficiency style of organizational ethical climate in JFMEs

Ethical Standards	Analytic Approach		
	Individual	**Organization**	**World**
Self-interest	Self-interest (instrumental)	Company profit (instrumental)	Efficiency
Mercy	Friendship (caring)	Team interest (caring)	Social responsibility
Principles	Personal morality (independence)	Rules and procedures (rules)	Laws and professional codes (law and code)

JFMEs in China, the prevalence of the caring-efficiency style of organizational ethical climate is to some extent directly attributable to the influence of their leaders (Table 4.6).

Principal component 3 therefore represents a caring-efficiency style of organizational ethical climate, whose primary measuring loading factors include BC3, BI2, BI3, EC2, BI1, and EC3. The descriptive statistics of the principal component 3 payload factors are as follows:

Variable	Obs	Mean	Std. dev.	Min	Max
BC3	11050	4.519	0.616	1	5
BI2	11044	4.237	0.777	1	5
BI3	11049	3.836	0.992	1	5
EC2	11031	3.363	1.204	1	5
BI1	11022	3.932	0.904	1	5
EC3	11043	3.936	0.940	1	5

Again, these observed indexes have all been shown by SEM to be highly consistent with the coefficients in the loading matrix, and can therefore be said to contribute to this caring-efficiency style of organizational ethical climate with a high degree of reliability (Figs. 4.5 and 4.6).

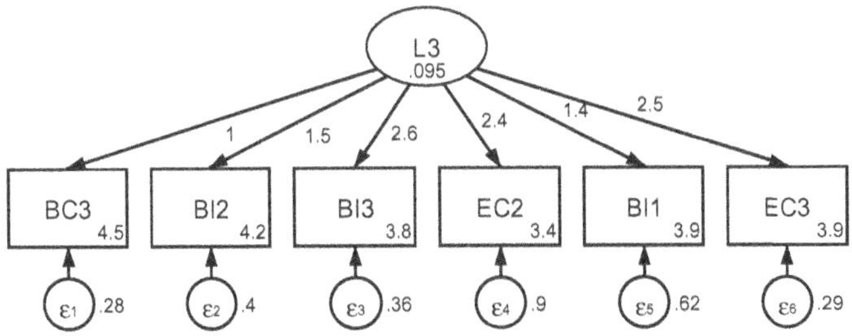

Fig. 4.5 Non-standardized loading factors of principal component 3 for ethical climate

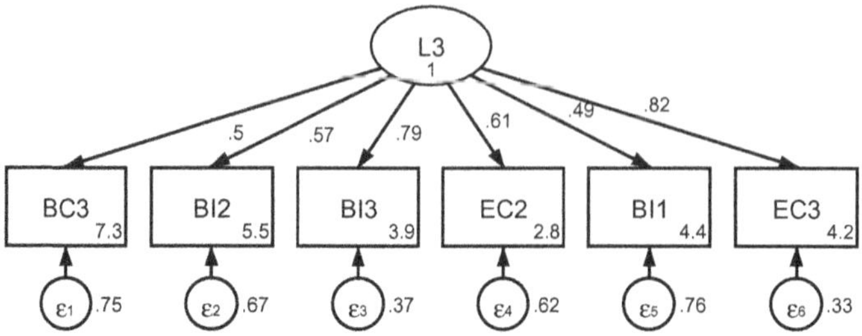

Fig. 4.6 Standardized loading factors of principal component 3 for ethical climate

4.2 An Empirical Analysis of Organizational Commitment in JFMEs

As discussed above, this study uses the PCA method to investigate samples of organizational commitment in JFMEs. As is shown in Table 4.7, only two characteristic roots are higher than 1, which means that the organizational commitment of JFMEs can be categorized into two principal components accounting for 71.1% of the information across all metrics.

Moreover, as shown in Table 4.8, since the results for almost all observed questions measuring organizational commitment are higher than 0.9 (average value of 0.922), the data passes the KMO validity test and the PCA results have high credibility.

As shown in Table 4.9, an analysis of the loading factor matrix of the two principal components yields the following feature vectors. Principal component 1 has larger coefficients for the observed indexes gf3, gf1, gf2, gf4, gf5, and gf6, thereby suggesting a high level of normative commitment in JFMEs in China.

Normative commitment refers to the commitment to social responsibility within an organization due to long-standing social factors, including but not necessarily limited to the level of social equity among employees, the degree of employee satisfaction with respect to their ability to rely on colleagues, and the collective working spirit of the organization. Based on the aforementioned analysis, JFMEs in China are particularly focused on fostering team spirit as part of an effort to cultivate a caring

Table 4.7 Principal components of organizational commitment in JFMEs

Principal component	Characteristic root	Characteristic root difference	Percentage	Cumulative percentage
1	5.381	4.365	0.598	0.598
2	1.016	0.494	0.113	0.711
Observed value	11083			

Table 4.8 Validity test of the questionnaire for organizational commitment in JFMEs

Variable	Kmo
gf4	0.934
jj1	0.923
gf5	0.904
gf6	0.915
jj2	0.939
jj3	0.903
gf2	0.899
gf1	0.943
gf3	0.945
jh1	0.921
jh2	0.923
jh3	0.933
gq1	0.923
gq2	0.899
lx1	0.942
lx2	0.922
Overall	0.922

Note The questionnaire for observed variables of organizational commitment is available in the appendix

Table 4.9 Loading factor matrix of principal components for organizational commitment of JFMEs

Observed variables	Principal component 1	Principal component 2
jj1	0.267	0.549
jj2	0.286	0.629
jj3	0.31	0.534
gf1	0.644	0.0477
gf2	0.701	-0.375
gf3	0.634	-0.186
gf4	0.725	-0.0905
gf5	0.522	-0.245
gf6	0.734	-0.283
jh1	0.377	0.317
jh2	0.365	-0.275
jh3	0.186	-0.133
gq1	0.105	-0.305
gq2	0.245	-0.145
lx1	0.273	-0.182
lx2	0.233	-0.071

organizational ethical climate. At the same time, however, the operational philosophies of these enterprises continue to prioritize self-interest, and it is this mixture of competing priorities, which has led to the Golden Mean style of organizational ethical climate.

Specifically, the operational philosophies and business environments of JFMEs in China are focused on the following three factors: employee satisfaction, team spirit, and fairness of wages. In order to strengthen organizational commitment, which is a necessary prerequisite for the long-term development of JFMEs in China, they also seek to instill a sense of fairness and belonging among Chinese employees while making a concerted effort to enhance their corporate image by strengthening corporate social responsibility (CSR) activities.

In sum, principal component 1 represents a normative organizational commitment, whose primary measuring loading factors include gf3, gf1, gf2, gf4, gf5, and gf6. The descriptive statistics of the principal component 1 payload factors are as follows:

Variable	Obs	Mean	Std. dev.	Min	Max
gf1	11032	3.705	1.038	1	5
gf2	11036	4.081	0.914	1	5
gf3	11025	3.630	1.052	1	5
gf4	11023	4.046	0.964	1	5
gf5	11024	4.060	0.930	1	5
gf6	11035	3.799	1.070	1	5

Again, the related observed indexes have all been shown by SEM to be highly consistent with the coefficients in the loading matrix, and can, therefore, be said to contribute to a normative organizational commitment with a high degree of reliability (Figs. 4.7 and 4.8).

Principal component 2 has larger coefficients for the observed indexes jj1, jj2, and jj3, which reflect economic organizational commitment. The descriptive statistics of the principal component 2 payload factors are as follows:

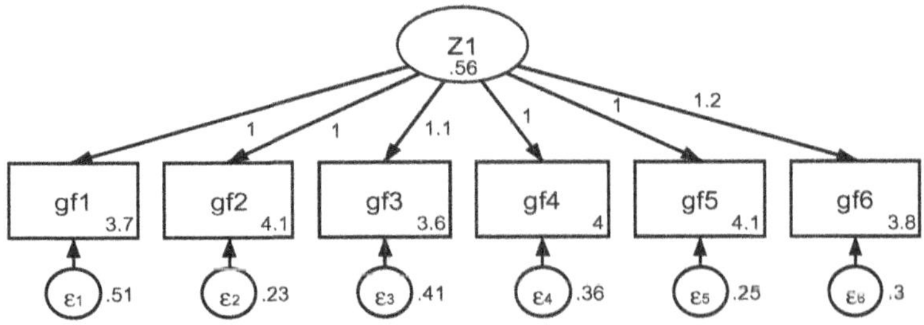

Fig. 4.7 Non-standardized loading factors of principal component 1 for organizational commitment

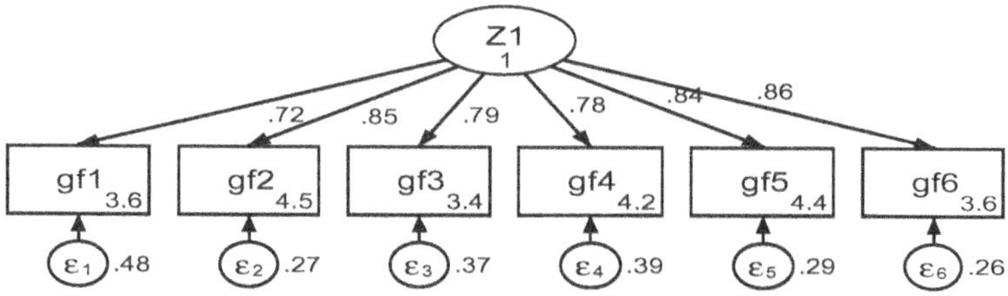

Fig. 4.8 Standardized loading factors of principal component 1 for organizational commitment

Variable	Obs	Mean	Std. dev.	Min	Max
jj1	11027	4.044	0.870	1	5
jj2	11026	3.684	0.951	1	5
jj3	11026	3.292	1.154	1	5

Again, there are practical reasons why economic commitment is prioritized by JFMEs in China. For one thing, the Chinese laborers from rural families with little or no education who tend to be employed by JFMEs care more about wages. China's transformation from a government-regulated to a market-oriented economy has caused considerable chaos in its system of labor. The opportunities available to rural laborers in urban areas are often restricted by education and domicile, which effectively excludes them from state enterprises, organs and institutions and forces them to accept lower wages in fringe markets. Rural and other fringe laborers therefore tend to seek jobs in private domestic enterprises, where the market is overcrowded and pay is significantly lower. Due in part to their technological advantage, however, foreign enterprises like JFMEs can afford to pay higher wages. And while income disparity among domestic and foreign enterprises in China has recently declined, the higher wages offered by the latter continue to appeal to workers on the front line of China's manufacturing industry.

The importance of economic commitment in JFMEs is also closely related to the national conditions of China as well as the organizational ethical climate of Japanese enterprises. As discussed above, research has shown that the organizational ethical climate of JFMEs in China comes in three types: the Golden Mean style, the social responsibility style, and the friendship-efficiency style, all of which serve to strengthen economic commitment. Both the Golden Mean and friendship-efficiency styles help JFMEs fulfill economic commitment insofar as economic output and efficiency are prioritized, while the social responsibility style ensures that they obey the law in order to protect their corporate image. As a result, their image as a good employer is an important incentive for the formation of economic commitment among employees.

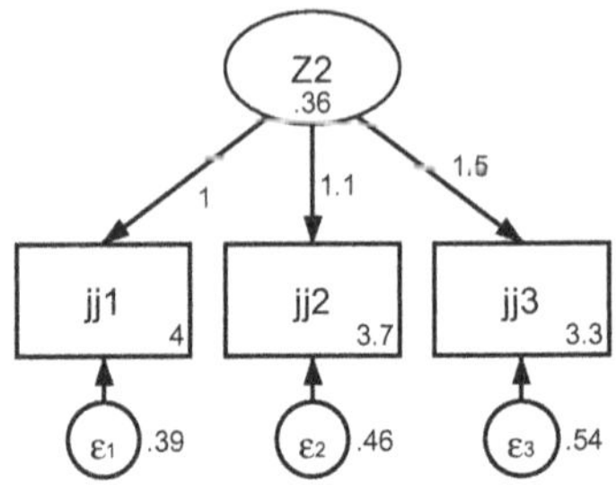

Fig. 4.9 Non-standardized loading factors of principal component 2 for organizational commitment

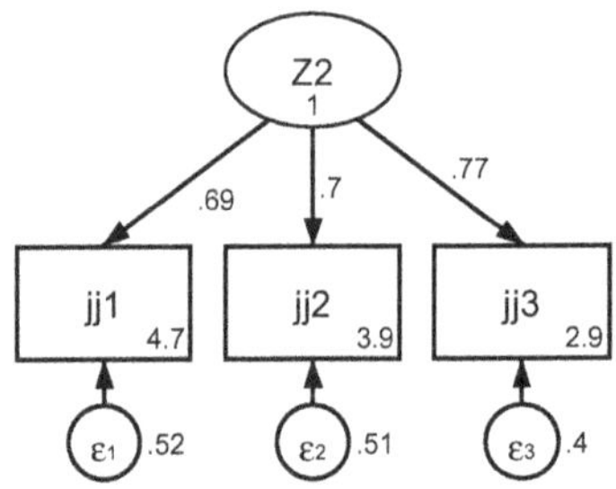

Fig. 4.10 Standardized loading factors of principal component 2 for organizational commitment

In sum, principal component 2 represents an economic organizational commitment, whose primary measuring loading factors include jj1, jj2, and jj3. As with the components above, the related observed indexes have all been shown by SEM to be highly consistent with the coefficients in the loading matrix, and can therefore be said to contribute to an economic organizational commitment with a high degree of reliability (Figs. 4.9 and 4.10).

4.3 An Empirical Analysis of Job Performance in JFMEs

This study also uses the PCA method to investigate samples of job performance in JFMEs. As shown in Table 4.10, only one characteristic root is higher than 1, suggesting that there is only one principal component for job performance accounting for 81.9% of the information across all metrics.

Table 4.10 The principal components of job performance in JFMEs

Principal component	Characteristic root	Characteristic root difference	Percentage	Cumulative percentage
1	4.474	3.555	0.819	0.819
Observed value	11,083			

Table 4.11 Validity test of the questionnaire for job performance in JFMEs

Variable	Kmo
rw1	0.929
rw2	0.917
rw3	0.918
rw4	0.880
gx1	0.869
gf4	0.758
xx1	0.758
xx2	0.813
xx3	0.781
cx1	0.771
cx2	0.759
cx3	0.758
Overall	0.856

Note The questionnaire for observed variables of job performance is available in the appendix

Moreover, as shown in Table 4.11, since the results for all observed questions measuring job performance are higher than 0.758 (average value of 0.856), the data passes the KMO validity test and the PCA results have high credibility.

As shown in Table 4.12, an analysis of the loading factor matrix of this principal component yields the following feature vectors. Principal component 1 has larger coefficients for the observed indexes rw1, rw2, rw3, and rw4, indicating that these indexes reflect task-based job performance.

Table 4.12 Loading factor matrix of principal components for the organizational commitment of JFMEs

Observed variables	Principal component 1
rw1	0.644
rw2	0.701
rw3	0.634
rw4	0.725
gx1	0.301
gf4	0.234
xx1	0.125
xx2	0.222
xx3	0.334
cx1	0.267
cx2	0.286
cx3	0.31

In sum, task-based job performance is defined as the efficiency, quantity, and quality of working behaviors as well as the performance achieved in completing a given task, whose primary measuring loading factors include rw1, rw2, rw3, and rw4. The descriptive statistics of the principal component 3 payload factors are as follows:

Variable	Obs	Mean	Std. dev.	Min	Max
rw1	11017	3.851	0.997	1	5
rw2	11023	3.994	0.928	1	5
rw3	11017	3.923	0.920	1	5
rw4	11008	3.968	0.850	1	5

The related observed indexes have all been shown by SEM to be highly consistent with the coefficients in the loading matrix, and can therefore be said to contribute to task-based job performance with a high degree of reliability (Figs. 4.11 and 4.12).

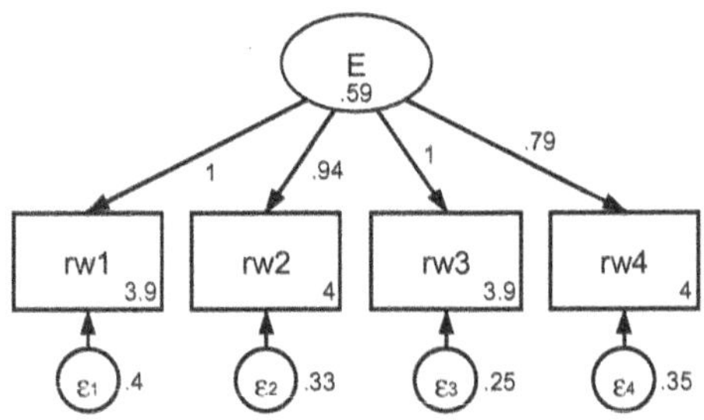

Fig. 4.11 Non-standardized loading factors of the principal component for job performance

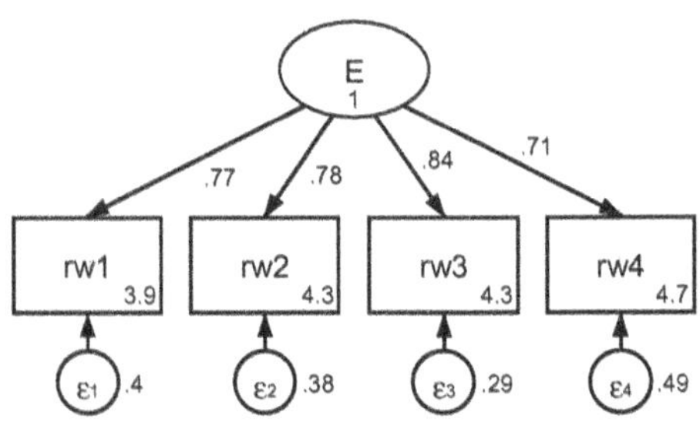

Fig. 4.12 Standardized loading factors of the principal component for job performance

4.4 Conclusions Regarding the Relationship Between Organizational Ethical Climate, Organizational Commitment, and Job Performance

As discussed above, JFMEs in China appear to exhibit three distinct types of organizational ethical climates: the Golden Mean style, the social responsibility style, and the friendship-efficiency style. The conclusions of this study are similar to the types of ethical climate of Chinese companies, but there are also differences. According to Li Bo, the organizational ethical climate in the context of Chinese culture should contain five dimensions: institutional, collectivist, profit-efficient, self-interested and caring ethical climate.[2] Chao and other researchers believe that the organizational ethical climate of Chinese-funded enterprises includes law-oriented, care-oriented, independent judgment-oriented, corporate interest-oriented and tool-oriented five organizational ethical climates.[3] In terms of dimensions, the structure of Japanese-funded enterprises in China is clearer and the complexity is far lower than that of Chinese-funded enterprises. In terms of content, in the context of Chinese culture, there are also similarities with Chinese-funded enterprises. For example, the friendship-efficient type of Japanese-funded enterprises in China includes the care type and profit-efficiency type of Chinese-funded enterprises. However, the organizational ethics of Japanese-funded enterprises in China emphasizes social responsibility. This has a lot to do with the social image that Japanese companies in China have to establish.

The Golden Mean style is closely related to the traditional Chinese notion of the Golden Mean as well as the Japanese managerial culture of staff-orientation. The social responsibility style is a product of the long-standing animosity between China and Japan, and a response to the resulting opposition faced by Japanese products in China as part of a larger effort to bolster their corporate image. And the prevalence of the friendship-efficiency style is at least partly attributable to the increasing tendency of JFMEs to act as MNCs in their focus on localization.

In the manufacturing industry, there are two typical organizational commitments in Japanese-funded enterprises in China, which are normative organizational commitments and economic organizational commitments. Whether it is a normative organizational commitment or an economic organizational commitment, it not only has a great relationship with China's objective reality but also is inextricably linked with the organizational ethical climate of Japanese companies in the manufacturing industry. In other words, the organizational ethic climate in Japanese-funded enterprises affects the organizational commitment or sense of belonging of employees.

In addition, two types of organizational commitment—normative and economic—have also been identified as a defining characteristic of JFMEs, both of which are

[2]Li Bo. A Study on the Structure and Amendment of Organizational Ethics Climates Questionnaire of Chinese Enterprises [D]. Shanxi University, 2008.

[3]Chao Gang, XiongYinzhu, Wang Lei, et al. An Empirical Study on Organizational Ethical Climate on Job Satisfaction and Employee Deviant Behavior[J]. Chinese Journal of Management, 2013, 10(11): 1611.

inextricable from the conditions of doing business in China as well as the organizational ethical climates discussed above. In fact, these organizational ethical climates have been shown to have a significant impact on the organizational commitment of individual employees.

Finally, task-based job performance is enhanced by JFMEs in two ways. First, production methods have been standardized in order to increase efficiency. Second, efficiency management techniques are used to incentivize and stimulate the low-wage laborers who tend to work in the manufacturing industry in accordance with the physiological and safety needs of the so-called "economic man." The following chapter analyzes the ways in which organizational ethical climates inform the cultivation of organizational commitment in JFMEs, and uses such analysis to propose certain HRM measures to enhance overall performance.

Therefore, in the measurement of the type of organizational ethical climate, the assumptions of the ethical atmosphere of Japanese-funded enterprises in the manufacturing industry in China include self-interest (self-interest-oriented), corporate profits (self-interested), efficiency, friendship (care-oriented), team interests (care-oriented), social responsibility, personal ethics (independent orientation), company rules and levels (rule-oriented), legal and professional norms (legal and regulatory) organizational ethics which are composed of nine dimensions that have not been fully verified. There are only three main ethical climates in the Japanese-funded enterprises in China, which are the moderate organizational ethics, the socially responsible organizational ethics, and the friendship-efficient organizational ethics. There is no verification of the organizational ethics of personal ethics (independent orientation), legal and professional norms (legal and regulatory orientation), team interests (care orientation) in organizational ethic climates. The other six organizational ethics climate have become a comprehensive organizational ethic atmosphere with a moderate organizational ethic atmosphere, a socially responsible organizational ethical climate, and a friendship-efficient organizational ethical climate.

The conclusions of this study and the types of organizational commitments of Chinese-funded enterprises are somewhat lacking. For example, Ling Wenquan (2001)'s research found that Chinese companies' organizational commitments include five factors: emotional commitment, normative commitment, ideal commitment, economic commitment, and opportunity commitment. In this study, we found that the main organizational commitment types of employees in Japanese-funded enterprises in China mainly include normative and economic organizational commitments. That is to say, there is a lack of emotional commitment and ideal commitment in Japanese-funded enterprises in China, which has a great relationship with the history of China and Japan. There are many political and cultural factors incorporated into it.

The definition of work performance definition and structure by Han Yi and Zhang Jing includes not only the two basic dimensions of task performance and relationship performance but also learning performance and innovation performance. Through the principal component analysis of the data of Japanese companies in the manufacturing industry in China, only one major component was obtained. According to the main load, the main component is task-based work performance.

Chapter 5
The Impact of Organizational Ethical Climate on Organizational Commitment in JFMEs in China

Insofar as the effectiveness of corporate HRM largely depends on the organizational ethical climate, a better understanding of the relationship between the two should help improve employee management. This chapter focuses on the impact of organizational ethical climate on organizational commitment in JFMEs in China, with a particular emphasis on the interaction between different types of ethical climates and organizational commitments.

5.1 The Impact of the Golden Mean Style of Organizational Ethical Climate on Normative Commitment in JFMEs

As discussed above, the main loading factors of the Golden Mean style of organizational ethical climate in JFMEs are EC4, EI1, EI3, BI4, EL1, BL3, BL2, and PI1, while the main loading factors of normative commitment are gf1, gf2, gf3, gf4, gf5, and gf6. As shown in Figs. 5.1 and 5.2, and as calculated by Stata, SEM has been used to determine the degree to which this Golden Mean style affects normative commitment.

The panes in the bottom half of the figures represent observed variables of the Golden Mean style of organizational ethical climate, which are also the main loading factors of the loading matrix, whereby L1 stands for the Golden Mean style as an endogenous latent variable measured through various observed variables (EC4, EI1, EI3, BI4, EL1, BL3, BL2, and PI1). The panes in the upper half of the figures represent observed variables of normative commitment, whereby Z1 stands for normative commitment as an exogenous latent variable. Finally, the error terms of each variable are set forth in the circles next to each pane. Generally speaking, the results suggest that the Golden Mean style of organizational ethical climate has a significantly positive impact on normative commitment with an influence coefficient value of 0.75 and a standard error of $p < 0.01$.

© Science Press and Springer Nature Singapore Pte Ltd. 2020

K. Ryu, *The Impact of Organizational Ethical Climate on Organizational Commitment and Job Performance*, https://doi.org/10.1007/978-981-15-2813-2_5

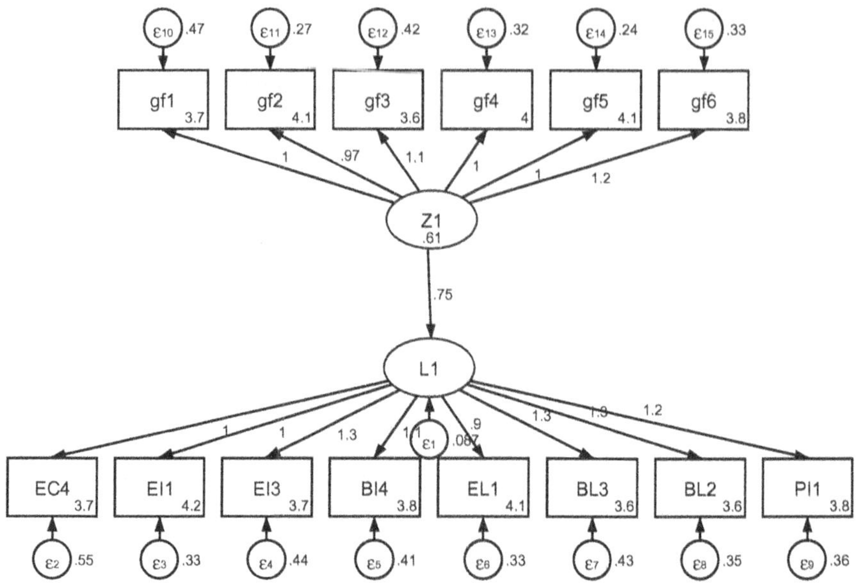

Fig. 5.1 Non-standardized structural figure of the impact of the Golden Mean style of organizational ethical climate on normative commitment in JFMEs

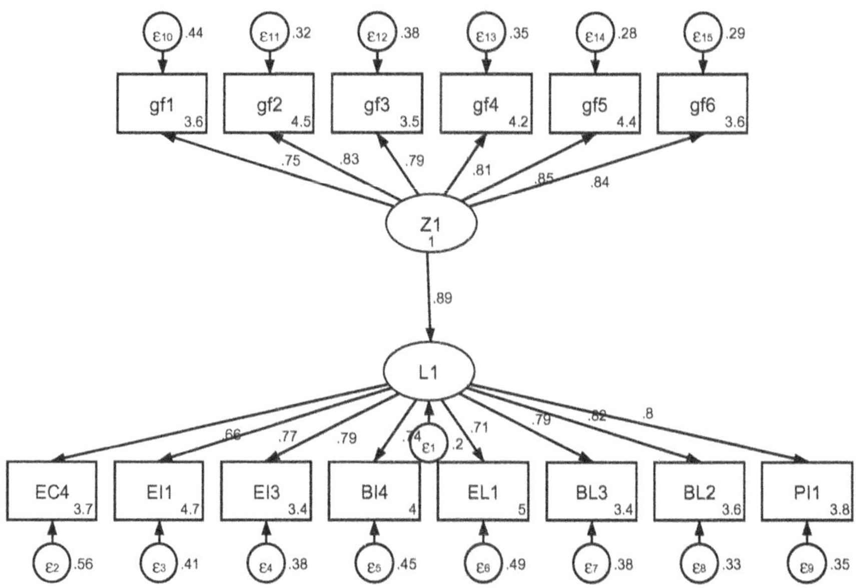

Fig. 5.2 Standardized structural figure of the impact of the Golden Mean style of organizational ethical climate on normative commitment in JFMEs

In addition, the following SEM regression tables reflect the significance of other observed variables, as well as the impact of the endogenous variables on the exogenous latent variables. The results clearly show that the Golden Mean style of organizational ethical climate (the endogenous latent variable) exerts a significant impact on normative commitment (the exogenous latent variable) as well as the measurement of the observed variables of the Golden Mean style of organizational commitment. The variances of these observed variables are shown in Tables 5.3 and 5.4, reflecting high significance in the variances of both the observed and latent variables (Tables 5.1, 5.2).

There are various explanations for this significant positive correlation between the Golden Mean style of organizational ethical climate and normative commitment. First, in terms of cultural influences; Chinese ideology maintains a strong influence on the operational philosophy of JFMEs, which is reflected in both their ethical climate and normative commitment. Traditional Chinese philosophy, as well as China's political and economic systems, remains strong determinants with respect to JFMEs' tendency to prioritize collectivism and national interest in dealing with employer-employee relationships. When the two sides are in conflict, employers, therefore, act on behalf of the organization (community), or in state-owned enterprises (SOEs), on behalf of the government, thereby subordinating employees' individual interests to those of the majority. The Chinese government also tends to favor the owners of private enterprises because their performance is often cited as a form of political achievement. Unlike in China, however, where management invariably has the upper hand, Japanese managers tend to assign a greater value to labor as necessary for the survival and development of enterprises, which means greater importance is placed on the individual interests of employees. It is the combination of this implicit contract between management and labor along with the impact of Chinese ideology and culture, which has led JFMEs in China to adopt the Golden Mean style of management.

Normative commitment in JFMEs is also affected by the social equity among employees, the level of employee satisfaction with their colleagues and the collective working spirit of the organization. The above analysis suggests that while JFMEs in China are strongly focused on the cultivation of team spirit and a caring organizational ethical climate, there is also no lack of self-interest in their operational philosophies, which contributes to the formation of a Golden Mean style discussed above. Generally speaking, therefore, the business administration of JFMEs typically takes three factors into account: employee satisfaction, team spirit, and fairness in wages—all of which are representative of the perceived need to cultivate a sense of fairness and belonging in their Chinese employees for the sake of long-term development. In the end, the Golden Mean style of organizational ethical climate ultimately leads to normative organizational commitment.

Table 5.1 Impact of the Golden Mean style of organizational ethical climate on normative commitment in JFMEs

Variables	(1) L1	(2) EC4	(3) EI1	(4) EI3	(5) BI4	(6) EL1	(7) BL3	(8) BL2	(9) PI1
L1		1 (0)	1.049*** (0.0149)	1.300*** (0.0181)	1.080*** (0.0156)	0.896*** (0.0133)	1.281*** (0.0175)	1.278*** (0.0172)	1.244*** (0.0168)
Z1	0.750*** (0.0114)								
Constant		3.658*** (0.00949)	4.173*** (0.00860)	3.659*** (0.0104)	3.847*** (0.00917)	4.126*** (0.00789)	3.589*** (0.0102)	3.637*** (0.00982)	3.797*** (0.00972)
Observations	11,083	11,083	11,083	11,083	11,083	11,083	11,083	11,083	11,083

Standard errors in parentheses
***$p < 0.01$, **$p < 0.05$, *$p < 0.1$

Table 5.2 (5.1 Cont.) Impact of the Golden Mean style of organizational ethical climate on normative commitment in JFMEs

(10) gf1	(11) gf2	(12) gf3	(13) gf4	(14) gf5	(15) gf6
1 (0)	0.969*** (0.0110)	1.065*** (0.0125)	1.004*** (0.0116)	1.013*** (0.0111)	1.154*** (0.0126)
3.704*** (0.00996)	4.084*** (0.00878)	3.631*** (0.0101)	4.045*** (0.00928)	4.060*** (0.00893)	3.802*** (0.0103)
11,083	11,083	11,083	11,083	11,083	11,083

Standard errors in parentheses
***$p < 0.01$, **$p < 0.05$, *$p < 0.1$

5.2 The Impact of the Golden Mean Style of Organizational Ethical Climate on Economic Commitment in JFMEs

Because data limitations prevent the use of SEM to analyze the impact of the Golden Mean style of organizational ethical climate on economic commitment in JFMEs, the relationship between the two has been examined through the covariance between endogenous latent variables of the Golden Mean style and economic commitment. The resulting covariance coefficient of 0.42 indicates that the two share the same direction of deviance and can therefore be said to be closely correlated and even mutually reinforcing (Fig. 5.3).

There are several possible explanations for the ability of the Golden Mean style of organizational ethical climate to reinforce economic commitment. While many Chinese enterprises have adopted Taylor's scientific management theory based on the ideology of the "economic man," Chinese employees of JFMEs find such a philosophy hard to accept, which leads to inefficiency. But such inefficiency is more attributable to historical stereotypes rather than any self-interested style of leadership, as corroborated by the fact that organizational climates under entirely altruistic leadership tend to fail as well. In fact, front-line employees in China, particularly those in the manufacturing industry who are marginalized by the labor market, earn such low wages that they attach great importance to economic in centives, which tends to render an altruistic management philosophy ineffective. In addition, China has long been influenced by the traditional notion of the Golden Mean, under which a management philosophy that merges self-interest and altruism is expected to yield results. This can also be explained by Fiedler's contingency theory of management. All of this supports the conclusion that the Golden Mean style of organizational ethical climate tends to encourage economic commitment.

Table 5.3 (5.1 Cont.) Impact of the Golden Mean style of organizational ethical climate on normative commitment in JFMEs

(16) var(e.EC4)	(17) var(e.EI1)	(18) var(e.EI3)	(19) var(e.BI4)	(20) var(e.EL1)	(21) var(e.BL3)	(22) var(e.BL2)	(23) var(e.PI1)	(24) var(e.gf1)
0.548*** (0.00792)	0.330*** (0.00517)	0.441*** (0.00693)	0.411*** (0.00613)	0.331*** (0.00486)	0.433*** (0.00666)	0.346*** (0.00563)	0.362*** (0.00570)	0.469*** (0.00705)
11,083	11,083	11,083	11,083	11,083	11,083	11,083	11,083	11,083

Standard errors in parentheses
***$p < 0.01$, **$p < 0.05$, *$p < 0.1$

Table 5.4 (5.1 Cont.) Impact of the Golden Mean style of organizational ethical climate on normative commitment in JFMEs

(25) var(e.gf2)	(26) var(e.gf3)	(27) var(e.gf4)	(28) var(e.gf5)	(29) var(e.gf6)	(30) var(e.L1)	(31) var(Z1)
0.266*** (0.00432)	0.418*** (0.00645)	0.322*** (0.00511)	0.241*** (0.00404)	0.335*** (0.00557)	0.0869*** (0.00298)	0.606*** (0.0135)
11,083	11,083	11,083	11,083	11,083	11,083	11,083

Standard errors in parentheses
***p < 0.01, **p < 0.05, *p < 0.1

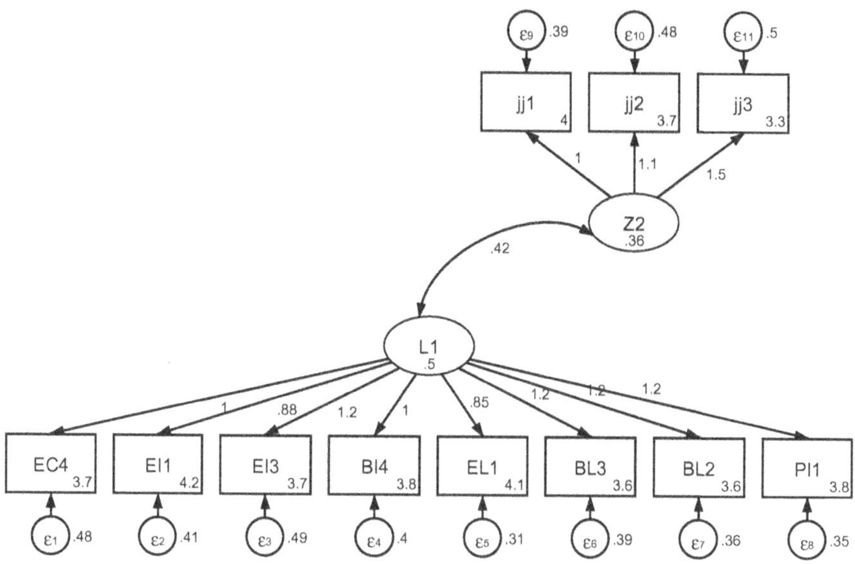

Fig. 5.3 Standardized structural figure of the impact of the Golden Mean style of organizational ethical climate on economic commitment in JFMEs

5.3 The Impact of the Social Responsibility Style of Organizational Ethical Climate on Normative Commitment in JFMEs

As discussed above, the main loading factors of the social responsibility style of organizational ethical climate adopted by JFMEs are BC3, BI2, BI3, EC2, BI1, and EC3, while the main loading factors of normative commitment are gf1, gf2, gf3, gf4, gf5, and gf6. As shown in the structural figures below, and as calculated by Stata, SEM has been used to determine the degree to which this social responsibility style affects normative commitment (Figs. 5.4, 5.5).

The panes in the bottom half of the figures represent observed variables of the social responsibility style of organizational ethical climate, which are also the main

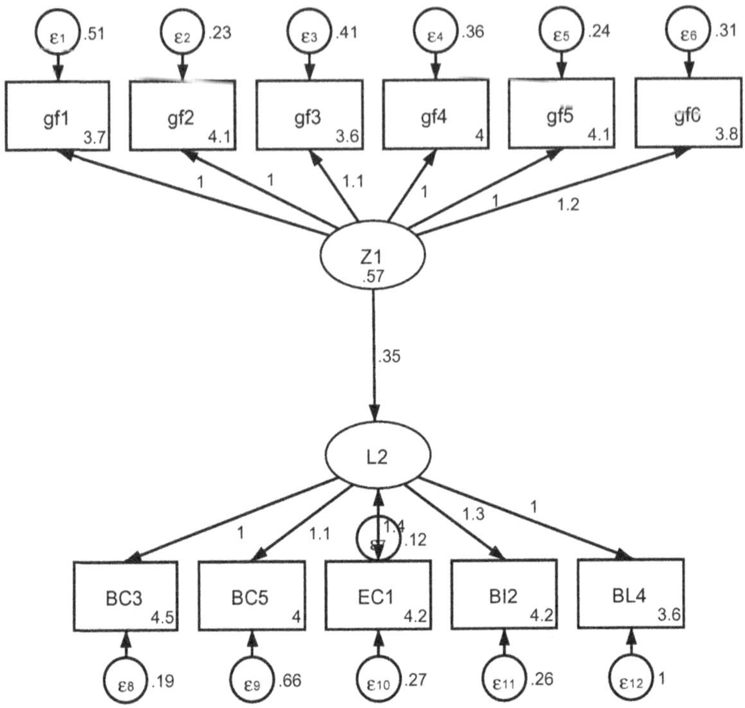

Fig. 5.4 Non-standardized structural figure of the impact of the social responsibility style of organizational ethical climate on normative commitment in JFMEs

loading factors of the loading matrix, whereby L2 stands for the social responsibility style as an endogenous latent variable measured through various observed variables (BC3, BI2, BI3, EC2, BI1, and EC3). The panes in the upper half of the figures represent observed variables of normative commitment, whereby Z1 stands for normative commitment as an exogenous latent variable. Finally, the error terms of each variable are set forth in the circles next to each pane.

As evident in the SEM regression data in Table 5.5 (showing an influence coefficient value of 0.35 and a standard error of $p < 0.01$), the results clearly show that the observed variables associated with the social responsibility style of organizational ethical climate (the endogenous latent variable) exerts a significant positive impact on normative commitment (the exogenous latent variable), as well as on the measurement of the observed variables of social responsibility and organizational commitment. Moreover, as shown in Tables 5.6 and 5.7, the variances of the observed and both latent variables also reflect high significance.

In sum, it is clear that the social responsibility style of organizational ethical climate can help JFMEs enhance their corporate image while encouraging normative commitment among employees by instilling in them a sense of fairness. That said,

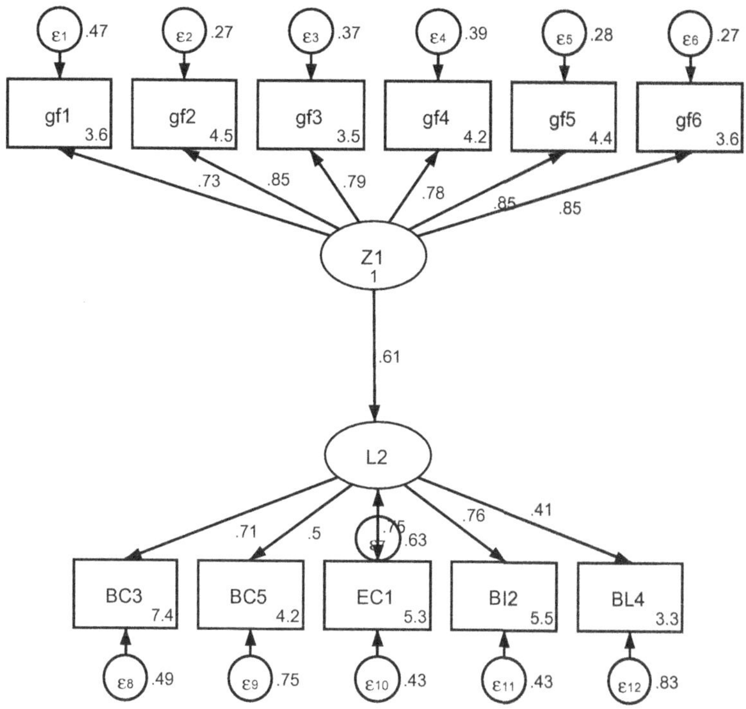

Fig. 5.5 Standardized structural figure of the impact of the social responsibility style of organizational ethical climate on normative commitment in JFMEs

insofar as the fulfillment of social responsibility necessarily requires higher profits, JFMEs must at the same time set up effective regulations and adopt scientific management techniques to enhance operational efficiency.

5.4 The Impact of the Social Responsibility Style of Organizational Ethical Climate on Economic Commitment in JFMEs

The main loading factors of the social responsibility style of organizational ethical climate adopted by JFMEs are BC3, BI2, BI3, EC2, BI1, and EC3, while the main loading factors of economic commitment are jj1, jj2 and jj3. As shown in the structural figures below, and as calculated by Stata, SEM has been used to determine the degree to which this social responsibility style affects economic commitment (Figs. 5.6, 5.7).

As evident in the SEM regression data in the following tables, the results clearly show that the social responsibility style of organizational ethical climate (the endogenous latent variable) exerts a significant positive impact on economic commitment

Table 5.5 Impact of the social responsibility style of organizational ethical climate on normative commitment in JFMEs

Variables	(1) L2	(2) BC3	(3) BC5	(4) EC1	(5) BI2	(6) BL4	(7) gf1	(8) gf2	(9) gf3	(10) gf4	(11) gf5	(12) gf6
L2		1 (0)	1.060*** (0.0232)	1.364*** (0.0196)	1.342*** (0.0201)	1.034*** (0.0288)						
Z1	0.353*** (0.00716)						1 (0)	1.037*** (0.0119)	1.108*** (0.0135)	1.004*** (0.0125)	1.046*** (0.0121)	1.212*** (0.0137)
Constant		4.520*** (0.00590)	3.953*** (0.00898)	4.165*** (0.00760)	4.237*** (0.00745)	3.594*** (0.0105)	3.705*** (0.00993)	4.083*** (0.00876)	3.630*** (0.0101)	4.046*** (0.00925)	4.060*** (0.00891)	3.799*** (0.0103)
Observations	11,083	11,083	11,083	11,083	11,083	11,083	11,083	11,083	11,083	11,083	11,083	11,083

Standard errors in parentheses
***$p < 0.01$, **$p < 0.05$, *$p < 0.1$

Table 5.6 (5.5 Cont.) Impact of the social responsibility style of organizational ethical climate on normative commitment in JFMEs

Variables	(13) var(e.BC3)	(14) var(e.BC5)	(15) var(e.EC1)	(16) var(e.BI2)	(17) var(e.BL4)	(18) var(e.gf1)	(19) var(e.gf2)
	0.185*** (0.00330)	0.661*** (0.00966)	0.270*** (0.00532)	0.257*** (0.00495)	0.995*** (0.0144)	0.507*** (0.00759)	0.226*** (0.00394)
Observations	11,083	11,083	11,083	11,083	11,083	11,083	11,083

Standard errors in parentheses
***p < 0.01, **p < 0.05, *p < 0.1

Table 5.7 (5.5 Cont.) Impact of the social responsibility style of organizational ethical climate on normative commitment in JFMEs

Variables	(20) var(e.EI4)	(21) var(e.gf4)	(22) var(e.gf5)	(23) var(e.gf6)	(24) var(e.L2)	(25) var(Z1)
	0.412*** (0.00652)	0.359*** (0.00563)	0.244*** (0.00424)	0.313*** (0.00547)	0.122*** (0.00357)	0.566*** (0.0132)
Observations	11,083	11,083	11,083	11,083	11,083	11,083

Standard errors in parentheses
***p < 0.01, **p < 0.05, *p < 0.1

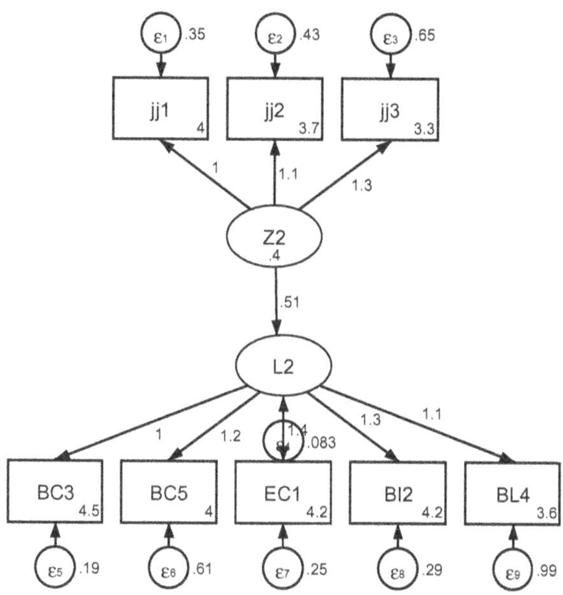

Fig. 5.6 Non-standardized structural figure of the impact of the social responsibility style of organizational ethical climate on economic commitment in JFMEs

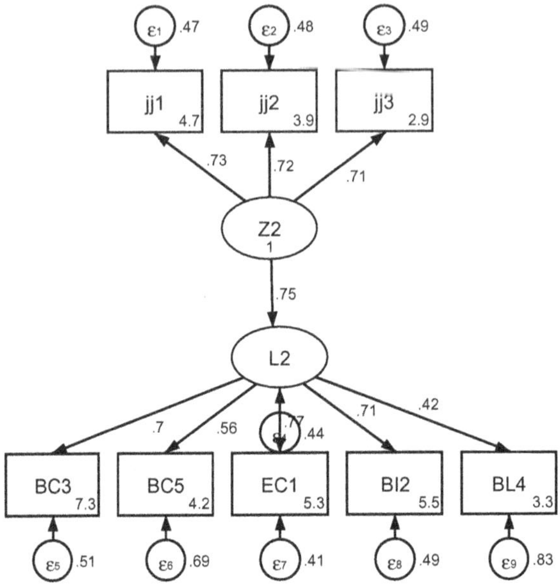

Fig. 5.7 Standardized structural figure of the impact of the social responsibility style of organizational ethical climate on economic commitment in JFMEs

(the exogenous latent variable) as well as on the measurement of the observed variables of social responsibility and organizational commitment. As shown in the tables below, the variances of the observed and both latent variables also reflect high significance (Table 5.8, 5.9 and 5.10).

Generally speaking, assuming greater social responsibility benefits JFMEs in two ways. First, it reduces opposition from Chinese consumers and employees, thereby enhancing operational efficiency. Second, it helps win much-needed support from local governments, which is especially important given how Chinese society works today. Although China's modern enterprise management system is based on market economics, China is still largely a socialist country dominated by state-owned enterprises (SOEs), and because SOEs are managed by the Communist Party, government functions are inseparable from enterprise management. An effective corporate culture thereby requires not just operational efficiency, but also a certain level of support from the government in order to remain competitive. By attracting this support while cultivating a sense of fairness and team spirit among employees, the social responsibility style of organizational ethical climate is an effective tool for enhancing operational efficiency and economic commitment. Accordingly, though the significant time and money necessary to develop such a climate does not necessarily yield any tangible results as with R&D, the potential benefits for corporate branding, marketing, recruitment, and morale all help strengthen normative commitment.

Table 5.8 Impact of the social responsibility style of organizational ethical climate on economic commitment in JFMEs

Variables	(1) L2	(2) BC3	(3) BC5	(4) EC1	(5) BI2	(6) BL4	(7) jj1	(8) jj2	(9) jj3
L2		1 (0)	1.208*** (0.0251)	1.417*** (0.0202)	1.285*** (0.0197)	1.058*** (0.0296)			
Z2	0.510*** (0.00973)						1 (0)	1.088*** (0.0182)	1.304*** (0.0210)
Constant		4.519*** (0.00590)	3.950*** (0.00898)	4.164*** (0.00759)	4.236*** (0.00743)	3.592*** (0.0105)	4.045*** (0.00831)	3.683*** (0.00909)	3.291*** (0.0110)
Observations	11,083	11,083	11,083	11,083	11,083	11,083	11,083	11,083	11,083

Standard errors in parentheses
***$p < 0.01$, **$p < 0.05$, *$p < 0.1$

Table 5.9 (5.8 Cont.) Impact of the social responsibility style of organizational ethical climate on economic commitment in JFMEs

Variables	(10) var(e.BC3)	(11) var(e.BC5)	(12) var(e.EC1)	(13) var(e.BI2)	(14) var(e.BL4)	(15) var(e.jj1)
	0.194*** (0.00340)	0.607*** (0.00931)	0.255*** (0.00522)	0.295*** (0.00520)	0.994*** (0.0144)	0.355*** (0.00689)
Observations	11,083	11,083	11,083	11,083	11,083	11,083

Standard errors in parentheses
***p < 0.01, **p < 0.05, *p < 0.1

Table 5.10 (5.8 Cont.) Impact of the social responsibility style of organizational ethical climate on economic commitment in JFMEs

Variables	(16) var(e.jj2)	(17) var(e.jj3)	(18) var(e.L2)	(19) var(Z2)
Constant	0.431*** (0.00828)	0.652*** (0.0122)	0.0828*** (0.00319)	0.398*** (0.0103)
Observations	11,083	11,083	11,083	11,083

Standard errors in parentheses
***p < 0.01, **p < 0.05, *p < 0.1

5.5 The Impact of the Friendship-Efficiency Style of Organizational Ethical Climate on Normative Commitment in JFMEs

As for the friendship-efficiency style of organizational ethical climate which has been shown to exist in JFMEs, the main loading factors include BC3, BI2, BI3, EC2, EI4, BI1, and EC3, while the main loading factors of normative commitment include gf1, gf2, gf3, gf4, gf5, and gf6. As shown in the structural figures below, and as calculated by Stata, SEM has again been used to determine the degree to which this social responsibility style affects normative commitment (Figs. 5.8, 5.9).

The panes in the bottom half of the figures represent observed variables of the friendship-efficiency style of organizational ethical climate, which are also the main loading factors of the loading matrix, whereby L3 stands for the friendship-efficiency style of organizational ethical climate as an endogenous latent variable measured through various observed variables (EC4, EI1, EI3, BI4, EL1, BL3, BL2, and PI1). The panes in the upper half of the figures represent observed variables of normative commitment, with Z1 standing for normative commitment as an exogenous latent variable. Finally, the error terms of each variable are set forth in the circles next to each pane. Generally speaking, the results suggest that the friendship-efficiency style of organizational ethical climate has a significantly positive impact on normative commitment with an influence coefficient value of 0.31 and a standard error of $p < 0.01$. In addition, the following SEM regression tables reflect the significance of

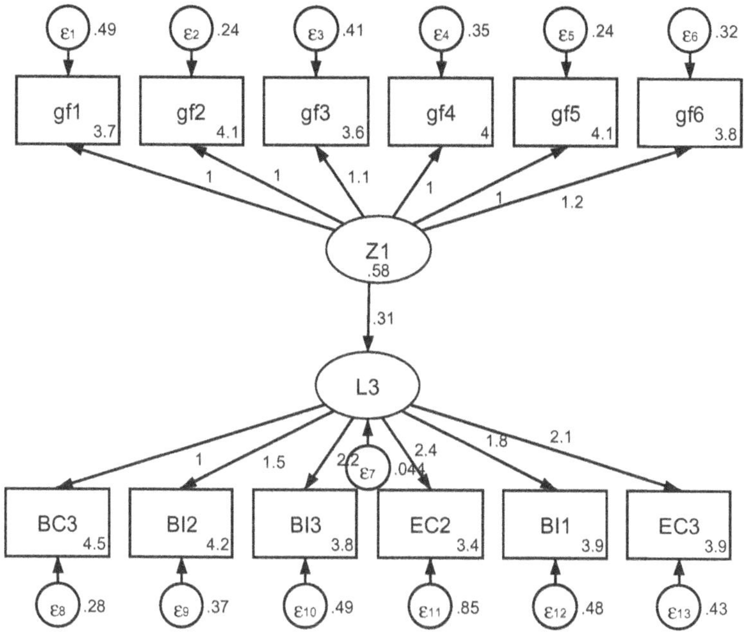

Fig. 5.8 Non-standardized structural figure of the impact of the friendship-efficiency style of organizational ethical climate on normative commitment in JFMEs

other observed variables, as well as the impact of the endogenous variables on the exogenous latent variables (Tables 5.11, 5.12, 5.13 and 5.14).

The management philosophies of JFMEs are necessarily influenced by Japanese culture and based on the belief that self-interest and efficiency should ultimately be grounded in altruism. As a result, the tendency of Japanese enterprises to place a special emphasis on employee and consumer satisfaction leads to the development of a friendship-efficiency style of organizational climate, under which loyalty is fostered through training, investment and the cultivation of an overall sense of belonging (Fig. 5.10).

5.6 The Impact of the Friendship-Efficiency Style of Organizational Ethical Climate on Economic Commitment in JFMEs

As with the various other styles of organizational ethical climate discussed above, SEM has also been used to determine the degree to which the friendship-efficiency style of organizational ethical climate affects economic commitment in JFMEs.

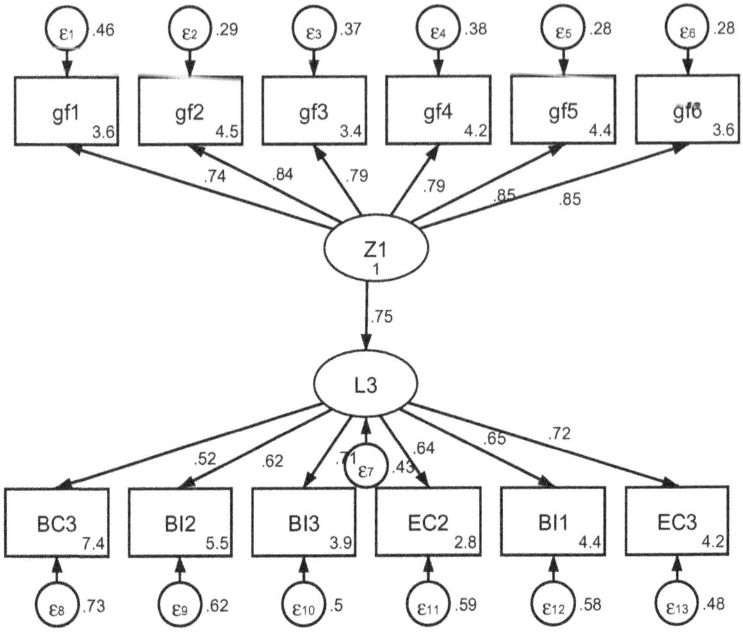

Fig. 5.9 Standardized structural figure of the impact of the friendship-efficiency style of organizational ethical climate on normative commitment in JFMEs

Table 5.11 Impact of the friendship-efficiency style of organizational ethical climate on normative commitment in JFMEs

Variables	(1) L1	(2) BC3	(3) BI2	(4) BI3	(5) EC2	(6) BI1	(7) EC3
L1		1 (0)	1.514*** (0.0321)	2.202*** (0.0467)	2.430*** (0.0541)	1.836*** (0.0420)	2.124*** (0.0445)
Z1	0.315*** (0.00703)						
Constant		4.521*** (0.00589)	4.237*** (0.00746)	3.836*** (0.00953)	3.364*** (0.0115)	3.933*** (0.00867)	3.936*** (0.00902)
Observations	11,083	11,083	11,083	11,083	11,083	11,083	11,083

Standard errors in parentheses
***p < 0.01, **p < 0.05, *p < 0.1

Structural figures showing the results of this analysis, as calculated by Stata, are set forth below.

In addition, the following SEM regression tables reflect the significance of other observed variables, as well as the impact of the endogenous variables on the exogenous latent variables. With an influence coefficient value of 0.46 and a standard error

Table 5.12 (5.11 Cont.) Impact of the friendship-efficiency style of organizational ethical climate on normative commitment in JFMEs

Variables	(8) gf1	(9) gf2	(10) gf3	(11) gf4	(12) gf5	(13) gf6
L1						
Z1	1 (0)	1.011*** (0.0115)	1.094*** (0.0131)	1.000*** (0.0122)	1.031*** (0.0117)	1.191*** (0.0133)
Constant	3.706*** (0.00994)	4.084*** (0.00876)	3.630*** (0.0101)	4.046*** (0.00926)	4.060*** (0.00891)	3.801*** (0.0103)
Observations	11,083	11,083	11,083	11,083	11,083	11,083

Standard errors in parentheses
***p < 0.01, **p < 0.05, *p < 0.1

Table 5.13 (5.11 Cont.) Impact of the friendship-efficiency style of organizational ethical climate on normative commitment in JFMEs

Variables	(14) var(e.BC3)	(15) var(e.BI2)	(16) var(e.BI3)	(17) var(e.EC2)	(18) var(e.BI1)	(19) var(e.EC3)	(20) var(e.gf1)
	0.276*** (0.00404)	0.372*** (0.00577)	0.495*** (0.00940)	0.849*** (0.0133)	0.475*** (0.00849)	0.427*** (0.00844)	0.492*** (0.00739)
Observations	11,083	11,083	11,083	11,083	11,083	11,083	11,083

Standard errors in parentheses
***p < 0.01, **p < 0.05, *p < 0.1

Table 5.14 (5.11 Cont.) Impact of the friendship-efficiency style of organizational ethical climate on normative commitment in JFMEs

Variables	(21) var(e.569)	(22) var(e.572)	(23) var(e.698)	(24) var(e.463)	(25) var(e.gf6)	(26) var(e.L1)	(27) var(Z1)
	0.356*** (0.00668)	0.332*** (0.00523)	0.408*** (0.00810)	0.312*** (0.0123)	0.317*** (0.00549)	0.0436*** (0.00190)	0.581*** (0.0133)
Observations	11,083	11,083	11,083	11,083	11,083	11,083	11,083

Standard errors in parentheses
***p < 0.01, **p < 0.05, *p < 0.1

of $p < 0.01$, the results clearly show that the friendship-efficiency style of organizational ethical climate has a significant positive impact on economic commitment (Fig. 5.11, Tables 5.15, 5.16, 5.17 and 5.18).

Generally speaking, while the type of ethical climate cultivated by an organization does not directly change employee behavior, it does serve to regulate the relationship of the four stages set forth in Fig. 2.2 above, under which rules and professional codes climates have a moderating effect on individual moral judgments and behavioral intentions (Tim 2000). In addition, a positive ethical climate necessarily entails regulation between individuals and organizations, whereby positive interaction between the two helps to strengthen members' perception of organizational ethical climate and thereby enhance their level of commitment. In addition,

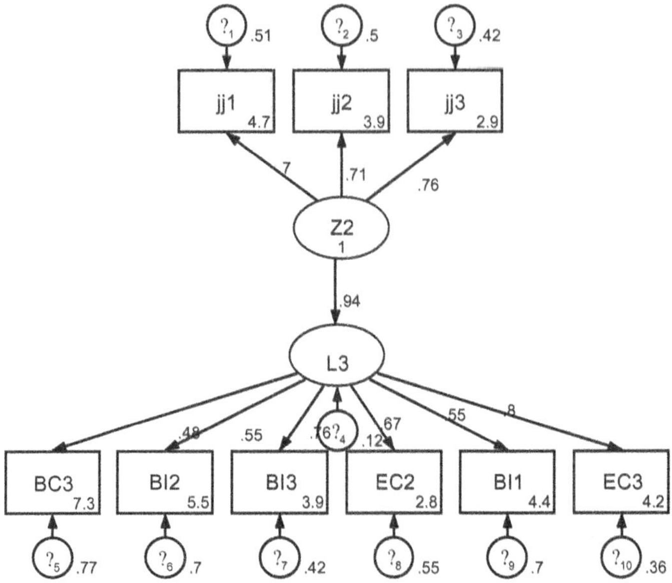

Fig. 5.10 Non-standardized structural figure of the impact of the friendship-efficiency style of organizational ethical climate on economic commitment in JFMEs

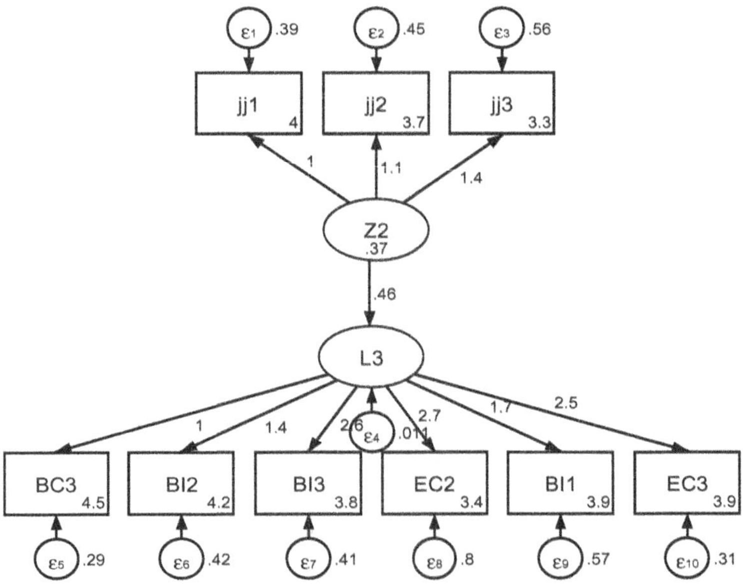

Fig. 5.11 Standardized structural figure of the impact of the friendship-efficiency style of organizational ethical climate on economic commitment in JFMEs

Table 5.15 Impact of the friendship-efficiency style of organizational ethical climate on economic commitment in JFMEs

	(1) L3	(2) BC3	(3) BI2	(4) BI3	(5) EC2	(6) BI1	(7) EC3
L3		1 (0)	1.449*** (0.0343)	2.555*** (0.0538)	2.716*** (0.0614)	1.686*** (0.0416)	2.549*** (0.0524)
Z2	0.456*** (0.0102)						
Constant		4.519*** (0.00590)	4.236*** (0.00745)	3.836*** (0.00950)	3.362*** (0.0115)	3.933*** (0.00866)	3.936*** (0.00900)
Observations	11,083	11,083	11,083	11,083	11,083	11,083	11,083

Standard errors in parentheses
***p < 0.01, **p < 0.05, *p < 0.1

Table 5.16 (5.15 Cont.) Impact of the friendship-efficiency style of organizational ethical climate on economic commitment in JFMEs

	(8) jj1	(9) jj2	(10) jj3
L3			
Z2	1 (0)	1.110*** (0.0170)	1.440*** (0.0207)
Constant	4.044*** (0.00832)	3.683*** (0.00910)	3.292*** (0.0110)
Observations	11,083	11,083	11,083

Standard errors in parentheses
***p < 0.01, **p < 0.05, *p < 0.1

Table 5.17 (5.15 Cont.) Impact of the friendship-efficiency style of organizational ethical climate on economic commitment in JFMEs

Variables	(11) var(e.BC3)	(12) var(e.BI2)	(13) var(e.BI3)	(14) var(e.EC2)	(15) var(e.BI1)	(16) var(e.EC3)	(17) var(e.jj1)
	0.292*** (0.00415)	0.420*** (0.00610)	0.413*** (0.00717)	0.803*** (0.0124)	0.567*** (0.00830)	0.315*** (0.00595)	0.385*** (0.00628)
Observations	11,083	11,083	11,083	11,083	11,083	11,083	11,083

Standard errors in parentheses
***p < 0.01, **p < 0.05, *p < 0.1

Table 5.18 (5.15 Cont.) Impact of the friendship-efficiency style of organizational ethical climate on economic commitment in JFMEs

Variables	(18) var(e.jj2)	(19) var(e.jj3)	(20) var(e.L3)	(21) var(Z2)
	0.448*** (0.00738)	0.563*** (0.0102)	0.0106*** (0.000870)	0.369*** (0.00945)
Observations	11,083	11,083	11,083	11,083

Standard errors in parentheses
***p < 0.01, **p < 0.05, *p < 0.1

the identification of organizational ethical climate also enables a higher degree of coordination between members and organizations.

Finally, to some extent at least, the impact of the friendship-efficiency style of organizational ethical climate on organizational commitment is necessarily determined by the underlying values and priorities of individual employees. As discussed above, most front-line employees of JFMEs are comprised of economically marginalized Chinese laborers suffering from low wages and job insecurity who tend to attach greater importance to economic commitment. Fortunately, the results of this research show that a friendship-efficiency style of organizational ethical climate has a significant positive impact on economic commitment, thereby suggesting that then eeds and priorities of these employees are satisfied.

5.7 Conclusions Concerning the Impact of Organizational Ethical Climate on Organizational Commitment in JFMEs

As discussed above, the Golden Mean style of organizational ethical climate has been shown to have a strong impact on normative commitment in JFMEs with an influence coefficient of 0.75, the influence coefficient for the impact of social responsibility climate on normative and economic commitment is 0.35 and 0.51, respectively, while the influence coefficient for the impact of friendship-efficiency climate on normative and economic commitment is 0.31 and 0.46, respectively. These results clearly indicate that the Golden Mean style of organizational ethical climate has the greatest impact on normative commitment and that social responsibility climate has the greatest impact on economic commitment, both of which are rooted in the unique characteristics of Chinese and Japanese culture as well as the management philosophy of Japan (Table 5.19).

The findings demonstrate the hypothesis H2 that organizational ethics is positively related to organizational commitment. The sub-hypotheses H2.1–H2.6 have also been verified on the dimensions of the organizational ethical climate and the actual

Table 5.19 Influence coefficient of organizational ethics on organizational commitment

Organizational commitment type organizational ethic type	Normative organizational commitment Z1	Economic organization commitment Z2
Moderate organizational ethics, L1	0.75	0.42
Social responsibility organization ethics, L2	0.35	0.51
Friendship-efficient organizational ethics, L3	0.31	0.46

measured dimensions of organizational commitment of Japanese-funded enterprises in the manufacturing industry in China.

In fact, Japanese enterprises have long engaged in social responsibility efforts. As Konosuke Matsushita said during the "Commemorative Day of Business" in 1932, "I have known the duty of an industrialist: overcoming poverty and making society richer. The purpose of production is to enrich our daily life with the necessities and expand the content of life. Such is the ultimate duty of our nationals."[1] Japanese enterprises therefore tend to be people-oriented insofar as they view corporations as a collective of individuals, whose needs must come first so that employee productivity can be increased, thereby generating more wealth for the enterprise and society as a whole. Under this worldview, the value of corporations is to make society prosperous while making itself appreciated by employees. Therefore, while Japanese enterprises continue to value family-style loyalty under which core employees are granted absolute discretion to manage the affairs of the enterprise, they also strive to develop positive living and working conditions for all employees.[2]

When these enterprises come to China, this focus on social responsibility is sustained not just by tradition but also by Chinese policies with respect to Japan. As China expects more social responsibility from Japanese enterprises, JFMEs have been forced to contribute more to society in order to enhance their corporate image and counteract the historical animosity between the two countries. Moreover, while the task or work-oriented management philosophies adopted by JFMEs tend to be more efficient, the effectiveness of such philosophies is necessarily undermined by hostility from Chinese laborers. At the same time, however, if JFMEs are completely employee-oriented, productivity can also be negatively impacted. This is why JFMEs in China appear to favor a Golden Mean style of organizational ethical climate while cultivating normative and economic commitment through a social responsibility style of organizational ethical climate.

In order to localize CSR, some Japanese-funded enterprises will summarize the social contribution made by the company, establish a CSR plan for the year, and include this plan into the company's development strategy for the coming year to ensure the smooth development of the company's CSR localization activities. At the same time, Japanese-funded enterprises in China are actively carrying out a variety of social welfare activities that are highly relevant to Chinese society, such as donating money to underdeveloped or underfunded areas, organizing environmental protection activities to plant trees, and building elementary schools. In addition, CSR awards were established to recognize the outstanding performance of CSR localization activities in Japanese companies' Chinese branches.

---

[1]Li. Ping Japan is "taking a shortcut" in building up corporate ethics[J]. Chinese and Foreign Corporate Culture, 2003(3):48–50.

[2]Huiying Hou, Changsheng Zhang. The Sovereign Phenomenon of Japanese Operators and the Reform of Corporate Governance Structure [J]. Contemporary Economy of Japan, 2005(4):51–54. Yan Zhang. Reflections on the Current New Humanistic Management Model—Taking the Experience of Japanese Enterprise Management as a Case [J]. Business Week, 2004(7):42–43.

Chapter 6
The Relationship Between Organizational Ethical Climate, Organizational Commitment, and Job Performance in JFMEs in China

Organizational ethical climate refers to a shared perception among organization members about how to address ethical questions. As such, it underlies the decisions of the organization and its members and has a significant effect on their behavior. In fact, research has shown that different organizational ethical climates impact individual members in different ways: the more positive a climate is, the more it encourages ethical behavior and organizational performance, while negative climates tend to be associated with unethical and deviant behaviors such as lying, stealing, rule-breaking, and other misconduct. Through its impact on individual behavior, the organizational ethical climate has also been shown to affect job performance.

At the same time, in today's modern knowledge economy, the key to sustainable development lies in making good use of human resources within the organization, which in turn hasbeen shown to have a positive influence on job performance and the development of the core competence. While much research has focused on job performance in terms of working attitude, this study approaches job performance as a product of organizational commitment and interprets the results to propose various practical HRM measures designed to boost organizational commitment and individual performance. The underlying aim is to model the impact of organizational commitment on job performance in China, which can then be used as a reference for the enhancement of HRM.

6.1 The Golden Mean Style of Organizational Ethics, Normative Commitment, and Job Performance

As prior research has shown that organizational ethical climate can enhance job performance by encouraging positive work behaviors, this study is focused on the relationship between organizational ethical climate, organizational commitment and job performance in JFMEs in China. Moreover, insofar as the organizational ethical climate has been shown to impact job performance both directly and indirectly (i.e. by

© Science Press and Springer Nature Singapore Pte Ltd. 2020

K. Ryu, *The Impact of Organizational Ethical Climate on Organizational Commitment and Job Performance*, https://doi.org/10.1007/978-981-15-2813-2_6

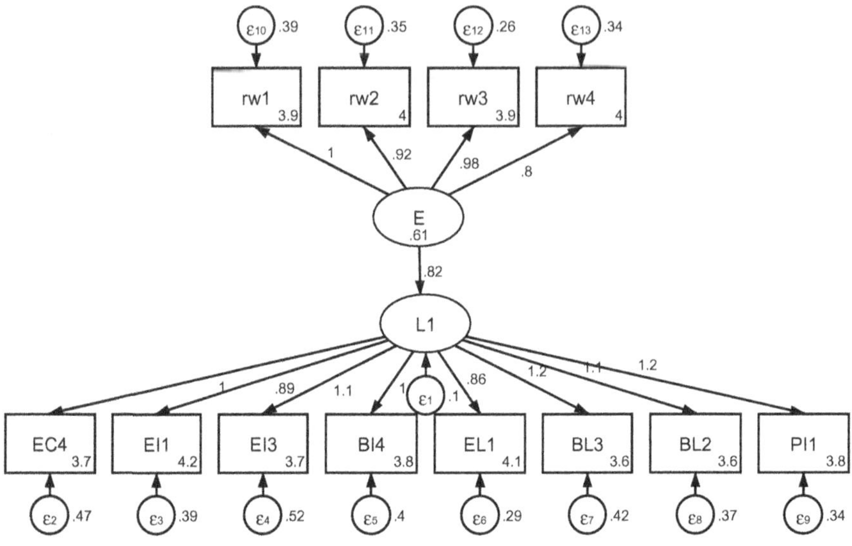

Fig. 6.1 Non-standardized effect of the influence of the Golden Mean style of the organizational ethical climate on job performance

strengthening organizational commitment), this study seeks to explore the dynamics between organizational ethical climate and job performance, organizational commitment and job performance, as well as organizational ethical climate, organizational commitment, and job performance (Figs. 6.1 and 6.2).

As a preliminary matter, the results suggest that the Golden Mean style of organizational ethical climate can, to some extent, influence work behaviors (and in turn job performance) through its focus on employees and tasks. As indicated by the SEM results set forth in Table 6.1, the path coefficient of the Golden Mean style of organizational ethical climate and job performance is as high as 0.82, suggesting that the former can significantly enhance the latter (Figs. 6.3 and 6.4, Tables 6.2 and 6.3).

To the extent that SEM shows a correlation between ethical climate and job performance as well as normative commitment and job performance, these results also confirm the findings of prior research that the Golden Mean style of organizational ethical climate has the potential to impact job performance both directly and indirectly, i.e. through its effect on normative commitment. Specifically, the path coefficient for the direct impact of the Golden Mean style of organizational ethical climate on job performance was found to be 0.47, while the path coefficient between the Golden Mean style of organizational ethical climate and organizational commitment, as well as organizational commitment and job performance, was 0.48 and 0.68, respectively.

Moreover, while related empirical surveys on JFMEs have indicated that the path coefficient for the impact of the Golden Mean style of organizational ethical climate on normative commitment is 0.75, the path coefficient for its impact on organizational commitment in this study was found to be much lower at 0.48. This suggests that the impact of the Golden Mean style of organizational ethical climate assumes

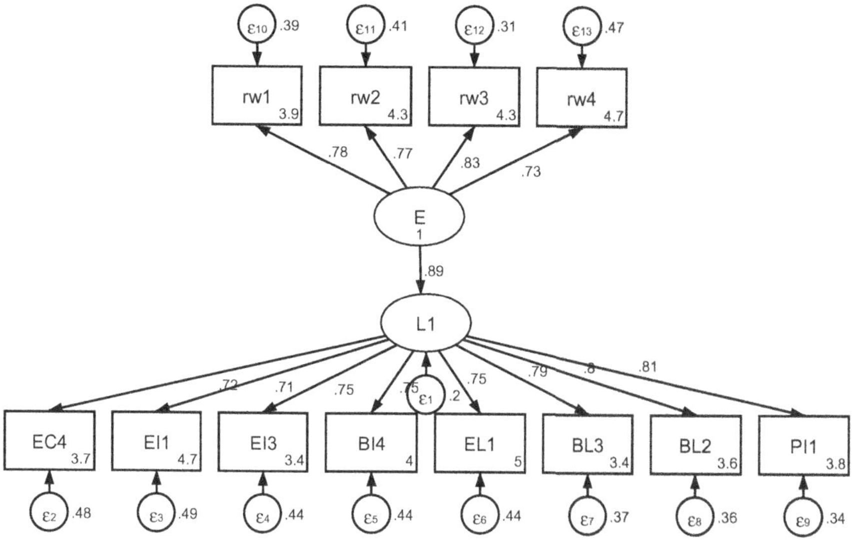

Fig. 6.2 Standardized effect of the impact of the Golden Mean style of the organizational ethical climate on job performance

two distinct paths. At the same time, the influential coefficient for the impact of the Golden Mean style of organizational ethical climate on job performance was found to be 0.82, with a path coefficient of 0.47 for the direct path and 0.68 for the indirect path. Generally speaking, this supports previous findings that the Golden Mean style of organizational ethical climate has both a direct and indirect impact on job performance (Tables 6.4, 6.5, 6.6 and 6.7).

As discussed above, the Golden Mean style of organizational ethical climate represents a combination of both caring and instrumental climates. A caring climate is focused primarily on the well-being of employees and tends to encourage an atmosphere of "solidarity and mutual assistance" whereby employees view team interest as a means to promote self-interest. When faced with ethical dilemmas, research has shown that such employees are less likely to engage in unethical behavior, which serves to further enhance job performance. An instrumental climate, on the other hand, is characterized by extreme individualism whereby employees prioritize their own self-interest above all else. Taken to its logical extreme, such a climate can lead to the wholesale neglect of organizational interest along with rampant unethical behavior, which would necessarily have an adverse effect on job performance.

Therefore, while the Golden Mean style of organizational ethics has the potential to negatively affect job performance by promoting instrumentalism, it can also serve to serve the interests of both employees and the organization while facilitating stronger relationships and team building, both of which are conducive to the development of a more caring climate and stronger job performance.

Table 6.1 Impact of the Golden Mean style of organizational ethical climate on job performance

Variables	(1)	(2)	(3)	(4)	(5)	(6)	(7)	(8)	(9)
	m19								
	L1	EC4	EI1	EI3	BI4	EL1	BL3	BL2	PI1
L1		1 (0)	0.895*** (0.0124)	1.128*** (0.0153)	1.004*** (0.0131)	0.864*** (0.0113)	1.185*** (0.0146)	1.147*** (0.0143)	1.155*** (0.0140)
E	0.818*** (0.0117)								
Constant		3.660*** (0.00951)	4.174*** (0.00860)	3.661*** (0.0104)	3.849*** (0.00916)	4.127*** (0.00788)	3.591*** (0.0102)	3.639*** (0.00981)	3.800*** (0.00972)
Observations	11,083	11,083	11,083	11,083	11,083	11,083	11,083	11,083	11,083

Standard errors in parentheses
***$p < 0.01$, **$p < 0.05$, *$p < 0.1$

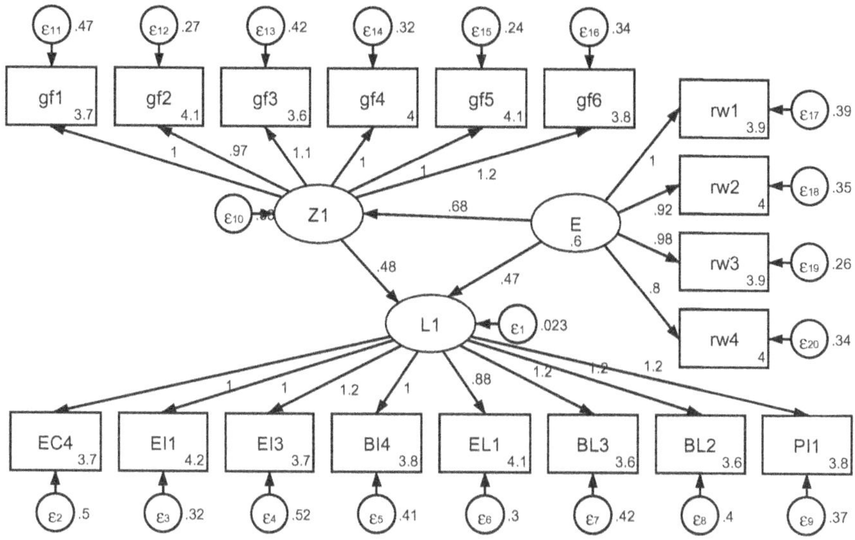

Fig. 6.3 Non-standardized effect of the Golden Mean style of organizational ethical climate, normative commitment, and job performance

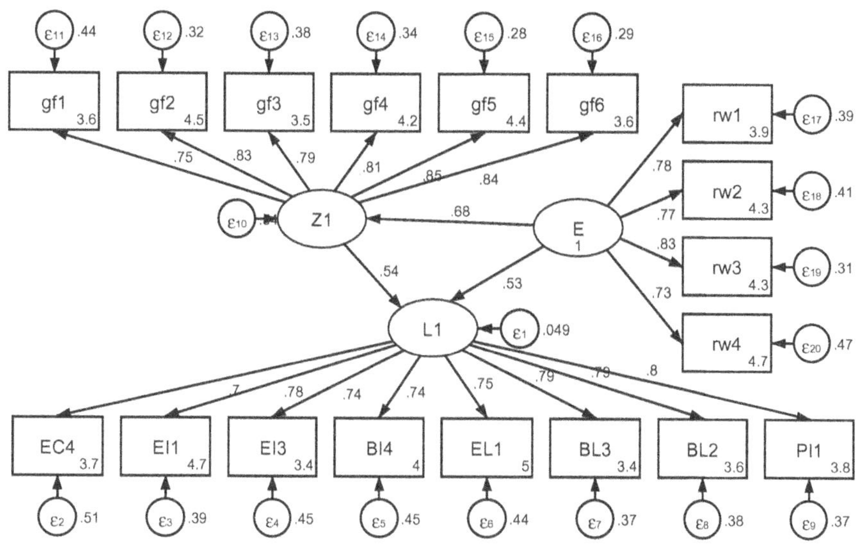

Fig. 6.4 Standardized effect of the Golden Mean style of organizational ethical climate, normative commitment, and job performance

Table 6.2 (6.1 Cont.) Impact of the Golden Mean style of organizational ethical climate on job performance

Variables	(10)	(11)	(12)	(13)	(14)	(15)	(16)	(17)	(18)
	rw1	rw2	rw3	rw4	var(e.EC4)	var(e.EI1)	var(e.EI3)	var(e.BI4)	var(e.EL1)
L1									
E	1 (0)	0.917*** (0.0110)	0.983*** (0.0108)	0.796*** (0.0101)					
Constant	3.851*** (0.00958)	3.996*** (0.00890)	3.923*** (0.00884)	3.967*** (0.00817)	0.469*** (0.00701)	0.392*** (0.00578)	0.515*** (0.00797)	0.396*** (0.00595)	0.293*** (0.00444)
Observations	11,083	11,083	11,083	11,083	11,083	11,083	11,083	11,083	11,083

Standard errors in parentheses
***$p < 0.01$, **$p < 0.05$, *$p < 0.1$

Table 6.3 (6.1 Cont.) Impact of the Golden Mean style of organizational ethical climate on job performance

(19)	(20)	(21)	(22)	(23)	(24)	(25)	(26)	(27)
var(e.BL3)	var(e.BL2)	var(e.PI1)	var(e.rw1)	var(e.rw2)	var(e.rw3)	var(e.rw4)	var(e.L1)	var(E)
0.416*** (0.00651)	0.373*** (0.00603)	0.344*** (0.00550)	0.388*** (0.00641)	0.348*** (0.00569)	0.261*** (0.00479)	0.339*** (0.00528)	0.104*** (0.00345)	0.605*** (0.0130)
11,083	11,083	11,083	11,083	11,083	11,083	11,083	11,083	11,083

Standard errors in parentheses
***$p < 0.01$, **$p < 0.05$, *$p < 0.1$

Table 6.4 Impact of the Golden Mean style of organizational ethical climate on normative commitment and job performance

Variables	(1)	(2)	(3)	(4)	(5)	(6)	(7)	(8)	(9)	(10)
	m18									
	L1	Z1	EC4	EI1	EI3	BI4	EL1	BL3	BL2	PI1
Z1	0.479*** (0.00846)									
E	0.472*** (0.00899)	0.676*** (0.0116)								
L1			1 (0)	1.005*** (0.0131)	1.154*** (0.0158)	1.022*** (0.0138)	0.882*** (0.0118)	1.218*** (0.0154)	1.159*** (0.0149)	1.161*** (0.0147)
Constant			3.659*** (0.00953)	4.174*** (0.00863)	3.660*** (0.0104)	3.849*** (0.00919)	4.127*** (0.00791)	3.590*** (0.0103)	3.638*** (0.00985)	3.799*** (0.00976)
Observations	11,083	11,083	11,083	11,083	11,083	11,083	11,083	11,083	11,083	11,083

Standard errors in parentheses
***$p < 0.01$, **$p < 0.05$, *$p < 0.1$

Table 6.5 (6.4 Cont.) Impact of the Golden Mean style of organizational ethical climate on normative commitment and job performance

(11)	(12)	(13)	(14)	(15)	(16)	(17)	(18)	(19)	(20)
gf1	gf2	gf3	gf4	gf5	gf6	rw1	rw2	rw3	rw4
1 (0)	0.972*** (0.0111)	1.067*** (0.0126)	1.007*** (0.0117)	1.016*** (0.0112)	1.157*** (0.0128)				
						1 (0)	0.916*** (0.0110)	0.983*** (0.0108)	0.797*** (0.0102)
3.705*** (0.00998)	4.084*** (0.00881)	3.631*** (0.0101)	4.047*** (0.00931)	4.061*** (0.00895)	3.803*** (0.0103)	3.850*** (0.00961)	3.995*** (0.00893)	3.922*** (0.00888)	3.967*** (0.00819)
11,083	11,083	11,083	11,083	11,083	11,083	11,083	11,083	11,083	11,083

Standard errors in parentheses
***$p < 0.01$, **$p < 0.05$, *$p < 0.1$

Table 6.6 (6.4 Cont.) Impact of the Golden Mean style of organizational ethical climate on normative commitment and job performance

(21)	(22)	(23)	(24)	(25)	(26)	(27)	(28)	(29)	(30)
var(e.EC4)	var(e.EI1)	var(e.EI3)	var(e.BI4)	var(e.EL1)	var(e.BL3)	var(e.BL2)	var(e.PI1)	var(e.gf1)	var(e.gf2)
0.496*** (0.00719)	0.316*** (0.00486)	0.522*** (0.00784)	0.406*** (0.00595)	0.299*** (0.00438)	0.419*** (0.00629)	0.397*** (0.00612)	0.375*** (0.00574)	0.470*** (0.00707)	0.266*** (0.00433)
11,083	11,083	11,083	11,083	11,083	11,083	11,083	11,083	11,083	11,083

Standard errors in parentheses
***$p < 0.01$, **$p < 0.05$, *$p < 0.1$

Table 6.7 (6.4 Cont.) Impact of the Golden Mean style of organizational ethical climate on normative commitment and job performance

(31)	(32)	(33)	(34)	(35)	(36)	(37)	(38)	(39)	(40)	(41)
var(e.EI4)	var(e.gf4)	var(e.gf5)	var(e.gf6)	var(e.rw1)	var(e.rw2)	var(e.rw3)	var(e.rw4)	var(e.L1)	var(e.Z1)	var(E)
0.421*** (0.00651)	0.321*** (0.00511)	0.239*** (0.00401)	0.336*** (0.00559)	0.389*** (0.00642)	0.349*** (0.00572)	0.262*** (0.00481)	0.337*** (0.00526)	0.0233*** (0.00154)	0.326*** (0.00785)	0.605*** (0.0130)
11,083	11,083	11,083	11,083	11,083	11,083	11,083	11,083	11,083	11,083	11,083

Standard errors in parentheses
***$p < 0.01$, **$p < 0.05$, *$p < 0.1$

6.2 The Social Responsibility Style of Organizational Ethics, Normative Organizational Commitment, and Job Performance

As shown in Fig. 6.5, a significant positive correlation was also found between the social responsibility style of organizational ethical climate and job performance. Specifically, SEM shows that the path coefficient between the two is 0.42, suggesting that the social responsibility style of organizational ethical climate can significantly enhance job performance (Fig. 6.6, Tables 6.8 and 6.9).

Though the path coefficient for the impact of the social responsibility style of organizational ethical climate on job performance was found to be 0.42, slightly lower than the Golden Mean style, the results once again suggest that this type of ethical climate can affect job performance both directly and indirectly, i.e. through its effect on normative commitment. Specifically, the path coefficient for the direct impact of the social responsibility style of organizational ethical climate on job performance was found to be 0.33, while the path coefficient between the social responsibility style of organizational ethical climate and organizational commitment, as well as organizational commitment and job performance, was 0.12 and 0.67, respectively. (Figs. 6.7 and 6.8, Tables 6.10, 6.11, 6.12 and 6.13).

Moreover, while related empirical surveys on JFMEs have indicated that the path coefficient for the impact of the social responsibility style of organizational ethical climate on normative commitment is 0.35, the path coefficient for its impact on organizational commitment in this study was found to be much lower at 0.12. This

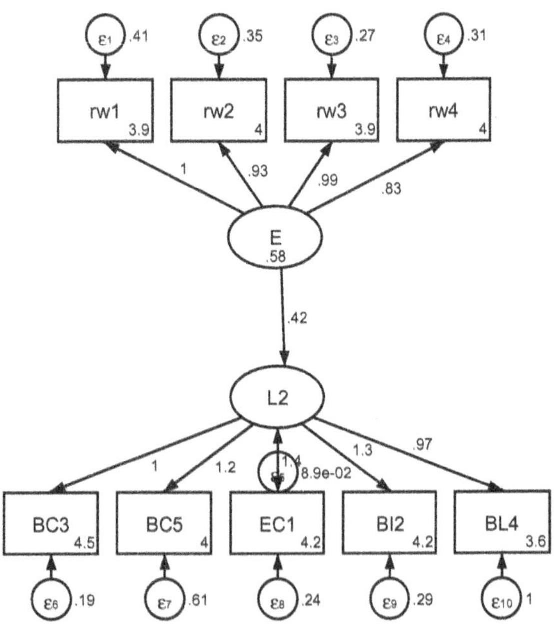

Fig. 6.5 Non-standardized effect of the impact of the social responsibility style of organizational ethical climate on job performance

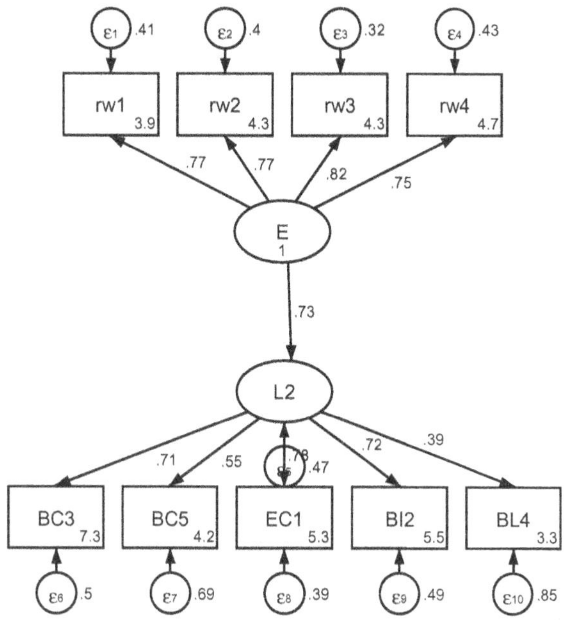

Fig. 6.6 Standardized effect of the impact of the social responsibility style of the organizational ethical climate on job performance

suggests that the impact of the social responsibility style of organizational ethical climate assumes two distinct paths. At the same time, the influential coefficient for the impact of the social responsibility style of organizational ethical climate on job performance was 0.42, with a path coefficient of 0.33 for the direct path and 0.67 for the indirect path. Generally speaking, this supports the earlier findings that the social responsibility style of organizational ethical climate has both a direct and indirect impact on job performance.

The notion of social responsibility generally refers to those responsibilities an organization assumes in order to maintain and improve the welfare of society as a whole. In its obligation to fulfill the long-term betterment of society, it is more closely related to philosophies of ethics and morality than legal regulations and economic benefits. From an organization's perspective, assuming greater social responsibility not only enhances its reputation and the sense of belonging of its employees but also acts as a positive reflection of its cultural norms and values. From the perspective of society, socially responsible organizations help mitigate the adverse effects of social change while lowering its associated costs.

Some have expressed concern that assuming greater social responsibility necessarily harms an organization's short-term business interests, insofar as its costs tend to outweigh its benefits. But studies have shown that this is in fact not the case and that the assumption of greater social responsibility acts as a powerful investment in the future. For while business performance may temporarily suffer in the short term, the resulting long-term gains with respect to the enhancement of an organization's reputation as well as its ability to attract talent are more than enough to offset any

Table 6.8 Impact of the social responsibility style of organizational ethics on job performance

Variables	(1)	(2)	(3)	(4)	(5)	(6)	(7)	(8)	(9)	(10)
	m21									
	L2	BC3	BC5	EC1	BI2	BL4	rw1	rw2	rw3	rw4
L2		1 (0)	1.191*** (0.0242)	1.419*** (0.0199)	1.276*** (0.0193)	0.969*** (0.0279)				
E	0.415*** (0.00735)						1 (0)	0.934*** (0.0117)	0.987*** (0.0116)	0.834*** (0.0108)
Constant		4.519*** (0.00591)	3.953*** (0.00900)	4.165*** (0.00760)	4.237*** (0.00746)	3.597*** (0.0105)	3.852*** (0.00956)	3.998*** (0.00888)	3.924*** (0.00882)	3.969*** (0.00814)
Observations	11,083	11,083	11,083	11,083	11,083	11,083	11,083	11,083	11,083	11,083

Standard errors in parentheses
***p < 0.01, **p < 0.05, *p < 0.1

Table 6.9 (6.8 Cont.) Impact of the social responsibility style of organizational ethics on job performance

(11)	(12)	(13)	(14)	(15)	(16)	(17)	(18)	(19)	(20)	(21)
var(e.BC3)	var(e.BC5)	var(e.EC1)	var(e.BI2)	var(e.BL4)	var(e.rw1)	var(e.rw2)	var(e.rw3)	var(e.rw4)	var(e.L2)	var(E)
0.189*** (0.00327)	0.609*** (0.00924)	0.245*** (0.00496)	0.294*** (0.00512)	1.020*** (0.0145)	0.407*** (0.00699)	0.345*** (0.00602)	0.274*** (0.00541)	0.313*** (0.00537)	0.0891*** (0.00295)	0.585*** (0.0130)
11,083	11,083	11,083	11,083	11,083	11,083	11,083	11,083	11,083	11,083	11,083

Standard errors in parentheses
***$p < 0.01$, **$p < 0.05$, *$p < 0.1$

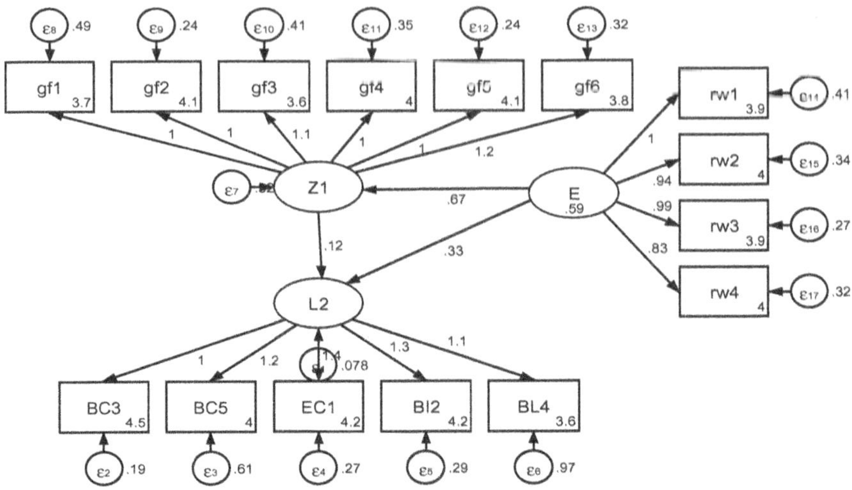

Fig. 6.7 Non-standardized effect of the impact of the social responsibility style of organizational ethics on normative commitment and job performance

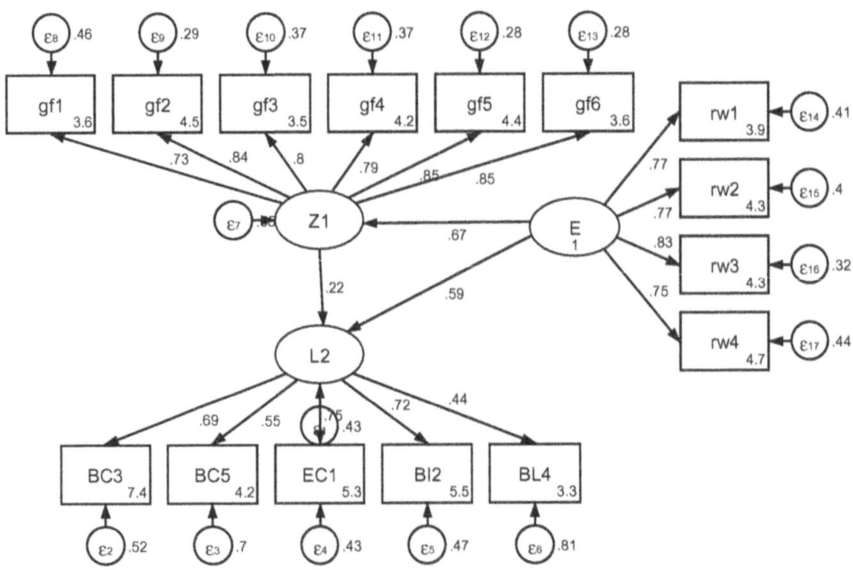

Fig. 6.8 Standardized effect of the impact of the social responsibility style of organizational ethics on normative commitment and job performance

Table 6.10 Impact of the social responsibility style of organizational ethics on normative commitment and job performance

Variables	(1)	(2)	(3)	(4)	(5)	(6)	(7)
	m20						
	L2	Z1	BC3	BC5	EC1	BI2	BL4
Z1	0.122*** (0.00759)						
E	0.330*** (0.00862)	0.666*** (0.0119)					
L2			1 (0)	1.209*** (0.0252)	1.399*** (0.0204)	1.320*** (0.0203)	1.120*** (0.0308)
Constant			4.520*** (0.00591)	3.954*** (0.00902)	4.165*** (0.00762)	4.237*** (0.00748)	3.596*** (0.0105)
Observations	11,083	11,083	11,083	11,083	11,083	11,083	11,083

Standard errors in parentheses
***$p < 0.01$, **$p < 0.05$, *$p < 0.1$

additional costs. In this sense, efforts to benefit others serve to benefit the interests of the organization itself, and studies have shown a strong positive correlation between engagement in social responsibility and business performance.

6.3 The Friendship-Efficiency Style of Organizational Ethics, Normative Commitment, and Job Performance

As shown in Fig. 6.9, a significant positive correlation was also found between the friendship-efficiency style of organizational ethical climate and job performance. Specifically, SEM shows that the path coefficient between the two is 0.34, suggesting that this type of ethical climate can significantly enhance job performance (Fig. 6.10, Tables 6.14, 6.15 and 6.16).

With a path coefficient for the impact of the friendship-efficiency style of organizational ethical climate on job performance of 0.27, the results once again suggest that this type of ethical climate can affect job performance both directly and indirectly, i.e. through its effect on normative commitment. Specifically, the path coefficient for the direct impact of the friendship-efficiency style of organizational ethical climate on job performancewas found to be 0.27, while the path coefficient between the friendship-efficiency style of organizational ethical climate and organizational commitment, as well as organizational commitment and job performance, was 0.11 and 0.67, respectively (Figs. 6.11 and 6.12).

Moreover, while related empirical surveys on JFMEs have indicated that the path coefficient for the impact of the friendship-efficiency style of organizational ethical climate on normative commitment is 0.31, the path coefficient for its impact on organizational commitment in this study was found to be much lower at 0.11. This

Table 6.11 (6.10 Cont.) Impact of the social responsibility style of organizational ethics on normative commitment and job performance

Variables	(8)	(9)	(10)	(11)	(12)	(13)	(14)	(15)	(16)	(17)
	rw1	rw2	rw3	rw4	gf1	gf2	gf3	gf4	gf5	gf6
Z1					1 (0)	1.015*** (0.0117)	1.103*** (0.0133)	1.007*** (0.0123)	1.033*** (0.0119)	1.138*** (0.0135)
E	1 (0)	0.936*** (0.0116)	0.992*** (0.0115)	0.827*** (0.0107)						
L2										
Constant	3.851*** (0.00959)	3.996*** (0.00891)	3.923*** (0.00885)	3.969*** (0.00816)	3.706*** (0.00996)	4.084*** (0.00879)	3.631*** (0.0101)	4.047*** (0.00928)	4.060*** (0.00893)	3.801*** (0.0103)
Observations	11,083	11,083	11,083	11,083	11,083	11,083	11,083	11,083	11,083	11,083

Standard errors in parentheses
***$p < 0.01$, **$p < 0.05$, *$p < 0.1$

Table 6.12 (6.10 Cont.) Impact of the social responsibility style of organizational ethics on normative commitment and job performance

Variables	(19)	(20)	(21)	(22)	(23)	(24)	(25)	(26)
	var(e.BC5)	var(e.EC1)	var(e.BI2)	var(e.BL4)	var(e.rw1)	var(e.rw2)	var(e.rw3)	var(e.rw4)
Z1								
E								
L2								
Constant	0.611*** (0.00926)	0.270*** (0.00535)	0.287*** (0.00512)	0.970*** (0.0144)	0.406*** (0.00688)	0.344*** (0.00590)	0.269*** (0.00522)	0.319*** (0.00532)
Observations	11,083	11,083	11,083	11,083	11,083	11,083	11,083	11,083

Standard errors in parentheses
***$p < 0.01$, **$p < 0.05$, *$p < 0.1$

Table 6.13 (6.10 Cont.) Impact of the social responsibility style of organizational ethics on normative commitment and job performance

Variables	(27)	(28)	(29)	(30)	(31)	(32)	(33)	(34)	(35)
	var(e.gf1)	var(e.gf2)	var(e.gf3)	var(e.gf4)	var(e.gf5)	var(e.gf6)	var(e.L2)	var(e.Z1)	var(E)
Z1									
E									
L2									
Constant	0.494*** (0.00745)	0.241*** (0.00411)	0.407*** (0.00646)	0.346*** (0.00550)	0.245*** (0.00424)	0.316*** (0.00551)	0.0783*** (0.00282)	0.316*** (0.00781)	0.585*** (0.0130)
Observations	11,083	11,083	11,083	11,083	11,083	11,083	11,083	11,083	11,083

Standard errors in parentheses
***$p < 0.01$, **$p < 0.05$, *$p < 0.1$

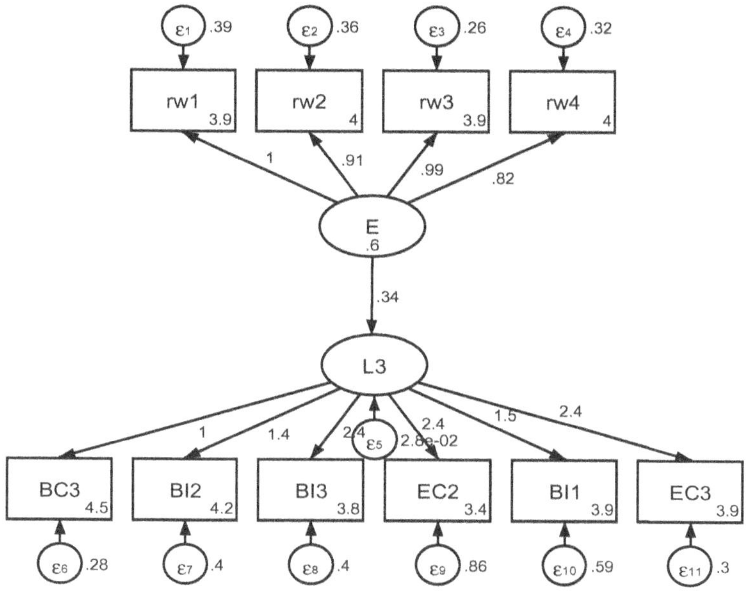

Fig. 6.9 Non-standardized effect of the impact of the friendship-efficiency style of organizational ethical climate on job performance

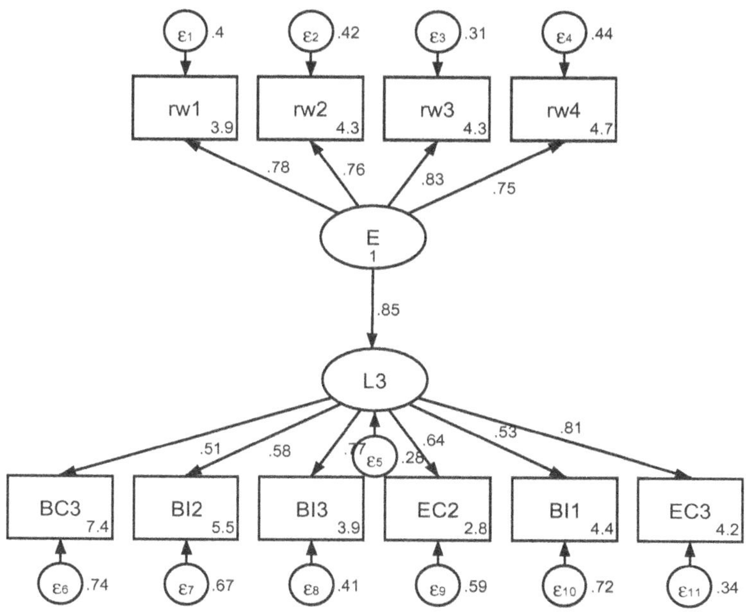

Fig. 6.10 Standardized effect of the impact of the friendship-efficiency style of organizational ethical climate on job performance

Table 6.14 Impact of the friendship-efficiency style of the organizational ethical climate on job performance

Variables	(1)	(2)	(3)	(4)	(5)	(6)	(7)	(8)	(9)
	m22								
	L3	BC3	BI2	BI3	EC2	BI1	EC3	rw1	rw2
L3		1 (0)	1.430*** (0.0317)	2.432*** (0.0488)	2.444*** (0.0537)	1.520*** (0.0368)	2.428*** (0.0475)		
E	0.343*** (0.00724)							1 (0)	0.913*** (0.0113)
Constant		4.520*** (0.00590)	4.237*** (0.00747)	3.838*** (0.00952)	3.366*** (0.0115)	3.934*** (0.00867)	3.938*** (0.00902)	3.852*** (0.00956)	3.996*** (0.00890)
Observations	11,083	11,083	11,083	11,083	11,083	11,083	11,083	11,083	11,033

Standard errors in parentheses
***p < 0.01, **p < 0.05, *p < 0.1

Table 6.15 (6.14 Cont.) Impact of the friendship-efficiency style of organizational ethical climate on job performance

Variables	(10)	(11)	(12)	(13)	(14)	(15)	(16)	(17)
	rw3	rw4	var(e.BC3)	var(e.BI2)	var(e.BI3)	var(e.EC2)	var(e.BI1)	var(e.EC3)
L3								
E	0.989*** (0.0112)	0.817*** (0.0104)						
Constant	3.924*** (0.00884)	3.970*** (0.00814)	0.280*** (0.00403)	0.404*** (0.00596)	0.404*** (0.00712)	0.859*** (0.0130)	0.588*** (0.00854)	0.304*** (0.00589)
Observations	11,083	11,083	11,083	11,083	11,083	11,083	11,083	11,083

Standard errors in parentheses
***$p < 0.01$, **$p < 0.05$, *$p < 0.1$

Table 6.16 (6.14 Cont.) Impact of the friendship-efficiency style of organizational ethical climate on job performance

(18)	(19)	(20)	(21)	(22)	(23)
var(e.rw1)	var(e.rw2)	var(e.rw3)	var(e.rw4)	var(e.L3)	var(E)
0.394*** (0.00668)	0.361*** (0.00601)	0.262*** (0.00508)	0.320*** (0.00523)	0.0277*** (0.00123)	0.597*** (0.0130)
11,083	11,083	11,083	11,083	11,083	11,083

Standard errors in parentheses
***$p < 0.01$, **$p < 0.05$, *$p < 0.1$

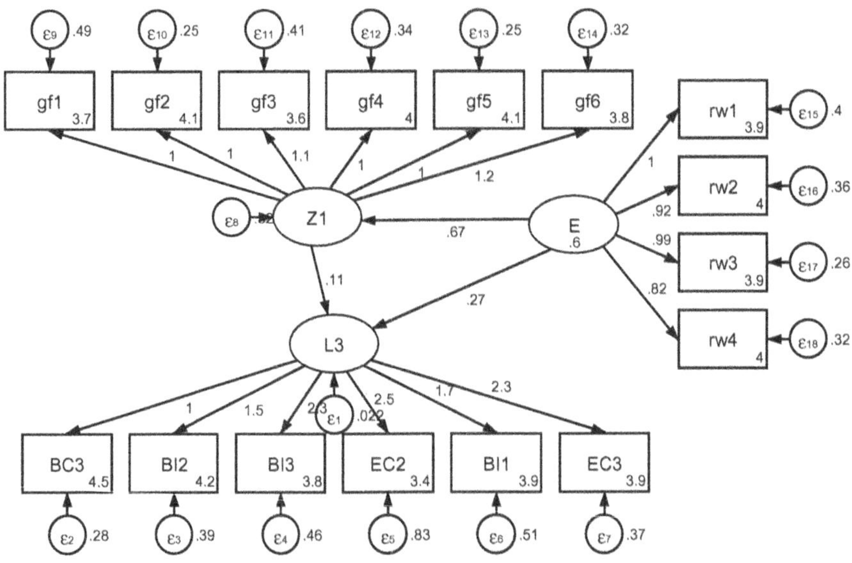

Fig. 6.11 Non-standardized effect of the impact of the friendship-efficiency style of organizational ethics on normative commitment and job performance

suggests that the impact of the friendship-efficiency style of organizational ethical climate assumes two distinct paths. At the same time, the influential coefficient for the impact of the friendship-efficiency style of organizational ethical climate on job performance was found to be 0.34, with a path coefficient of 0.27 for the direct path and 0.67 for the indirect path. Generally speaking, this supports previous findings that the friendship-efficiency style of organizational ethical climate has both a direct and indirect impact on job performance (Tables 6.17, 6.18, 6.19 and 6.20).

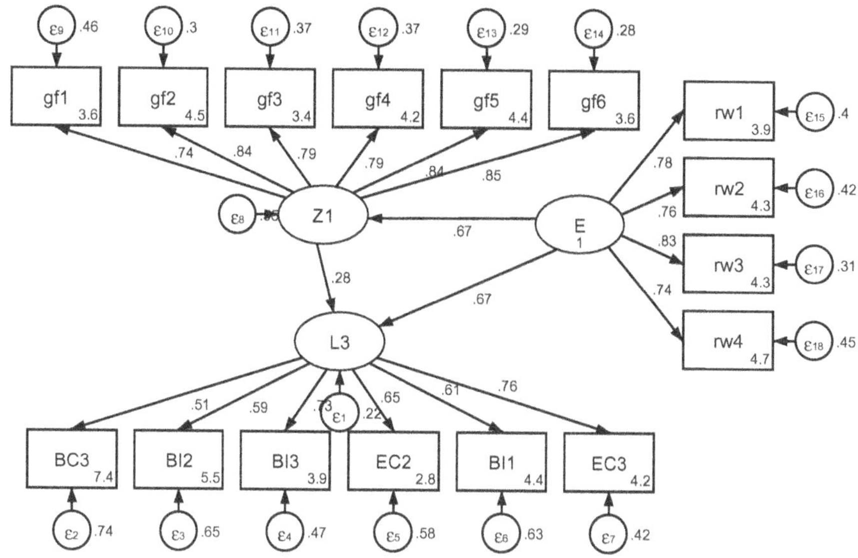

Fig. 6.12 Standardized effect of the impact of the friendship-efficiency style of organizational ethics on normative commitment and job performance

6.4 The Golden Mean Style of Organizational Ethics, Economic Organizational Commitment, and Job Performance

Perhaps surprisingly, no significant correlation was found between economic commitment and job performance, nor was there an obvious coefficient relationship in the path regression of the two. There was also no significant correlation in the path between Golden Mean style of organizational ethical climate and economic commitment, though a significant correlation was found between the Golden Mean style of organizational ethical climate and job performance, with a path coefficient of 0.82, which increases to 0.89 when the path coefficient is standardized (Figs. 6.13 and 6.14).

As discussed above, the Golden Mean style of organizational ethical climate represents a combination of both caring and instrumental climates. While caring climates are focused primarily on the well-being of employees, instrumental climates are characterized by extreme individualism based on the prioritization of self-interest. Taken to its logical extreme, such a climate can lead to the neglect of organizational interest along with rampant unethical behavior. This is why the Golden Mean style of organizational ethical climate tends to have a weak impact on economic commitment and is ultimately powerless in affecting job performance through economic commitment. Therefore, unlike some of the other climate, the Golden Mean style of organizational ethical climate only has a direct impact on job performance (Tables 6.21, 6.22 and 6.23).

Table 6.17 Impact of the friendship-efficiency style of organizational ethics on normative commitment and job performance

Variables	(1)	(2)	(3)	(4)	(5)	(6)	(7)	(8)	(9)	(10)
	m23									
	L3	Z1	BC3	BI2	BI3	EC2	BI1	EC3	gf1	gf2
Z1	0.114*** (0.00533)								1 (0)	1.003*** (0.0115)
E	0.275*** (0.00691)	0.666*** (0.0117)								
L3			1 (0)	1.467*** (0.0318)	2.293*** (0.0467)	2.482*** (0.0536)	1.746*** (0.0397)	2.262*** (0.0450)		
Constant			4.521*** (0.00591)	4.237*** (0.00749)	3.837*** (0.00956)	3.366*** (0.0116)	3.933*** (0.00870)	3.937*** (0.00905)	3.707*** (0.00997)	4.084*** (0.00879)
Observations	11,083	11,083	11,083	11,083	11,083	11,083	11,083	11,083	11,083	11,083

Standard errors in parentheses
***$p < 0.01$, **$p < 0.05$, *$p < 0.1$

Table 6.18 (6.17 Cont.) Impact of the friendship-efficiency style of organizational ethics on normative commitment and job performance

Variables	(11)	(12)	(13)	(14)	(15)	(16)	(17)	(18)	(19)	(20)
	EI4	gf4	gf5	gf6	rw1	rw2	rw3	rw4	var(e.BC3)	var(e.BI2)
Z1	1.096*** (0.0131)	1.004*** (0.0121)	1.026*** (0.0117)	1.188*** (0.0133)						
E					1 (0)	0.918*** (0.0113)	0.992*** (0.0112)	0.817*** (0.0104)		
L3										
Constant	3.631*** (0.0101)	4.047*** (0.00930)	4.061*** (0.00893)	3.802*** (0.0103)	3.851*** (0.00959)	3.995*** (0.00893)	3.923*** (0.00887)	3.970*** (0.00816)	0.276*** (0.00399)	0.390*** (0.00581)
Observations	11,083	11,083	11,083	11,083	11,083	11,083	11,083	11,083	11,083	11,083

Standard errors in parentheses
***$p < 0.01$, **$p < 0.05$, *$p < 0.1$

Table 6.19 (6.17 Cont.) Impact of the friendship-efficiency style of organizational ethics on normative commitment and job performance

Variables	(21)	(22)	(23)	(24)	(25)	(26)	(27)	(28)
	var(e.BI3)	var(e.EC2)	var(e.BI1)	var(e.EC3)	var(e.gf1)	var(e.gf2)	var(e.EI4)	var(e.gf4)
Z1								
E								
L3								
Constant	0.463***	0.833***	0.512***	0.374***	0.487***	0.246***	0.408***	0.343***
	(0.00819)	(0.0127)	(0.00818)	(0.00710)	(0.00736)	(0.00415)	(0.00647)	(0.00546)
Observations	11,083	11,083	11,083	11,083	11,083	11,083	11,083	11,083

Standard errors in parentheses
***p < 0.01, **p < 0.05, *p < 0.1

Table 6.20 (6.17 Cont.) Impact of the friendship-efficiency style of organizational ethics on normative commitment and job performance

Variables	(29)	(30)	(31)	(32)	(33)	(34)	(35)	(36)	(37)
	var(e.gf5)	var(e.gf6)	var(e.rw1)	var(e.rw2)	var(e.rw3)	var(e.rw4)	var(e.L3)	var(e.Z1)	var(E)
Z1									
E									
L3									
Constant	0.246***	0.318***	0.396***	0.357***	0.262***	0.321***	0.0219***	0.319***	0.595***
	(0.00424)	(0.00552)	(0.00666)	(0.00595)	(0.00501)	(0.00521)	(0.00106)	(0.00783)	(0.0130)
Observations	11,083	11,083	11,083	11,083	11,083	11,083	11,083	11,083	11,083

Standard errors in parentheses
***p < 0.01, **p < 0.05, *p < 0.1

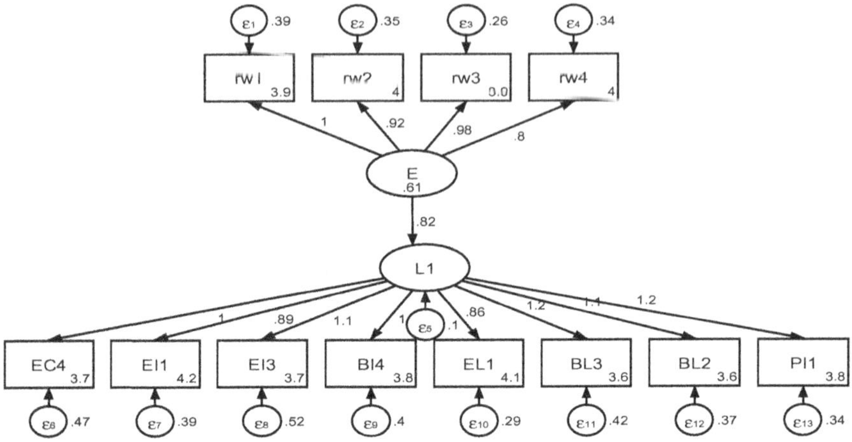

Fig. 6.13 Non-standardized effect of the impact of the Golden Mean style of organizational ethics on job performance

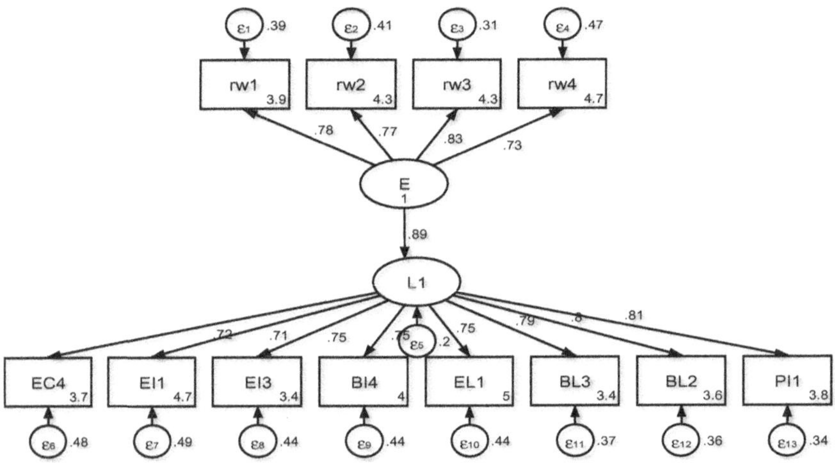

Fig. 6.14 Standardized effect of the impact of the Golden Mean style of organizational ethics on job performance

6.5 The Social Responsibility Style of Organizational Ethics, Economic Organizational Commitment, and Job Performance

As shown in Fig. 6.15, a significant positive correlation was also found between the social responsibility style of organizational ethical climate and job performance. Specifically, SEM shows that the path coefficient between the two is 0.42, suggesting

Table 6.21 Impact of the Golden Mean style of organizational ethics on economic commitment and job performance

Variables	(1)	(2)	(3)	(4)	(5)	(6)	(7)	(8)	(9)
	m116								
	L1	EC4	EI1	EI3	BI4	EL1	BL3	BL2	PI1
L1		1 (0)	0.895*** (0.0124)	1.128*** (0.0153)	1.004*** (0.0131)	0.864*** (0.0113)	1.185*** (0.0146)	1.147*** (0.0143)	1.155*** (0.0140)
E	0.818*** (0.0117)								
Constant		3.660*** (0.00951)	4.174*** (0.00860)	3.661*** (0.0104)	3.849*** (0.00916)	4.127*** (0.00788)	3.591*** (0.0102)	3.639*** (0.00981)	3.800*** (0.00972)
Observations	11,083	11,083	11,083	11,083	11,083	11,083	11,083	11,083	11,083

Standard errors in parentheses
***$p < 0.01$, **$p < 0.05$, *$p < 0.1$

Table 6.22 (6.21 Cont.) Impact of the Golden Mean style of organizational ethics on economic commitment and job performance

Variables	(10)	(11)	(12)	(13)	(14)	(15)	(16)	(17)	(18)
	rw1	rw2	rw3	rw4	var(e.EC4)	var(e.EI1)	var(e.EI3)	var(e.BI4)	var(e.EL1)
L1									
E	1 (0)	0.917*** (0.0110)	0.983*** (0.0108)	0.796*** (0.0101)					
Constant	3.851*** (0.00958)	3.996*** (0.00890)	3.923*** (0.00884)	3.967*** (0.00817)	0.469*** (0.00701)	0.392*** (0.00578)	0.515*** (0.00797)	0.396*** (0.00595)	0.293*** (0.00444)
Observations	11,083	11,083	11,083	11,083	11,083	11,083	11,083	11,083	11,083

Standard errors in parentheses
***$p < 0.01$, **$p < 0.05$, *$p < 0.1$

Table 6.23 (6.21 Cont.) Impact of the Golden Mean style of organizational ethics on economic commitment and job performance

Variables	(19)	(20)	(21)	(22)	(23)	(24)	(25)	(26)	(27)
	var(e.BL3)	var(e.BL2)	var(e.PI1)	var(e.rw1)	var(e.rw2)	var(e.rw3)	var(e.rw4)	var(e.L1)	var(E)
L1									
E									
Constant	0.416***	0.373***	0.344***	0.388***	0.348***	0.261***	0.339***	0.104***	0.605***
	(0.00651)	(0.00603)	(0.00550)	(0.00641)	(0.00569)	(0.00479)	(0.00528)	(0.00345)	(0.0130)
Observations	11,083	11,083	11,083	11,083	11,083	11,083	11,083	11,083	11,083

Standard errors in parentheses
***p < 0.01, **p < 0.05, *p < 0.1

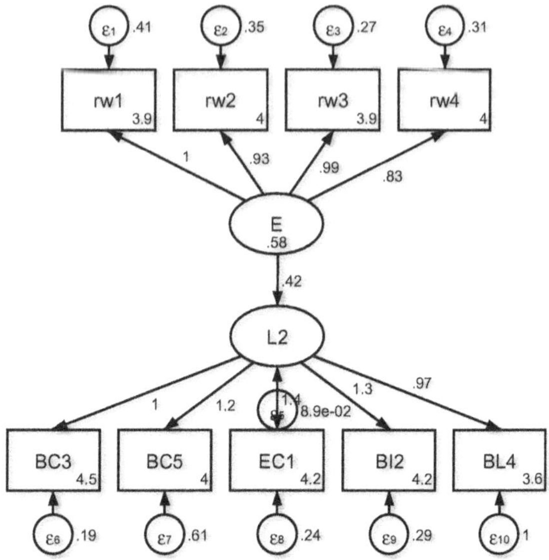

Fig. 6.15 Non-standardized effect of the impact of the social responsibility style of organizational ethics on job performance

that the social responsibility style of organizational ethical climate can significantly enhance job performance (Fig. 6.16, Tables 6.24 and 6.25).

With a path coefficient between the social responsibility style of organizational ethical climate and job performance of 0.42, the results of SEM again show that this type of ethical climate has the potential to affect job performance along two distinct

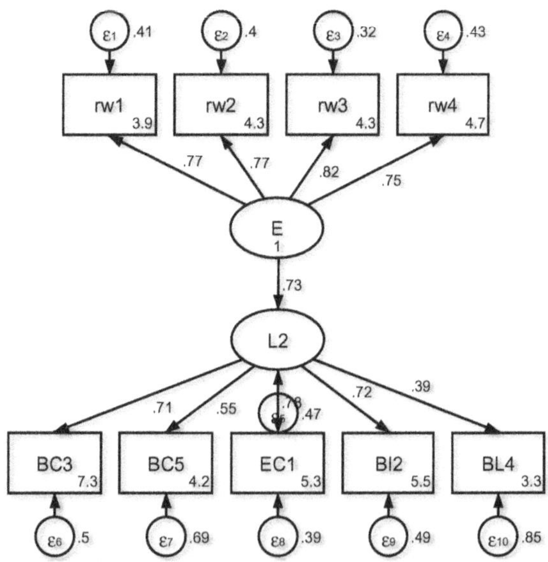

Fig. 6.16 Standardized effect of the impact of the social responsibility style of organizational ethics on job performance

Table 6.24 Impact of the social responsibility style of organizational ethics on job performance

Variables	(1)	(2)	(3)	(4)	(5)	(6)	(7)	(8)	(9)	(10)
	m113									
	L2	BC3	BC5	EC1	BI2	BL4	rw1	rw2	rw3	rw4
L2		1 (0)	1.191*** (0.0242)	1.419*** (0.0199)	1.276*** (0.0193)	0.969*** (0.0279)				
E	0.415*** (0.00735)						1 (0)	0.934*** (0.0117)	0.987*** (0.0116)	0.834*** (0.0108)
Constant		4.519*** (0.00591)	3.953*** (0.00900)	4.165*** (0.00760)	4.237*** (0.00746)	3.597*** (0.0105)	3.852*** (0.00956)	3.998*** (0.00888)	3.924*** (0.00882)	3.969*** (0.00814)
Observations	11,083	11,083	11,083	11,083	11,083	11,083	11,083	11,083	11,083	11,083

Standard errors in parentheses
***$p < 0.01$, **$p < 0.05$, *$p < 0.1$

Table 6.25 (6.24 Cont.) Impact of the social responsibility style of organizational ethics on job performance

(11)	(12)	(13)	(14)	(15)	(16)	(17)	(18)	(19)	(20)	(21)
var(e.BC3)	var(e.BC5)	var(e.EC1)	var(e.BI2)	var(e.BL4)	var(e.rw1)	var(e.rw2)	var(e.rw3)	var(e.rw4)	var(e.L2)	var(E)
0.189***	0.609***	0.245***	0.294***	1.020***	0.407***	0.345***	0.274***	0.313***	0.0891***	0.585***
(0.00327)	(0.00924)	(0.00496)	(0.00512)	(0.0145)	(0.00699)	(0.00602)	(0.00541)	(0.00537)	(0.00295)	(0.0130)
11,083	11,083	11,083	11,083	11,083	11,083	11,083	11,083	11,083	11,083	11,083

Standard errors in parentheses
***p < 0.01, **p < 0.05, *p < 0.1

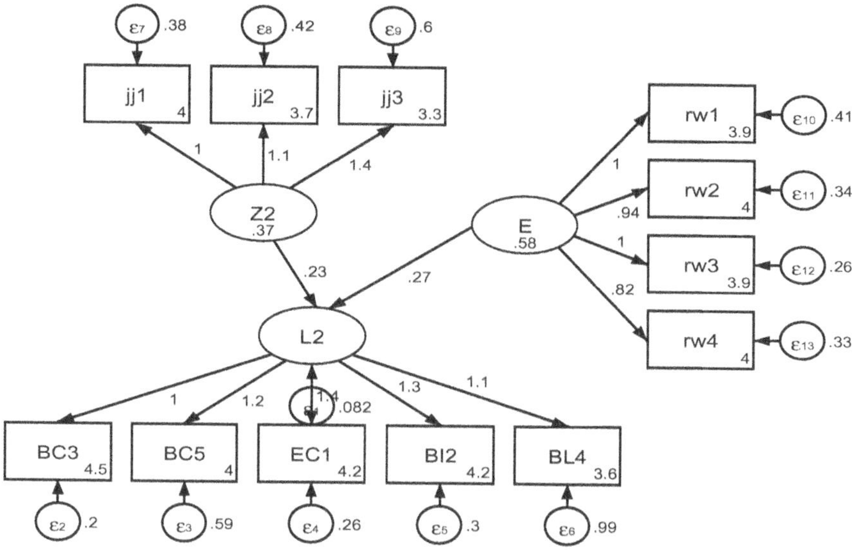

Fig. 6.17 Non-standardized effect of the impact of the social responsibility style of organizational ethics on economic commitment and job performance

paths, one direct and the other through its effect on economic commitment. That said, while the path between the social responsibility style of ethical climate and economic commitment is strong, the results also suggest a lack of causality between economic commitment and job performance, which means that the impact of the social responsibility style of ethical climate on job performance is primarily direct in nature (Figs. 6.17 and 6.18).

When the impact of the social responsibility style of organizational ethical climate on economic commitment is taken into account, the path coefficient between the two drops to 0.27, which indicates some sort of non-causal correlation between economic commitment and job performance. Moreover, when the impact of the social responsibility style of organizational ethical climate on job performance is accounted for, the coefficient between the two decreases from 0.51 to 0.22. (Tables 6.26, 6.27 and 6.28).

6.6 The Friendship-Efficiency Style of Organizational Ethics, Economic Commitment, and Job Performance

As shown in Fig. 6.19, a significant positive correlation was also found between the friendship-efficiency style of organizational ethical climate and job performance. Specifically, SEM shows that the path coefficient between the two is 0.34, suggesting that this type of climate can significantly enhance job performance (Fig. 6.20, Tables 6.29, 6.30 and 6.31).

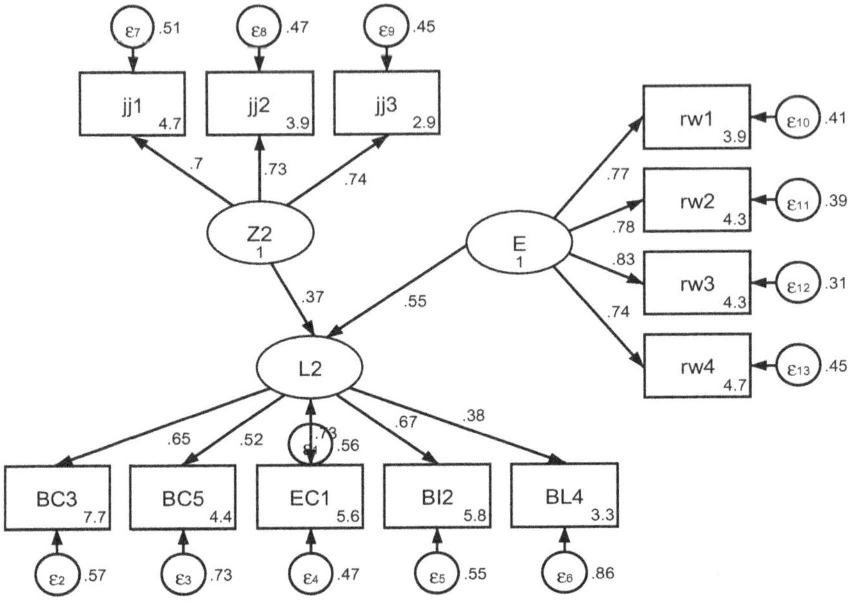

Fig. 6.18 Standardized effect of the impact of the social responsibility style of organizational ethics on economic commitment and job performance

With a path coefficient for the impact of the friendship-efficiency style of organizational ethical climate on job performance of 0.54, the results once again suggest that this type of ethical climate can affect job performance both directly and indirectly, i.e. through its effect on economic commitment. Yet while the path coefficient for the impact of economic commitment on job performance was found to be 0.84, the path coefficient for the direct impact of the friendship-efficiency style of organizational ethical climate on job performancewas only 0.4, suggesting that the only significant effect of this type of ethical climate on job performance is indirect (Figs. 6.21 and 6.22, Tables 6.32, 6.33 and 6.34).

Generally speaking, these results indicate that a certain significance can be seen in the path coefficient of the friendship-efficiency style of organizational ethical climate and economic commitment. This suggests that individual members are able to perceive the ethical climate of their organization in terms of both profit efficiency and friendship and that organizations are concerned not only with earnings but also social efficiency. It also suggests that JFMEs with operations in China have tended to cultivate an ethical climate focused on profit and efficiency as well as humanism. Based on the results of this study, managers would therefore do well to focus on the developmental and other needs of their employees as part of an effort to improve job performance by cultivating a caring climate.

Under the influence of a friendship-efficiency style of organizational ethical climate, studies have also shown that employees care not only about the members of the organization but also about the various outside stakeholders who are affected

Table 6.26 Impact of the social responsibility style of organizational ethics on economic commitment and job performance

Variables	(1)	(2)	(3)	(4)	(5)	(6)	(7)	(8)	(9)	(10)
	m112									
	L2	BC3	BC5	EC1	BI2	BL4	jj1	jj2	jj3	rw1
Z2	0.231*** (0.0122)						1 (0)	1.141*** (0.0209)	1.410*** (0.0244)	
E	0.275*** (0.00949)									1 (0)
L2		1 (0)	1.243*** (0.0257)	1.420*** (0.0204)	1.286*** (0.0199)	1.064*** (0.0300)				
Constant		4.519*** (0.00562)	3.952*** (0.00871)	4.165*** (0.00713)	4.236*** (0.00707)	3.595*** (0.0103)	4.046*** (0.00834)	3.685*** (0.00913)	3.293*** (0.0111)	3.851*** (0.00957)
Observations	11,083	11,083	11,083	11,083	11,083	11,083	11,083	11,083	11,083	11,083

Standard errors in parentheses
***$p < 0.01$, **$p < 0.05$, *$p < 0.1$

Table 6.27 (6.26 Cont.) Impact of the social responsibility style of organizational ethics on economic commitment and job performance

Variables	(11)	(12)	(13)	(14)	(15)	(16)	(17)	(18)	(19)
	rw2	rw3	rw4	var(e.BC3)	var(e.BC5)	var(e.EC1)	var(e.BI2)	var(e.BL4)	var(e.jj1)
Z2									
E	0.942*** (0.0118)	0.995*** (0.0119)	0.819*** (0.0109)						
L2									
Constant	3.997*** (0.00889)	3.923*** (0.00884)	3.969*** (0.00815)	0.196*** (0.00343)	0.595*** (0.00924)	0.257*** (0.00521)	0.299*** (0.00524)	0.991*** (0.0144)	0.385*** (0.00755)
Observations	11,083	11,083	11,083	11,083	11,083	11,083	11,083	11,083	11,083

Standard errors in parentheses
***$p < 0.01$, **$p < 0.05$, *$p < 0.1$

Table 6.28 (6.26 Cont.) Impact of the social responsibility style of organizational ethics on economic commitment and job performance

Variables	(20)	(21)	(22)	(23)	(24)	(25)	(26)	(27)	(28)
	var(e.jj2)	var(e.jj3)	var(e.rw1)	var(e.rw2)	var(e.rw3)	var(e.rw4)	var(e.L2)	var(Z2)	var(E)
Z2									
E									
L2									
Constant	0.424*** (0.00924)	0.599*** (0.0135)	0.406*** (0.00712)	0.337*** (0.00604)	0.265*** (0.00550)	0.327*** (0.00560)	0.0817*** (0.00295)	0.367*** (0.0103)	0.584*** (0.0131)
Observations	11,083	11,083	11,083	11,083	11,083	11,083	11,083	11,083	11,083

Standard errors in parentheses
***$p < 0.01$, **$p < 0.05$, *$p < 0.1$

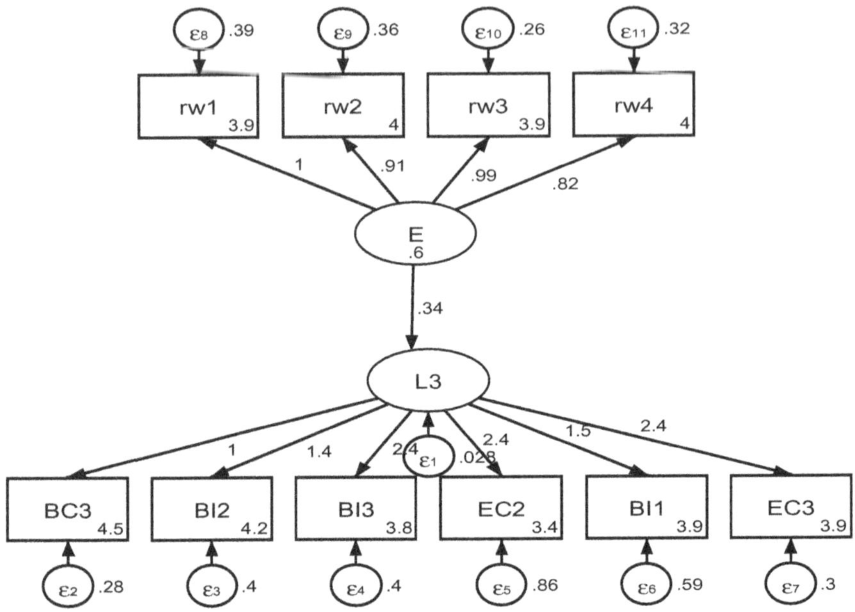

Fig. 6.19 Non-standardized effect of the impact of the friendship-efficiency style of organizational ethics on job performance

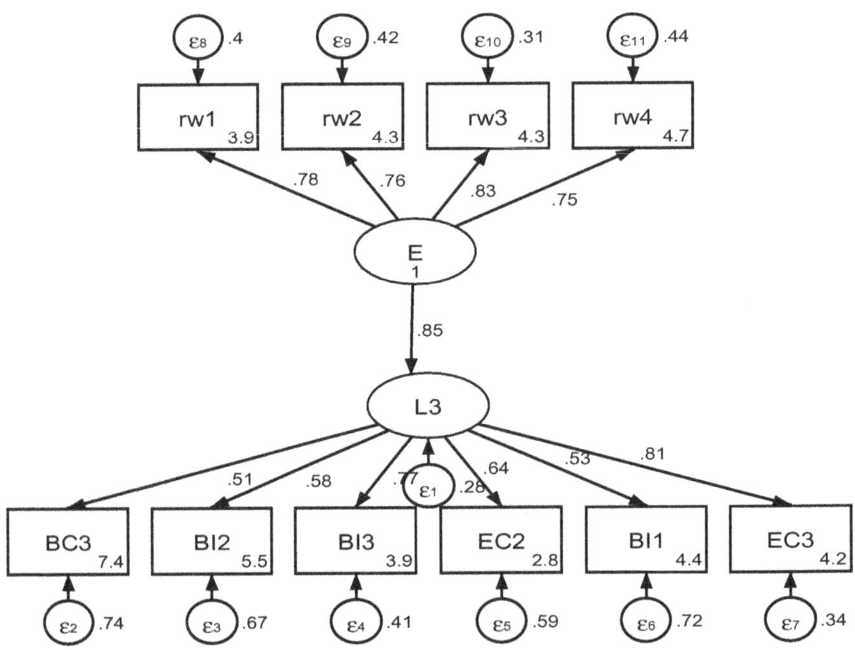

Fig. 6.20 Standardized effect of the impact of the friendship-efficiency style of organizational ethics on job performance

Table 6.29 Impact of the friendship-efficiency style of organizational ethics on job performance

Variables	(1)	(2)	(3)	(4)	(5)	(6)	(7)
	m115						
	L3	BC3	BI2	BI3	EC2	BI1	EC3
L3		1 (0)	1.430*** (0.0317)	2.432*** (0.0488)	2.444*** (0.0537)	1.520*** (0.0368)	2.428*** (0.0475)
E	0.343*** (0.00724)						
Constant		4.520*** (0.00590)	4.237*** (0.00747)	3.838*** (0.00952)	3.366*** (0.0115)	3.934*** (0.00867)	3.938*** (0.00902)
Observations	11,083	11,083	11,083	11,083	11,083	11,083	11,083

Standard errors in parentheses
***$p < 0.01$, **$p < 0.05$, *$p < 0.1$

by its decisions, all of which has a positive impact on the organization. This type of ethical climate is also associated with a higher degree of organizational commitment and camaraderie among members. From the perspective of social exchange theory, individuals tend to seek opportunities, which will allow them to maximize personal gain via negotiated exchanges. As applied to enterprises and their employees, the enterprise thereby offers greater consideration for employees' needs and wishes in exchange fora higher level of satisfaction and organizational commitment. Once employees find that their abilities, values, and beliefs resonate with the perceived ethical climate of the organization, they will actively seek to fulfill their duties, responsibilities, and commitments in order to repay the organization. In this respect, it should also be noted that employees have the option to terminate such an exchange relationship with their employer for a more advantageous relationship with another employer in order to increase their personal value. Therefore, another incentive for organizations to cultivate a friendship-efficiency style of ethical climate would be to counteract this desire to switch companies while strengthening an overall sense of commitment and belonging. In order to further explore the reasons for the conclusions of the study, we need to do further interviews or research based on grounded theory.

6.7 The Relationship Between Organizational Ethical Climate, Organizational Commitment and Job Performance in JFMEs

1. Moderate Organizational Ethics, Normative Organizational Commitment, and Job Performance

Although the path coefficient of the moderate organizational ethics impact on job performance is 0.82 (As Fig. 6.23), through the SEM structural equation, the moderate

Table 6.30 (6.29 Cont.) Impact of the friendship-efficiency style of organizational ethics on job performance

Variables	(8)	(9)	(10)	(11)	(12)	(13)	(14)	(15)
	rw1	rw2	rw3	rw4	var(e.BC3)	var(e.BI2)	var(e.BI3)	var(e.EC2)
L3								
E	1 (0)	0.913*** (0.0113)	0.989*** (0.0112)	0.817*** (0.0104)				
Constant	3.852*** (0.00956)	3.996*** (0.00890)	3.924*** (0.00884)	3.970*** (0.00814)	0.280*** (0.00403)	0.404*** (0.00596)	0.404*** (0.00712)	0.859*** (0.0130)
Observations	11,083	11,083	11,083	11,083	11,083	11,083	11,083	11,083

Standard errors in parentheses
***$p < 0.01$, **$p < 0.05$, *$p < 0.1$

Table 6.31 (6.29 Cont.) Impact of the friendship-efficiency style of organizational ethics on job performance

Variables	(16)	(17)	(18)	(19)	(20)	(21)	(22)	(23)
	var(e.BI1)	var(e.EC3)	var(e.rw1)	var(e.rw2)	var(e.rw3)	var(e.rw4)	var(e.L3)	var(E)
L3								
E								
Constant	0.588*** (0.00854)	0.304*** (0.00589)	0.394*** (0.00668)	0.361*** (0.00601)	0.262*** (0.00508)	0.320*** (0.00523)	0.0277*** (0.00123)	0.597*** (0.0130)
Observations	11,083	11,083	11,083	11,083	11,083	11,083	11,083	11,083

Standard errors in parentheses
***$p < 0.01$, **$p < 0.05$, *$p < 0.1$

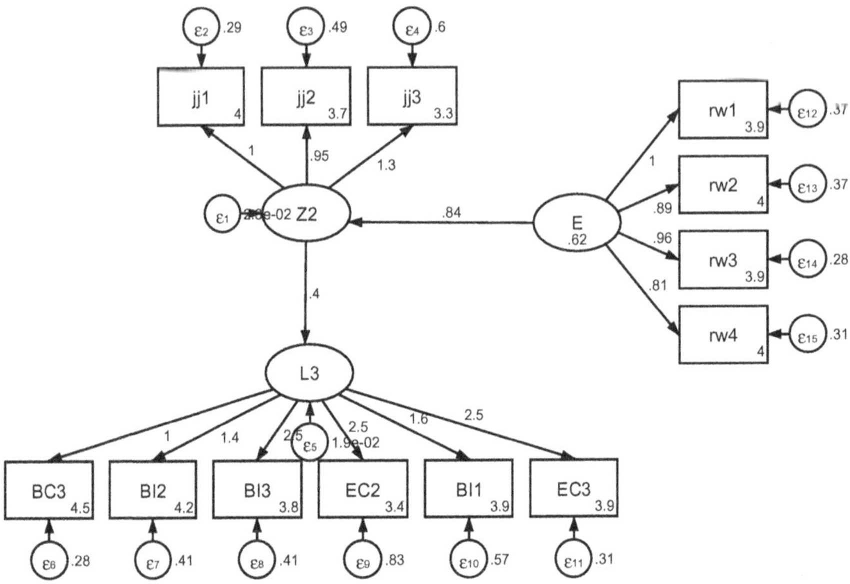

Fig. 6.21 Non-standardized effect of the impact of the friendship-efficiency style of organizational ethics on economic commitment and job performance

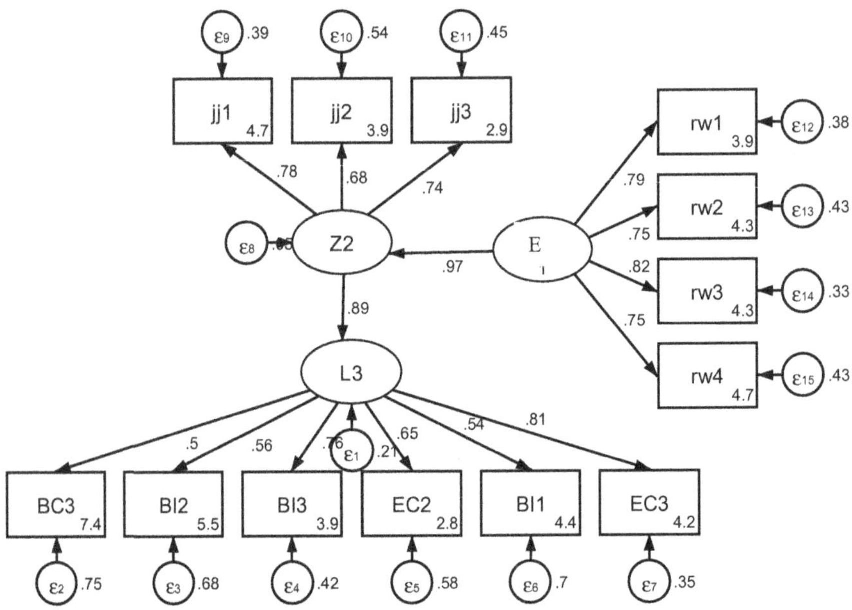

Fig. 6.22 Standardized effect of the impact of the friendship-efficiency style of organizational ethics on economic commitment and job performance

Table 6.32 Impact of the friendship-efficiency style of organizational ethics on economic commitment and job performance

Variables	(1)	(2)	(3)	(4)	(5)	(6)	(7)	(8)	(9)	(10)	(11)
	m114										
	L3	Z2	BC3	BI2	BI3	EC2	BI1	EC3	jj1	jj2	jj3
Z2	0.404*** (0.00838)								1 (0)	0.953*** (0.0134)	1.262*** (0.0160)
E		0.839*** (0.0102)									
L3			1 (0)	1.427*** (0.0325)	2.455*** (0.0498)	2.549*** (0.0560)	1.602*** (0.0385)	2.466*** (0.0487)			
Constant			4.519*** (0.00592)	4.236*** (0.00748)	3.837*** (0.00954)	3.364*** (0.0116)	3.934*** (0.00869)	3.938*** (0.00903)	4.046*** (0.00835)	3.685*** (0.00914)	3.294*** (0.0111)
Observations	11,083	11,083	11,083	11,083	11,083	11,083	11,083	11,083	11,083	11,083	11,083

Standard errors in parentheses
***$p < 0.01$, **$p < 0.05$, *$p < 0.1$

Table 6.33 (6.32 Cont.) Impact of the friendship-efficiency style of organizational ethics on economic commitment and job performance

Variables	(12)	(13)	(14)	(15)	(16)	(17)	(18)	(19)	(20)	(21)
	rw1	rw2	rw3	rw4	var(e.BC3)	var(e.BI2)	var(e.BI3)	var(e.EC2)	var(e.BI1)	var(e.EC3)
Z2										
E	1 (0)	0.886*** (0.0106)	0.957*** (0.0104)	0.813*** (0.00979)						
L3										
Constant	3.851*** (0.00958)	3.996*** (0.00891)	3.923*** (0.00886)	3.969*** (0.00816)	0.284*** (0.00406)	0.412*** (0.00601)	0.414*** (0.00711)	0.832*** (0.0126)	0.572*** (0.00833)	0.307*** (0.00577)
Observations	11,083	11,083	11,083	11,083	11,083	11,083	11,083	11,083	11,083	11,083

Standard errors in parentheses
***$p < 0.01$, **$p < 0.05$, *$p < 0.1$

Table 6.34 (6.32 Cont.) Impact of the friendship-efficiency style of organizational ethics on economic commitment and job performance

Variables	(22)	(23)	(24)	(25)	(26)	(27)	(28)	(29)	(30)	(31)
	var(e.jj1)	var(e.jj2)	var(e.jj3)	var(e.rw1)	var(e.rw2)	var(e.rw3)	var(e.rw4)	var(e.L3)	var(e.Z2)	var(E)
Z2										
E										
L3										
Constant	0.295*** (0.00483)	0.486*** (0.00735)	0.599*** (0.00948)	0.373*** (0.00608)	0.372*** (0.00590)	0.281*** (0.00490)	0.310*** (0.00485)	0.0194*** (0.000986)	0.0230*** (0.00265)	0.618*** (0.0129)
Observations	11,083	11,083	11,083	11,083	11,083	11,083	11,083	11,083	11,083	11,083

Standard errors in parentheses
***$p < 0.01$, **$p < 0.05$, *$p < 0.1$

organizational ethics atmosphere and work performance, the moderate organizational ethics atmosphere, the normative organizational commitment, and work performance are established. The paths between the two can be found that the moderate organizational ethics has two effects on job performance: the organizational ethics has a direct impact on job performance, and the moderate organizational ethics creates an indirect impact on job performance through organizational commitment. According to the empirical results, the moderate organizational ethics atmosphere reflects the organizational leadership style that focuses on the interests of employees, but also on the interests of the organization. At the same time, it also attaches great importance to the friendship and team-building of employees, which helps to cultivate the positive behavior of employees. In turn, it promotes the improvement of work performance.

2. Socially Responsible Organizational Ethics, Normative Organizational Commitment, and Job Performance

Through the SEM structural equations, two paths between social responsibility organizational ethics and work performance, social responsibility organizational ethics, normative organizational commitment, and job performance are established, and the social responsibility type organizational ethics can be found. The impact of job performance has two effects: the socially responsible organizational ethics has a direct impact on job performance, and the socially responsible organizational ethic atmosphere has an indirect impact on job performance through organizational commitment.

Organizational fulfillment of social responsibility means that companies have to pay more organizational costs and may reduce their performance in the short term. From the point of view of the accounting system, the short-term benefits of socially responsible activities can't make up for the cost of the enterprise, but in the long run, this is an effective, free, and far-reaching publicity campaign. A persuasive public relations activity organized by the organization. In the long run, the organization fulfills its social responsibility and can obtain a good job image, attract a large number of outstanding talents, and obtain additional sales growth. Therefore, most studies show that there is a positive correlation between organizational social responsibility participation and business performance (Fig. 6.24).

3. Friendship-Efficient Organizational Ethics, Normative Organizational Commitment, and Job Performance

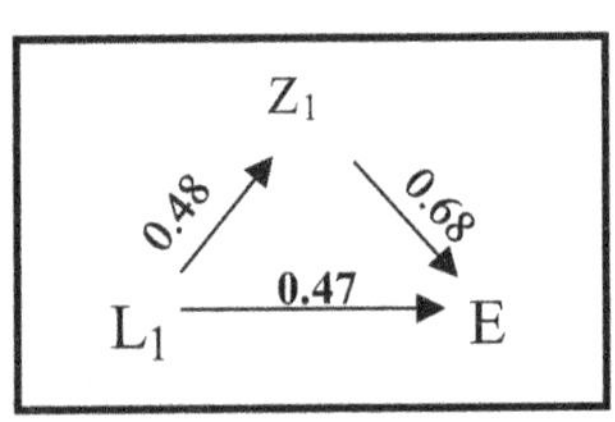

Fig. 6.23 Moderate organizational ethics ethic L1, Normative organization commitment Z1 and Job performance E

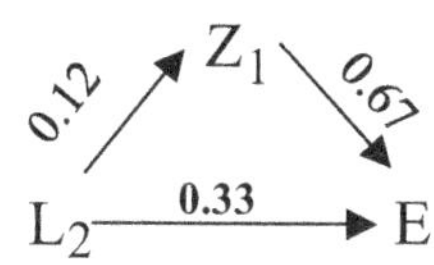

Fig. 6.24 Social responsibility organizational ethics atmosphere L2, Standard organizational commitment Z1, and job performance E

The path coefficient of friendship-efficient organizational ethics impact on job performance is 0.27 (As Fig. 6.25). Through the SEM structural equation, friendship-efficiency organizational ethics and work performance, friendship-efficient organizational ethics, normative organizational commitment, and work are established. The two paths between performance can be found that friendship-efficient organizational ethics has two effects on job performance: friendship-efficient organizational ethics has a direct impact on job performance and friendship-efficient organizational ethics Indirect impact on job performance through organizational commitment.

4. Moderate Organizational Ethics, Economic Organizational Commitment, and Job Performance

The moderate organizational ethics atmosphere includes a caring orientation and a self-interested organizational ethic atmosphere.

Care orientation is a comprehensive perception of organizational values and values of colleagues in the course of their work. In the course of work, employees can feel the concern and respect of employees through the policies and rules of the company, and they are advocating for labor ethics. This perception ultimately creates an identity, internalization, and ultimately the common goal of the value goals of employees and organizations. In turn, an organizational ethic atmosphere of high unity and cooperation is formed, which in turn helps improve work performance.

Utilitarian orientation is an individualism. To do things is generally to make self-interested choices under the company's framework and rules based on their own utility. This kind of organizational climate often has anti-ethical behaviors, that is, employees may improve their performance by destroying others' performance, or they may form a relatively independent action and refuse to cooperate with colleagues. Therefore, when cultivating the ethical atmosphere of the moderate organization, the impact on economic organizational commitment is weak. In the end, it is impossible to make a moderate organizational ethics atmosphere have an impact

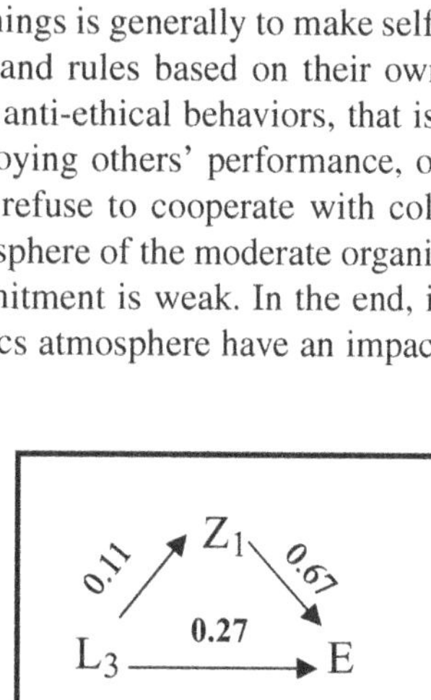

Fig. 6.25 Friendship-efficient organizational ethics atmosphere L3, Normative organizational commitment Z1, and Job performance E

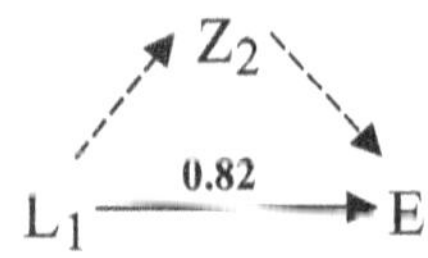

Fig. 6.26 Moderate organizational ethics ethical L1, Economic organization commitment Z2 and Job performance E

on job performance through economic organization commitment. The final performance is a modest organizational ethic atmosphere that has a direct impact on job performance (Fig. 6.26).

5. Socially Responsible Organizational Ethics, Economic Organizational Commitment, and Job Performance

Through the SEM structural equations, two paths between social responsibility organizational ethics and work performance, social responsibility organizational ethics, economic normative organizational commitment, and job performance are established, and economic organizational commitment can be found for job performance. The path between them is not obvious, so there is no obvious causal relationship between the two. However, the path between the socially responsible organizational ethic atmosphere and job performance is obvious, and there is also a clear path relationship between the socially responsible organizational ethical atmosphere and the economic organizational commitment (Fig. 6.27).

6. Friendship-Efficient Organizational Ethics, Economic Organizational Commitment, and Job Performance

The friendship-efficiency organizational ethics atmosphere and the economic organization commitment path coefficient have a certain significance, indicating that most members of Japanese-funded enterprises can perceive the ethical atmosphere of their organization in terms of profit efficiency and friendship. The most important characteristics of Japanese-funded enterprises in China are the pursuit of efficiency and profit. This corporate goal and value will undoubtedly assimilate the values of employees through the rules and regulations of the company. The main purpose of Chinese employees to work in Japanese-funded enterprises in China is to earn a living and obtain a higher return on wages. However, this kind of return is also the strengthening of the organizational ethic atmosphere advocated by Japanese-funded enterprises in China. However, due to the special history of Japan and China, in the construction of this efficient ethical atmosphere, it is necessary to have a high caring atmosphere, that is, care for employees, not only due to the special national conditions

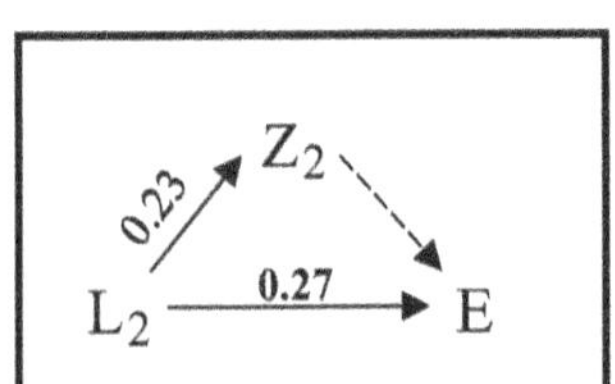

Fig. 6.27 Social responsibility organizational ethics climate L2, Economic organization commitment Z2 and Job performance E

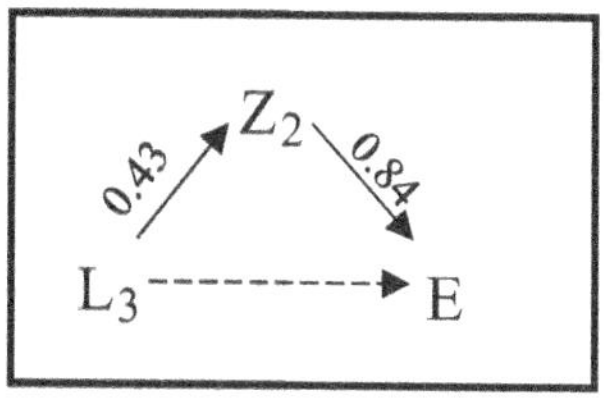

Fig. 6.28 Friendship-efficient organizational ethical atmosphere L3, economic organization commitment Z2 and job performance E

of China and Japan but also with Japan. Related to local culture, it eventually formed a profit-efficient ethical atmosphere with a humanistic spirit. Therefore, friendship-efficient organizational ethics can easily form a high economic commitment, which in turn encourages employees to work harder and improve work performance.

From this part of the study, the organizational ethic atmosphere is positively related to job performance H1 hypothesis, organizational theory, atmosphere, and organizational commitment are positively correlated with H2 hypothesis, organizational commitment and job performance are positively correlated with H3 hypothesis, and organizational commitment has a regulatory role. The H4 hypothesis has been verified. And the sub-hypothesis of each of the organizational ethical dimensions, organizational commitment, and job performance measured by Japanese companies in the manufacturing industry in China has also been verified.

In order to ensure the reproducibility of the research results, the sample data were still used, and 60, 70, and 80% of the sample size were randomly selected to perform the same empirical results. There was no significant difference in the conclusions, and the H1, H2, H3, and H4 hypotheses were all It was verified. Therefore, the empirical results are relatively stable and reliable. In order to be able to use other data to further verify this conclusion, the following points must be met when collecting data: first, collect Japanese-funded enterprise data in the manufacturing industry in China; second, ensure the sample of Japanese-funded enterprises in the manufacturing industry in China. The representativeness needs to collect samples in places where Japanese companies in the manufacturing industry in China are intensive. Third, the data obtained from the questionnaires should have good reliability and validity and ensure the quality of the data obtained by the questionnaire (Fig. 6.28).

Chapter 7
Research Conclusions, Contributions, and Prospects

7.1 Main Findings

7.1.1 The Main Types of Organizational Ethical Climates in JFMEs

JFMEs in China exhibit three main organizational ethical climates generally referred to as the "Golden Mean" style, the "social responsibility" style, and the "friendship-efficiency" style.

The "Golden Mean" style of ethical climate is derived from the idea of the golden mean, a concept of moderation in traditional Chinese philosophy, which has been incorporated into Japanese management practices. It combines focus on balancing friendship and self-interest, team interest and profit. The resulting tension between self-interest and profit on one hand and team interest and friendship on the other has been shown to result in an effective leadership style and a positive ethical climate.

The "social responsibility" style of organizational ethical climate also prioritizes self-interest, but is infused with a sense of altruism toward others and society at large. It has become increasingly prominent as the Chinese government's focus has shifted from economic growth to social welfare. While over the course of reform and opening-up efforts have been made to extricate the management and operations of enterprises from government oversight by focusing on macro-economic regulations, the Chinese government continues to intervene in economic activities of Chinese enterprises, and it has an outsized impact on organizational ethical climate. At the same time, the tendency of JFMEs to prioritize corporate social responsibility is also a product of the historically fraught relationship between China and Japan, as they aim to overcome Chinese hostility and opposition to Japanese products. Only with the positive image, which comes from assuming greater social responsibility, JFMEs are able to thrive in the Chinese market.

As for the "friendship-efficiency" style, JFMEs in China tend to act like multinational corporations in terms of their focus on international operations and increased

© Science Press and Springer Nature Singapore Pte Ltd. 2020

K. Ryu, *The Impact of Organizational Ethical Climate on Organizational Commitment and Job Performance*, https://doi.org/10.1007/978-981-15-2813-2_7

efficiency through localization. At the same time, however, Japanese leaders place great importance on the individual needs of their employees, and it positively impacts organizational ethical climate. In fact, prior research shows that leaders play a pivotal role in influencing the formation and development of ethical climate, and organizations' ethical standards are necessarily shaped by the psychological and behavioral makeup of its executives. This includes but is not necessarily limited to their distinctive approach to problems, the values reflected in their managerial practices, the ethical distinctions they make, as well as the way in which they manage employee expectations.[1] Therefore, to the extent that the management practices of JFMEs tend to emphasize both efficiency and friendship, the "friendship-efficiency" style of the organizational ethical climate remains widespread.

This research evaluated nine dimensions of organizational ethics climate in Japanese-funded enterprises in the manufacturing industry in China, including self-interest (self-interest-oriented), corporate profits (self-interest-oriented), efficiency, friendship (care-oriented), team interests (care-oriented), social responsibility, personal ethics (independent orientation), company rules and levels (rule-oriented), legal and professional norms (legal and regulatory orientation).

We find that three main ethical climates dominate in the Japanese-funded enterprises in China, which are the moderate organizational ethics ("Golden Mean"), the socially responsible organizational ethics, and the friendship-efficiency organizational ethics. From the nine dimensions, there is no evidence that personal ethics (independent orientation), legal and professional norms (legal and regulatory orientation), and team interests (care-orientation) would have significant impact on organizational ethic climate. The other six dimensions of organizational ethics climate have become comprehensive elements of the moderate , socially responsible, and friendship-efficient organizational ethical climates.

7.1.2 The Main Types of Organizational Commitment in JFMEs

In addition to the three dominating ethical climates discussed above, organizational commitment within JFMEs in China can also be categorized into two distinct types: 1) normative and 2) economic. Both of them are significantly affected by organizational ethical climate, as discussed in detail below.

The conclusions of this study indicate differences between the types of organizational commitments of Chinese-funded enterprises and JFMEs in China. Prior research has found that Chinese companies' organizational commitments include

[1] Yanfei Wang, Yu Zhu. An Overview of Innovative Climate in Foreign Organizations [J]. Foreign Economics & Management, 2005, 27(8): 26–32. In his study of the role of leaders in shaping ethical climates, Grojean (2004) has identified seven way sin which leaders influence the ethics and values of their employees. A study conducted by Sim and Brinkman (2002) has also outlined how effective leaders strengthen ethical climate.

five major factors: emotional commitment, normative commitment, ideals commitment, economic commitment, and opportunity commitment (Ling Wenquan, 2001). In this study, we found that the main organizational commitment types of employees in JFMEs in China mainly include normative and economic organizational commitments, and lack emotional commitment and ideals commitment. This difference could be related to the history of China and Japan, and impacted by many political and cultural factors.

7.1.3 The Relationship Between Organizational Ethical Climate, Organizational Commitment and Job Performance in JFMEs

1. *Organizational ethics, normative commitment, and job performance*

The results suggest that all three ethical climates have the potential to impact job performance both directly and indirectly through their effect on normative commitment. SEM analysis indicates a significant correlation between both the "Golden Mean", "social responsibility", and "friendship-efficiency" styles of organizational ethical climate and job performance as well as between normative commitment and job performance. Generally speaking, the "Golden Mean" style of organizational ethical climate represents the interests of both the organization and its employees and has been shown to enhance job performance by cultivating enthusiasm and focusing on friendship and team building. The "social responsibility" style of ethical climate has long-term positive impact on performance because of organization's reputation as well as its ability to attract talent. Those more than enough offset any related additional costs which could affect performance and business interests in the short term.

2. *Organizational ethics, economic commitment, and job performance*

The "Golden Mean" style of organizational ethical climate may lead to the neglect of organizational interest along with rampant unethical behavior, because it is a combination of both caring and instrumental climates focused on the well-being of employees, and it prioritizes self-interest. As a result, it tends to have a weak impact on economic commitment and only affects job performance directly. As for the "social responsibility" style, its effect on job performance and economic commitment are strong. However, the results also suggest lack of causality between economic commitment and job performance, which again means that this type of climate only affects job performance directly. Finally, there also appears to be a strong correlation between the "friendship-efficiency" style of ethical climate and economic commitment. It indicates that JFMEs in China are concerned not only with maximizing profit and efficiency but also nurturing friendship among employees. Based on these results, managers are advised to focus on the developmental and other needs of their employees as part of their effort to improve job performance by cultivating a caring climate.

It can be seen that all hypotheses been verified. From this study we see that the organizational ethical climate is positively related to job performance (H1 hypothesis),: organizational climate is positively correlated with organizational commitment (H2 hypothesis), organizational commitment is positively correlated with job performance (H3 hypothesis), and organizational commitment has a regulatory role (H4 hypothesis).

Also each sub-hypothesis related to the dimensions of the organizational ethical climate, the actual organizational commitment, and the measurement of job performance of Japanese companies in the manufacturing industry in China has been verified.

7.2 Major Contributions and Further Study

7.2.1 Major contributions of this study in terms of labor economics

Prior studies on organizational ethical climate and its effect on organizational commitment have approached the topic from an ethical, psychological, philosophical and/or sociological perspective. Yet relatively few have examined it from the perspective of economic ethics, which is what this research attempts to accomplish. It uses questionnaires to measure the impact of various ethical climates on organizational commitment and job performance of JFMEs in China.

As discussed above, three types of ethical climates have been identified along with two types of organizational commitments and at least one style of job performance. Those at least partially are the result of cultural differences between China and Japan and inform about the corporate management practices of the two countries. In addition to these theoretical distinctions, various practical recommendations have also been offered to promote the development of positive ethical climates from the perspective of economic ethics.

The limitation of this paper is that the dimensions L2 and L3 in measuring the organizational climate are latent variables, and observable variables BC3 and BI2 are included in both of them. It may, to some extent, cause the correlation between L2 and L3. Since we cannot judge the correlation between the two latent variables, the degree of correlation between L2 and L3 is not tested in the analysis. Therefore, the research of the impact of organizational ethical climate on job performance is based on the different dimensions of organizational ethical climate (L1, L2, L3 return to Z1, Z2 and E). This approach is used to minimize estimation errors may related to potential endogeneity. In addition, further research based on grounded theory is needed to strengthen conclusions of this research.

This study involves an evaluation of the organizational ethical climate, organizational commitment and job performance of JFMEs in China, with a particular focus on labor economics. It is based on a review of related research as well as an empirical analysis of the various types of organizational ethical climates of JFMEs in China. The major contribution of this study is the application of economic ethics perspective, which comprehensively analyzes the unity of economic and ethical issues. From the economic ethics perspective, the organizational ethical climate is analyzed in conjunction with theory of supply and demand in the labor market, dual labor market theory, and labor policy in labor economics.

7.2.2 Frameworks of Ethical Economics Through Empirical Research

Scholars in China and in the world have conducted less research on enterprises in China and Japan, and there are only few relevant studies from the perspective of organizational atmosphere and ethical economics, especially in countries with significant non-market factors such as in China. The framework of economics ethics helps to fill the research gap in the academic field. Economic ethics not only focuses on the growth of social wealth but also on the distribution of it, as well as on the harmonious development of society. This makes the framework suitable for explaining some of the phenomena present in China's economy and enterprises where strong emphasis on culture and ethics is prevalent.

For the first time, the measurement dimension of organizational ethics, organizational commitment, and job performance of Japanese-funded enterprises in China were measured. According to the research, the organizational ethic climate of Japanese-funded enterprises in China's manufacturing industry includes three types, namely, the "Golden Mean" or moderate organizational ethic climate, the "social responsibility" organizational ethic climate, and the "friendship-efficient" organizational ethic climate. Observed organizational commitments include economic commitment and normative commitment; and work performance is primarily measured by task performance.

For the first time, the relationship between organizational ethics, organizational commitment, and job performance were discussed from the perspective of economic ethics. During a comprehensive literature review was found, that few scholars have explained organizational ethics from the perspective of economic ethics. Also there is insufficient research on relationships between organizational ethics, organizational commitment, and job performance. This study illustrates the feasibility of studying the perspective of organizational ethics from the perspective of economic ethics. Also it lays out the theoretical basis for the feasibility of explaining the problem. Finally, this research provides the first example of exploring the organizational ethical climate and organization from the perspective of economic ethics.

This research further develops understanding about role and importance of the organizational climate in economic ethics framework. In prior research, there are few conjoint empirical studies on organizational ethical climate, organizational commitment, and work performance. Especially lacking is such research on Chinese and foreign organizations' ethical climate. This research synthesizes prior research and systematically sorts out the research focusing on organizational ethical climates globally. Focusing on organizational ethics, and ethical management issues in specific situations, this research contributes to the theoretical reproduction of existing research and encourage debate among scholars in the field.

Through integration of different less research cultures, multinational companies can better address and solve the cultural issues they face in their operations, and by integrating corresponding human resources can achieve good practical results. This means integration of existing internal and external resources of the enterprise and forming common values recognized by all employees of the enterprise. Such integration should be based on the basic principle of seeking common ground while reserving the room for differences. For achieving assimilation of relevant values, it is necessary to confirm them against the basis of common values and then transform into ones that are recognized by most employees. Therefore, cross-cultural integration is a long process and it is the goal of many efforts in China.

7.2.3 The Need for Further Study with Grounded Theory

The underlying concepts of organizational ethical climate, organizational commitment, and job performance used in this study are all based on definitions derived from prior research. Therefore, if these ideas are redefined using a new questionnaire, results could turn out to be very different. Therefore, further studies with grounded theory may be necessary to address this potential shortcoming.

The primary task of grounded theory is to establish a substantive theory somewhere between macro and micro-operational hypotheses (applicable to a specific time and place), at the same time leaving possibilities for a more formal universal theory which itself would be based on a substantive theory. According to grounded theory, knowledge is derived from the accumulation of facts, which then evolve into a substantive theory and ultimately into a formal theory. Constructing formal theories requires numerous sources of data as well as the development of a substantive theory to serve as an intermediary for eliminating any loopholes. Moreover, formal theories are often able to incorporate several substantive theories by integrating disparate and potentially unrelated concepts into something more than the sum of their parts able to explain a wider range of phenomena. Essentially, by comparing different data and theories, grounded theory enables discovery of previously hidden correlations with the potential to provide unexpected insight into a given subject.

As a practical matter, this would necessarily require further development of detailed surveys and interviews to be conducted of JFMEs in China in order to obtain enough data for purposes of comparison, especially, including their parent companies and branches. This comparison could use the following protocol: (i) encoding and grouping data by concept categories, separating observations into as many categories as possible, and then comparing categories to identify specific attributes; (ii) integrating related concept categories with their attributes, comparing them, considering their relationships and making connections between these relationships; (iii) presenting a preliminary outline of a theory, determining any potential applications or extensions, verifying the preliminary theory with the original data and refining it; and (iv) providing an answer to the original research questions by describing the theory in terms of the collected data, concept categories, categorical attributes and relationships between attributes.

Therefore, while the literature on a given subject can provide a useful theoretical framework for data analysis, care should be taken not to abuse prior theories, leading to considerable risk of being constrained by existing concepts and misconstruing data using unrelated or inappropriate theories. To conclude, these universal theories from this research should emphasize more on reflecting real circumstances rather than applying them theoretically.

Accordingly, in order to better understand the characteristics of the ethical climates currently exhibited by JFMEs in China, as well as their potential impact on organizational commitment and job performance, additional in-depth investigation needs to be conducted, and resulting data analyzed using grounded theory, as described above.

7.3 Future Outlook

The fact that organizational ethical climate is viewed almost exclusively in terms of ethics, and not economics, remains a major weakness in prior research. As studies of ethical climate are concerned with the behavior of employees in an organization while economic ethics research is focused on the behavior of the "rational man" in the market, the two necessarily share the same theoretical foundation. In the modern market economy, economic ethics also has the potential to offer reasonable and convincing theoretical explanations for employee behavior, as well as for impact of organization's ethical climate on such behavior. There can be no doubt that the field of economic ethics will play an increasingly important role in studies of organizational ethical climate.

In addition, as China's economy continues to become an important overseas market for foreign-funded enterprises, and as the government seeks a balance between economic and social development, the criteria for a successful business are no longer limited to economic indexes but will necessarily include such intangibles as contributions to society.[2]

---

[2]Changhui Yin: Enhance Corporate Citizenship Awareness. Enterprise Vitality, 2004, 7.

Therefore, if Japanese enterprises are to expand their market share, they not only have to compete with other Chinese enterprises and MNCs but also have to pay more attention to corporate social responsibility in order to cultivate a positive corporate image. Furthermore, to better understand the political, cultural and historical roots of the economic challenges currently faced by Japanese enterprises in China, non-market theories and methods should be used. Research to date on the organizational ethical climate of JFMEs has produced some interesting results, but practical and effective solutions can be found only by adopting new and innovative approaches.

Appendix A
Letter of Intent

Purpose of the Survey
Through this investigation of organizational ethical climate, organizational commitment, and employee performance, the purpose of the survey is to clarify the impact of organizational ethical climate on organizational commitment and job performance from the perspective of economic ethics. In doing so, we hope to derive the relevance between this research and practical situations.

Abstract of the Survey
As a professor at Ritsumeikan University in Japan, I am now focusing on the study of organizational ethical climate from the perspective of economic ethics. The essential part of the study is defined as the impact of organizational ethical climate on organizational commitment and job performance.

The organizational ethical climate is the embodiment of the environment of organizational ethics. It refers to the common experiences of the members of the organization on what is ethical behavior and how to solve ethical dilemmas. It is also the primary factor affecting the ethical behavior of employees. Therefore, we could assume that the stronger an organization's organizational ethical climate, the more effective its organizational commitment will be, and the better its employees will perform. By clarifying these relationships, we hope to not only accumulate knowledge but also to apply that knowledge to practical situations.

This survey could assist companies that get involved; after confirming the status of the organization's ethical climate, it will also be my honor to offer advice regarding your organization's current situation.

Methodology and Process of the Survey
The staff will respond to a paper questionnaire, and there will be a statistical analysis of the data collected through the survey.

(1) The paper form of the questionnaire will be sent to the person in charge of the company's involvement in the investigation.
(2) Questionnaires will be distributed to the company staff by the person who is assisting the investigation.

© Science Press and Springer Nature Singapore Pte Ltd. 2020

K. Ryu, *The Impact of Organizational Ethical Climate on Organizational Commitment and Job Performance*, https://doi.org/10.1007/978-981-15-2813-2

(3) The staff answers anonymously, and their answers will be enclosed in an envelope.
(4) There are several ways, listed below, to send the answers to us.

  a. Staff members mail their answers directly to the address below.
  b. The person in charge collects staff responses and mails them to the address below without opening them.

(5) Statistical analysis will be conducted using data from the collected questionnaires.
(6) We will report the results of the analysis of this study.
   Mailing Address: Ryu Keikoh

Period of the Survey
The questionnaire survey of this study is expected to be completed this year.

Request for Assistance in Investigation
Apologies for disturbing. Please assist our investigation by understanding the basis of the investigation. Thank you for your cooperation!

Appendix B
Sample of Confidentiality Agreement 1

Confidentiality Agreement
RYUKEIKOH (hereinafter referred to as "A") and Company ____________ (hereinafter referred to as "B") will conclude a confidentiality agreement on mutual information between the two parties.

Article 1 (Purpose)
The purpose of this agreement is to have both parties conduct an investigation of "The Survey on Organizational Ethical Climate." The purpose of each of A and B is as follows.

A: The results of the investigation will be used for academic research, or the results of the research will be published.

B: The survey results are disclosed within the company and used as a reference for organizational decisions.

Article 2 (Definitions of Confidential Information)

1. The confidential information referred to in this agreement, that is, in this agreement or its contents, that A and B (hereinafter referred to as the discloser) disclose to the other party are clearly stated as within the scope of technical or business confidentiality. Secret intelligence is not limited to either paper or oral form.
2. When the information displayed by the discloser is tangible information such as written information or a recording, if the information is designated as "secret" or "confidential," this information should be included into the confidential information.
3. When the information to be presented is verbal or visual information, the discloser must clearly indicate its confidentiality to the other party at the time of opening and send a written notification to the other party within 10 days of the disclosing of the information.
4. Regardless of the above-mentioned provisions, any of the following circumstances are not classified as confidential information.

   (1) Open information which has already been disclosed at the time of opening.
   (2) Information that the recipient had learned before the time of the opening.

© Science Press and Springer Nature Singapore Pte Ltd. 2020

K. Ryu, *The Impact of Organizational Ethical Climate on Organizational Commitment and Job Performance*, https://doi.org/10.1007/978-981-15-2813-2

(3) Open information resulting from the negligence of non-recipients after the opening.
(4) Information obtained from a third party without due obligation.
(5) Information discovered by the recipient but not by opening or disclosure.

Article 3 (Information Protection and Management)

1. To achieve the purposes in Article 1, recipients of information must disclose information to a minimum level, strictly fulfill the written commitments made to the discloser prior to the opening of the information, and not express the content of the information to a third party by explicating or implicating. Except for the purposes in Article 1 of this Agreement, the information shall not be used for other purposes.
2. To prevent the loss of confidential information, the recipient must have an appropriate way to keep the information.
3. The recipient should immediately contact the presenter if the information is lost.

Article 4 (Prohibition of Copying)
The recipient is not allowed to reproduce or copy confidential information without the consent of the informer. Copies made by the recipient are also defined as confidential information.

Article 5 (Returning of Confidential Information)
After the validity period of this agreement ends, the recipient must return all confidential information (including the duplicates and copies made by the recipient) or destroy it with the consent of the discloser.

Article 6 (Penalty for Damages)
In the situation that the discloser suffers a loss due to the violation of this agreement by the recipient, the discloser may make a claim for compensation.

Article 7 (Period of Agreement)
The validity period of this agreement is one year from the date of conclusion of the agreement. Even if the agreement is terminated, the contents specified in Article 3 of this Agreement are still valid.

Article 8 (Agreed Contents)
Any matters not stipulated in this agreement or any doubt as to the interpretation of this agreement shall be settled through negotiation between both parties.

A total of two copies of this agreement will be printed. Each of the two parties will have their signatures stamped and save one of them. This proves as evidence for the agreement.

Year Month Day

A:

B:

Appendix C
Sample of Confidentiality Agreement 2

The company (hereinafter referred to as "A") and RYU KEIKOH (hereinafter referred to as "B") will conduct research on organizational ethical climate (hereinafter referred to as the present investigation). Party B will conduct the research, and Party A and related companies will disclose confidential information to B. The two parties make the following agreement.

(Definition)
Article 1 The confidential information referred to in this agreement shall be all technical and business information held by Party A and Party A's intelligence obtained through Party B's investigation.

(Secret Protection Obligation)
Article 2 B must strictly protect confidential information and must not disclose it to third parties without the permission of A. However, if B can prove that the information is any of the following, then the information is not confidential information.

1. Open information which has already been disclosed at the time of opening.
2. Information that the recipient had learned before the time of the opening.
3. Open information resulting from the negligence of non-recipients after the opening.
4. Information obtained from a third party without due obligation.

(Purpose of Usage)
Article 3 B can only use confidential information for the investigation of this study, and it cannot be used for other purposes.

(Disclosure Range)
Article 4

1. B can only disclose the confidential information to the minimum number of relevant parties and disclose it within the minimum limit.
2. Based on the provisions of the preceding paragraph, Party B shall manage the relevant persons who disclose the information and assume full responsibility for the disclosure of information.

© Science Press and Springer Nature Singapore Pte Ltd. 2020

K. Ryu, *The Impact of Organizational Ethical Climate on Organizational Commitment and Job Performance*, https://doi.org/10.1007/978-981-15-2813-2

(Valid Period)

Article 5 This agreement is valid for one year from the date of conclusion. However, the contents specified in Article 2 shall be valid for 5 years after the end of the agreement.

A total of two copies of this agreement will be printed. Each of the two parties will have their signatures stamped and save one of them. This proves as evidence for the agreement.

Year Month Day

A:

B:

Appendix D
Request for Investigation

Dear Project Manager:
Thank you for assisting me in this investigation of the organization's ethical climate. This survey investigates organizational ethical climate, organizational commitment, and employee performance, and it clarifies the impact of organizational ethical climate on organizational commitment and job performance from the perspective of economic ethics. It is also expected to inspire practical situations. Please assist the investigation by understanding the basis of the investigation. Thank you for your cooperation!

RYU KEIKOH

Survey Methodology and Recollecting Deadline

We will send envelopes equal to the number of persons joining the survey to the project manager and ask them to distribute them to the participants. At the same time, please issue an order to "seal the envelope after answering, so your responses are not read by others." Please send the collected questionnaires to the following address in a sealed state.

Recollecting Deadline:
Recipient: RYU KEIKOH

If you have any questions, please contact:
RYU KEIKOH

© Science Press and Springer Nature Singapore Pte Ltd. 2020

K. Ryu, *The Impact of Organizational Ethical Climate on Organizational Commitment and Job Performance*, https://doi.org/10.1007/978-981-15-2813-2

Appendix E
Questionnaire of Personal Information

1. Sex
   Male
   Female
   Other
2. Age
   Your age is years old
3. Working years
   You have been working in this company for years
4. Educational Background
   Junior High School
   High School
   Specialized School/Junior College
   Bachelor
   Master or higher
5. Position in company
   Upper Management
   Management
   Conductor
   Regular employee
   Other
6. Department in the company
   Business
   Construction
   Development
   Management
   Maintenance
   Other

© Science Press and Springer Nature Singapore Pte Ltd. 2020

K. Ryu, *The Impact of Organizational Ethical Climate on Organizational Commitment and Job Performance*, https://doi.org/10.1007/978-981-15-2813-2

Appendix F
Questionnaire of Organizational Ethical Climate

	Organizational ethical climate	Strongly disagree	Disagree	Neither agree nor disagree	Agree	Strongly agree	Variable
Self-interest	1. Most employees in this enterprise just consider their own interests	1	2	3	4	5	EI1
	2. Employees in this enterprise do not have space for professional or personal ethics	1	2	3	4	5	EI2
	3. Employees in this enterprise place their self-interest above anything else	1	2	3	4	5	EI3
	4. The main concern of employees in this enterprise is what benefits them the most	1	2	3	4	5	EI4

(continued)

© Science Press and Springer Nature Singapore Pte Ltd. 2020

K. Ryu, *The Impact of Organizational Ethical Climate on Organizational Commitment and Job Performance*, https://doi.org/10.1007/978-981-15-2813-2

(continued)

	Organizational ethical climate	Strongly disagree	Disagree	Neither agree nor disagree	Agree	Strongly agree	Variable
Company profit	5. The enterprise expects every employee to do things that gain economic benefits and raise corporate status	1	2	3	4	5	EL1
	6. Employees in this enterprise only care about economic benefits and corporate image	1	2	3	4	5	EL2
Efficiency	7. The main duty of employees in this enterprise is to control cost	1	2	3	4	5	EC1
	8. In this enterprise, the cheapest approaches are always the best	1	2	3	4	5	EC2
	9. The enterprise expects every employee to work in cost recovery	1	2	3	4	5	EC3
	10. The enterprise always seeks cheap solutions to problems	1	2	3	4	5	EC4

(continued)

(continued)

	Organizational ethical climate	Strongly disagree	Disagree	Neither agree nor disagree	Agree	Strongly agree	Variable
Friendship	11. In this enterprise, good interpersonal relationships are of supreme importance	1	2	3	4	5	BI1
	12. The main concern of employees in this enterprise is what benefits others the most	1	2	3	4	5	BI2
	13. The main concern of the enterprise is how to do good to every single employee	1	2	3	4	5	BI3
	14. The decisions in this enterprise will consider every single employee	1	2	3	4	5	BI4
	15. The main concern of this enterprise is what benefits every single employee the most	1	2	3	4	5	BL2
	16. In this enterprise, employees think that team spirit is important	1	2	3	4	5	BL3

(continued)

(continued)

	Organizational ethical climate	Strongly disagree	Disagree	Neither agree nor disagree	Agree	Strongly agree	Variable
	17. The enterprise thinks that good and extensive cooperation among employees is important	1	2	3	4	5	BL4
	18. The employees in this enterprise all pay active attention to customers they directly contact	1	2	3	4	5	BC3
Personal morality (independence)	19. The enterprise expects employees to follow their moral faith and professional ethics	1	2	3	4	5	PI1
	20. In this enterprise, employees' behaviors are guided by personal ethics	1	2	3	4	5	PI3
Rules and procedures (rules)	21. In this enterprise, it is important to follow the regulation and procedures	1	2	3	4	5	PL1
	22. The enterprise expects every single employee to follow the regulation and procedures	1	2	3	4	5	PL2

(continued)

(continued)

	Organizational ethical climate	Strongly disagree	Disagree	Neither agree nor disagree	Agree	Strongly agree	Variable
Laws and professional codes (law and code)	23. The first concern of the enterprise is whether things are against the law or not	1	2	3	4	5	PC1
	24. The enterprise expects employees to take laws and professional codes as their working principle	1	2	3	4	5	PC2
	25. The enterprise expects employees to strictly follow laws and professional codes	1	2	3	4	5	PC1
	26. The enterprise mainly concerns public interest	1	2	3	4	5	BC5

Appendix G
Questionnaire of Organizational Commitment

	Organizational commitment	Strongly disagree	Disagree	Neither agree nor disagree	Agree	Strongly agree	Variable
Normative commitment	1. I think the current job deserves my full dedication	1	2	3	4	5	gf5
	2. I think this hotel deserves the same love as I love my home	1	2	3	4	5	gf6
	3. I think I should be loyal to this enterprise	1	2	3	4	5	gf2
	4. I think I should be obliged to contribute to the development of this enterprise	1	2	3	4	5	gf3
	5. I won't leave my enterprise even though there is a better job	1	2	3	4	5	gf4

(continued)

© Science Press and Springer Nature Singapore Pte Ltd. 2020

K. Ryu, *The Impact of Organizational Ethical Climate on Organizational Commitment and Job Performance*, https://doi.org/10.1007/978-981-15-2813-2

(continued)

	Organizational commitment	Strongly disagree	Disagree	Neither agree nor disagree	Agree	Strongly agree	Variable
	6. I think it is not ethical to leave my enterprise	1	2	3	4	5	gf1
Economic commitment	7. If I leave the enterprise now, I am afraid that I will lose my current welfare	1	2	3	4	5	Jj1
	8. If I leave the enterprise now, I am afraid that I will lose my current income	1	2	3	4	5	jj2
	9. The reason why I do not leave the enterprise is that I have dedicated too much	1	2	3	4	5	jj3
Choice commitment	10. I cannot enjoy many privileges if I do not stay working in this enterprise	1	2	3	4	5	jh1
	11. I stay in this enterprise because it is hard for me to find a better job	1	2	3	4	5	jh2
	12. I stay in this enterprise because the welfare here is good	1	2	3	4	5	jh3

(continued)

(continued)

	Organizational commitment	Strongly disagree	Disagree	Neither agree nor disagree	Agree	Strongly agree	Variable
Affective commitment	13. I won't leave this enterprise even if it downsizes and declines	1	2	3	4	5	gq1
	14. I am willing to serve the enterprise because I have feelings for it	1	2	3	4	5	gq2
Ideal commitment	15. I think the enterprise can offer me nice chances of personal development	1	2	3	4	5	lx1
	16. I think the enterprise can offer me nice chances fortraining	1	2	3	4	5	lx2

Appendix H
Questionnaire of Job Performance

	Job performance	Strongly disagree	Disagree	Neither agree nor disagree	Agree	Strongly agree	Variable
Task performance	1. I often finish my task efficiently	1	2	3	4	5	rw1
	2. I keep a high working efficiency	1	2	3	4	5	rw2
	3. The goal of my task can always be successfully achieved	1	2	3	4	5	rw3
	4. I often undertake tasks beyond my own task	1	2	3	4	5	rw4
Contextual performance	5. I have good interpersonal relationships to help colleagues undertake tasks	1	2	3	4	5	gx1

(continued)

© Science Press and Springer Nature Singapore Pte Ltd. 2020

K. Ryu, *The Impact of Organizational Ethical Climate on Organizational Commitment and Job Performance*, https://doi.org/10.1007/978-981-15-2813-2

(continued)

	Job performance	Strongly disagree	Disagree	Neither agree nor disagree	Agree	Strongly agree	Variable
	6. I often undertake tasks in a pleasant environment	1	2	3	4	5	gx2
Learning performance	7. I pay attention to learning to increase my working efficiency	1	2	3	4	5	xx3
	8. I often make use of new knowledge to solve difficulties in tasks	1	2	3	4	5	xx4
	9. I have high competence in learning and efficiency	1	2	3	4	5	xx5
Innovation performance	10. I learn new knowledge, approaches, and skills unceasingly	1	2	3	4	5	cx1
	11. I often propose innovative solutions to difficulties in tasks	1	2	3	4	5	cx2
	11. I have increased working efficiency by applying innovative ideas	1	2	3	4	5	cx3

Appendix I
Free Comment

Please write any comments or suggestions freely if you have any:

© Science Press and Springer Nature Singapore Pte Ltd. 2020

K. Ryu, *The Impact of Organizational Ethical Climate on Organizational Commitment and Job Performance*, https://doi.org/10.1007/978-981-15-2813-2

Appendix J
Interview Form

[1] Acquisition of recording permission
[2] About the department

a. Position of the department
b. Status of affiliates in the company (organization chart)
c. Assigned business content
d. Job content
e. Number of years of service, experience (changing jobs, etc.), family background (marital status, etc.)
f. Ideas for the company department

[3] About the questionnaire

a. What is the difference between answering the question of other people around and answering your own question? (Do you remember the contents of the questionnaire? How was the questionnaire?)
b. Questionnaires are anonymous. If they are registered, are the answers the same?

[4] About the organizational ethical climate

a. What do you think of when you hear words like "organizational ethical climate"?
b. Specifically:
    1. About selfishness
        1. Do the company's employees only care about their own interests?
        2. Does the employee have a personal ethical space?
    2. About company profits and efficiency
        1. Does the company expect employee's behavior could boost company profits?
        2. Do employees only pay attention to economic benefits and company image?
        3. Does the company expect the cheapest way to be the right one?

© Science Press and Springer Nature Singapore Pte Ltd. 2020

K. Ryu, *The Impact of Organizational Ethical Climate on Organizational Commitment and Job Performance*, https://doi.org/10.1007/978-981-15-2813-2

        4. Does the company expect employees to work in a cost-reduced manner?
    3. About friendship
        1. Are good relationships important to the company?
        2. Does the company mainly consider how to be good for every employee?
        3. Do employees think that teamwork is important?
    4. About ethics and regulations
        1. Does the company expect employees to follow personal moral beliefs and professional conduct?
        2. Do the company's actions first consider whether it violates the law?
        3. Does the company mainly consider the public interest?

[5] About organizational commitment

a. What do you think of when you hear words like "organizational commitment"?
b. How does this affect your behavior?
c. Specifically:
    1. About specification promise
        1. Do you feel comfortable in your current company?
        2. Do you feel obliged to take responsibility for your company's development?
        3. Do you think that job-hopping is an immoral thing?
    2. About economic commitment and opportunity commitment
        1. If you leave the company now, do you worry about personal loss?
        2. Could you enjoy the benefits without staying in your company?
        3. Are you staying in the company because you could not find a better job?
    3. About emotional commitment and ideal commitment
        1. Even if the company's economic efficiency deteriorates, will you leave?
        2. Do you have feelings for the company, and are you willing to serve the company?
        3. Do you think the company offers a good opportunity?

[6] Job Performance

a. Is there a clear definition of job performance?
b. Specifically:
    1. About the task
        1. Do you often complete your work efficiently?
        2. Are you always achieving your work goal successfully?
        3. Are you often taking extra work?

2. About the relationship
    1. Do you have good personal relationships and often help colleagues with their jobs?
    2. Is it often done in a pleasant atmosphere?
3. About learning
    1. Do you pay attention to studying and continuously improving your working ability?
    2. Do you frequently use new knowledge to solve problems?
    3. Do you have a high learning ability and efficiency?
4. About innovation
    1. Are you constantly acquiring new knowledge, new methods, and new skills?
    2. Are you working out innovative solutions for problems at work?
    3. Has your work efficiency improved due to the use of innovation?

[7] Others

a. Is the company's system of ideas, long-term plans, goals, etc. shared by the whole company?
b. Do you know the related activities of your company after you finished this survey?

Appendix K
The 71 Selected Manufacturing Enterprises in China

Ranking	Name of enterprise in China	Name of enterprise in Japan	Registered capital (US$, million)	Investment ratio (%)	Product category
1	DONGFENG MOTOR CO., LTD.	日産自動車	2017.6392	50	Conveying machine
2	NISSAN (CHINA) INVESTMENT CO., LTD.	日産自動車	1015	100	Conveying machine
3	SONY (CHINA) LTD.	ソニー	1006.935	100	Electrical equipment
4	PANASONIC CORPORATION OF CHINA	パナソニック	986.18	100	Electrical equipment
5	JIANGSU OJI PAPER CO., LTD.	王子製紙	911.51	90	Paper
6	SHANGHAI HUA HONG NEC ELECTRONICS CO., LTD.	日本電気	894.08	17.4	Electrical equipment
7	SHENZHEN QIANWAN GAS TURBINE POWER PLANT CO., LTD.	兼松	850		Electric power gas
8	SHANGHAI SVA NEC LIQUID CRYSTAL DISPLAY CO., LTD.	NEC液晶テクノロジー	643.0256	25	Electrical equipment
9	DONGGUAN BAOTIAN CHEMICAL CO., LTD.	興宝国際工業	430	90	Chemistry
10	SHANGHAI ZOTOS CITIC COSMETICS CO., LTD.	資生堂の関連会社	418.27	72.6	Chemistry
11	TIANJIN FAW TOYOTA MOTOR CO., LTD.	トヨタ自動車	408.03	40	Conveying machine
12	YKK (CHINA) INVESTMENT CO., LTD.	YKK	375	100	Others

(continued)

© Science Press and Springer Nature Singapore Pte Ltd. 2020

K. Ryu, *The Impact of Organizational Ethical Climate on Organizational Commitment and Job Performance*, https://doi.org/10.1007/978-981-15-2813-2

(continued)

Ranking	Name of enterprise in China	Name of enterprise in Japan	Registered capital (US$, million)	Investment ratio (%)	Product category
13	SHANGHAI BAOSTEEL-NSC/ARCELOR AUTOMOTIVE STEEL SHEETS CO., LTD.	新日本製鉄	361.1584	40	Steel
14	NINGBO BAOXIN STAINLESS STEEL CO., LTD.	三井物産	344.1413	7	Steel
15	XIAN DAIKIN QINGAN COMPRESSOR CO., LTD.	ダイキン工業	322.8	51	Electrical equipment
16	JIANGXI CHANGHE SUZUKI AUTOMOBILE CO., LTD.	スズキ	311.8	25.1	Conveying machine
17	GUANGZHOU HONDA AUTOMOBILE CO., LTD.	本田技研工業	283.29	40	Conveying machine
18	CHANGAN FORD MAZDA AUTOMOBILE CO., LTD.	マツダ	282.639	15	Conveying machine
19	TIANJIN FAW TOYOTA ENGINE CO., LTD.	トヨタ自動車	248	50	Conveying machine
20	MINEBEA ELECTRONICS & HI-TECH CONMPONENTS (SHANGHAI) LTD.	ミネベア	239.06	100	Machine
21	SUMIRUBBER (CHANGSHU) CO., LTD.	住友ゴム工業	231.6	99	Rubber products
22	BEIJING MATSUSHITA COLOR CRT CO., LTD.	MT 映像ディスプレイ	221.663	50	Electrical equipment
23	DENSO (CHINA) INVESTMENT CO., LIMITED	デンソー	221.4569	100	Electrical equipment
24	FUJIFILM (CHINA) INVESTMENT CO., LTD.	富士フイルム	213.397	100	Chemistry
25	EAGLE INDUSTRY (WUXI) CO., LTD.	イーグル工業	211	100	Machine
26	GUANGQI TOYOTA ENGINE CO., LTD.	トヨタ自動車	208.6	57.6	Machine
27	TORAY FIBERS (NANTONG) CO., LTD.	東レ	202.388	90	Fiber products
28	DONGFENG HONDA AUTOMOBILE (WUHAN) CO., LTD.	本田技研工業	200	40	Conveying machine
29	HITACHI AIR-CONDITIONING TECHNOLOGY (SUZHOU) CO., LTD.	日立製作所	200	100	Electrical equipment
30	GUANGQI HINO MOTORS CO., LTD.	日野自動車	198.75	50	Conveying machine
31	HITACHI CHINA LTD.	日立製作所	193	100	Electrical equipment

(continued)

(continued)

Ranking	Name of enterprise in China	Name of enterprise in Japan	Registered capital (US$, million)	Investment ratio (%)	Product category
32	CHONGQING CHANGAN SUZUKI AUTOMOBILE CO., LTD.	サントリー	190	25	Conveying machine
33	TORAY SAKAI WEAVING & DYEING (NANTONG) CO., LTD.	東レ	184.69	69.4	Fiber products
34	SUNTORY (CHINA) HOLDING CO., LTD.	サントリー	180	100	Foods
35	NANTONG COSCO KHI SHIP ENGINEERING CO., LTD.	川崎重工業	179.2434	50	Conveying machine
36	TOKUYAMA CHEMICALS (ZHEJIANG) CO., LTD.	トクヤマ	177	100	Chemistry
37	SHOUGUANG NEC ELECTRONICS CO., LTD.	NECエレクトロニクス	173.1	50.3	Electrical equipment
38	CHINA HUALU PANASONIC AVC NETWORKS CO., LTD.	パナソニック	169.61	26	Electrical equipment
39	PANASONIC PLASMA DISPLAY (SHANGHAI) CO., LTD.	パナソニック	165	26	Electrical equipment
40	CHENG SHIN-TOYO TIRE & RUBBER (CHINA) CO., LTD.	正新橡膠工業(台湾)	165	77.6	Rubber products
41	NEUSOFT CORPORATION(SHENYANG)	東芝	162.82		Others
42	GUANGZHOU TOYOTA MOTOR CO., LTD.	トヨタ自動車	157	30.5	Conveying machine
43	SHANGHAI MITSUBISHI ELEVATOR CO., LTD.	三菱電	155.269	32	Machine
44	SMC (CHINA) CO., LTD.CHINA	SMC	153.27	100	Machine
45	SUZHOU EPSON CO., LTD.	セイコーエプソン	151	19.35	Electrical equipment
46	KIRIN (CHINA) INVESTMENT CO., LTD.	キリンホールディングス	150	100	Foods
47	HONDA AUTO PARTS MANUFACTURING CO., LTD.	本田技研工業	150	100	Conveying machine
48	THK (CHINA) CO., LTD.	THK	142.3	100	Machine
49	SHANGHAI NISSHA CONSULTANTS	日本車両製造	140	100	Information and communication
50	CHANGAN FORD MAZDA ENGINE CO., LTD.	マツダ	139.2	15	Conveying machine

(continued)

(continued)

Ranking	Name of enterprise in China	Name of enterprise in Japan	Registered capital (US$, million)	Investment ratio (%)	Product category
51	SOUTH EAST (FUJIAN) MOTOR CO., LTD.	三菱自動車工業	138	25	Conveying machine
52	JIANGNAN-ONODA CEMENT CO., LTD.	太平洋セメント	134.337	88.5	Glass cement
53	SUNDIRO HONDA MOTORCYCLE CO., LTD.	本田技研工業	129.465		Conveying machine
54	SHANGHAI KYOCERA ELECTRONICS CO., LTD.	京セラ	128.46	100	Electrical equipment
55	NIPPON ELECTRIC GLASS (FUJIAN) CO., LTD.	日本電気硝子	127.85	91.4	Glass cement
56	EPSON (CHINA) CO., LTD.	セイコーエプソン	124.5	100	Electrical equipment
57	NINGBO MITSUBUSHI CHEMICAL CO., LTD.	寧波PTA投資公司	123	90	Chemistry
58	SUMITOMO CORPORATION (HONG KONG) LTD.	住友商事	122.125	100	Wholesale trade
59	DONGFENG HONDA ENGIN CO., LTD.	本田技研工業	121.583	40	Conveying machine
60	DONGFENG HONDA AUTO PARTS CO., LTD.	本田技研工業	121.58	46	Conveying machine
61	SHANGHAI HITACHI ELECTRICAL APPLIANCES CO., LTD.	日立アプライアンス	119.04	25	Electrical equipment
62	TOYOTA MOTOR (CHINA) INVESTMENT CO., LTD.	トヨタ自動車	118	100	Conveying machine
63	HONDA MOTOR (CHINA) INVESTMENT CO., LTD.	本田技研工業	115.946	100	Conveying machine
64	DAIKIN MOTOR SUZHOU CO., LTD.	ダイキン工業	115.12	90	Electrical equipment
65	DAIKIN FLUOROCHEMICALS (CHINA) CO., LTD.	三井物産	108.74	5	Chemistry
66	NEC (CHINA) CO., LTD.	日本電気	106.774	100	Electrical equipment
67	CANON DALIAN BUSINESS MACHINES, INC.	キャノン	105.12	85.6	Electrical equipment
68	BRIDGESTONE (HUIZHOU) TIRE CO., LTD.	ブリヂストン	105	90	Rubber products
69	AJINOMOTO (CHINA) CO., LTD.	味の素	102.83	100	Foods
70	SHANGHAI SUOGUANG ELECTRONICS CO., LTD.	ソニー	102.58	70	Electrical equipment
71	OMRON (CHINA) CO., LTD.	オムロン	100.6	100	Electrical equipment

References

English References

Adam S. The wealth of nations. In: Strahan W, Cadell T, editors. London;1776.
Alasdair M. After virtue. University of Notre Dame Press;1981.
Allen NJ, Meyer JP. The measurement and antecedents of affective, continuance and normative commitment to the organization. J Occup Psychol. 1990;63(1):1–18.
Armen AA, Harold D. Production, information costs, and economic organization. Am Econ Rev. 1972;62(5):777–795.
Arnaud A, Schminke M. Ethical work climate: a weather report and forecast. In: Gilliland SW, Steiner D, Skarlicki D, editors. Research in social issues in management: managing social and ethical issues in organizations. Charlotte, NC: Information Age Publishing;2007. pp. 181–227.
Babin BJ, Boles JS, Robin DP. Representing the perceived ethical work climate among marketing employees. J Acad Mark Sci. 2000;28(3):345–358.
Becker HS. Notes on the concept of commitment. Am J Sociol. 1960;66(1):32–40.
Becker TE, Billings RS, Eveleth DM, et al. Foci and bases of employee commitment: implications for job performance. Acad Manag J. 1996;39(2):464–482.
Blau G, Merriman K, Tatum DS, et al. Antecedents and consequences of basic versus career enrichment benefit satisfaction. J Organ Behav. 2001;22(6):669–688.
Borman WC, Motowidlo SJ. Task performance and contextual performance: the meaning for personnel selection research. Hum Perform. 1997;10(2):99–109.
Brinkman RL, Brinkman JE. Corporate power and the globalization process. Int J Soc Econ. 2002;29(9):730–752.
Brouthers KD. Market entry and expansion. Wiley: Wiley International Encyclopedia of Marketing;2010.
Bruce Buchanan II. Building organizational commitment: the socialization of managers' work in organizations. Adm Sci Q. 1974;19(4):N/A.
Chan MH. Job satisfaction and intent to leave. J Soc Psychol. 1997;137(6):677–689.
Chen ZX, Tsui AS, Farh JL. Loyalty to supervisor vs. organizational commitment: relationships to employee performance in China. J Occup Organ Psychol. 2011;75(3):339–356.
Denison DR. What is the difference between organizational culture and organizational climate? A native's point of view on a decade of paradigm wars. Acad Manag Rev. 1996;21(3):619–654.
Deshpande SP. The impact of ethical climate types on facets of job satisfaction: an empirical investigation. J Bus Ethics. 1996;15(6):655–660.
Dessler G. How to earn your employees' commitment. Acad Manag Exec. 1999;13(2):58–67.
Dickson MW, Aditya RN, Chhokar JS. Definition and interpretation in cross-cultural organizational culture research; some pointers from the GLOBE research program. In: Ashkanasy N, Wilderom

© Science Press and Springer Nature Singapore Pte Ltd. 2020

K. Ryu, *The Impact of Organizational Ethical Climate on Organizational Commitment and Job Performance*, https://doi.org/10.1007/978-981-15-2813-2

C, Petersen M, editors. Handbook of organizational culture and climate. Thousand Oaks: Sage; 2000.

Dessler, G. How to earn your employees' commitment. Acad Manage Executive. 1999;13(2):58–67.

Donaldson L, Davis JH. Stewardship theory or agency theory: CEO governance and shareholder returns. Aust J Manag. 1991;16(1):49–64.

Falkenberg L, Herremans I. Ethical behaviours in organizations: directed by the formal or informal systems? J Bus Ethics. 1995;14(2):133–143.

Francis F. Trust: The social virtues and the creation of prosperity. Free Press;1995.

Fritzsche DJ. Ethical climates and the ethical dimension of decision making. J Bus Ethics. 2000;24(2):125–140.

Grojean MW, Resick CJ, Dickson MW, Smith DB. Leaders, values and organizational climate: examining leadership strategies for establishing an organizational climate regarding ethics. J Bus Ethics. 2004;55(3):223–241.

Huselid MA. High performance work system and firm performance: A synthesis of research and management implication. Res Pers Hum Resour Manage. 1998;16:53–101.

Johnson RE, Chang CH, Lord RG. Moving from cognition to behavior: what the research says. Psychol Bull. 2006;132(3):381–415.

Joseph J, Deshpande SP. The impact of ethical climate on job satisfaction of nurses. Health Care Manag Rev. 1997;22(1):76–81.

Jr CHS. Understanding salespeople's intention to behave unethically: The effects of perceived competitive intensity, cognitive moral development and moral judgment. J Bus Ethics. 1999;21(4):303–316.

Keikoh RYU. Strategic localization for Japanese corporations in China: The nexus of harmonious society and public value creation. Rikkyo Bus Rev. 2010;3:53–59.

Keikoh RYU. Theoretical research on organizational ethical climate: Applications and practices of Japanese enterprises in China. Int J Econ Behav. 2017;7(1):51–62.

Keikoh RYU. The impact of organizational ethical climate on organizational commitment and job performance. A case study of Japanese-funded manufacturing enterprises in China. Rom J Econ. 2017;45(2(54)):5—2.

Keikoh RYU. An empirical analysis of organizational ethical climate and its impact on organizational commitment in Japanese funded enterprisers doing business in China. Rom J Econ. 2018;46(1(55)):5–39.

Konovsky MA. Understanding procedural justice and its impact on business organizations. J Manag. 2000;26(3):489–511.

Lee TW, Ashford SJ, Walsh JP, et al. Commitment propensity, organizational commitment, and voluntary turnover: a longitudinal study of organizational entry processes. J Manag Off J South Manag Assoc. 1992;18(1):15–32.

Lemmergaard J, Lauridsen J. The ethical climate of Danish firms: a discussion and enhancement of the ethical-climate model. J Bus Ethics. 2008;80(4):653–675.

Lengnick-Hall ML. Managing social and ethical issues in organizations. Pers Psychol. 2007;60(4):1064–1067.

Litwin GH, Stringer RA. Motivation and organizational climate. Boston, MA: Harvard University Press; 1968.

Malloy DC, Agarwal J. Ethical climate in nonprofit organizations: propositions and implications. Nonprofit Manag Leadership. 2001;12(1):39–54.

Martin KD, Cullen JB. Continuities and extensions of ethical climate theory: a meta-analytic review. J Bus Ethics. 2006;69(2):175–194.

Mathieu JE, Zajac DM. A review and meta-analysis of the antecedents, correlates, and consequences of organizational commitment. Psychol Bull. 1990;108(2):171–194.

Marx, K. Capital: A critique of political economy. In: Fowkes, B. editor. Trans, vol. 1. London: Penguin; 1976.

Mcdonald GM, Zepp RA. What should be done? A practical approach to business ethics. Manag Decis. 1967;28(28):9–14.

Meyer JP, Allen NJ. Commitment in the workplace: theory, research, and application. Sage Publications; 1997. p. 175.
Michael WG, Christian JR, Marcus WD, Smith DB. Leaders, values and organizational climate: examining leadership strategies for establishing an organizational climate regarding ethics. J Bus Ethics. 2004;55(3):223–241.
Moore HL, Moore TW. The effect of ethical climate on the organizational commitment of faculty members. J Acad Bus Ethics. 2014;(9):6–11.
Morrison EW. Role definitions and organizational citizenship behavior: the importance of the employee's perspective. Acad Manag J. 1994;37(6):1543–1567.
Mowday RT. Reflections on the study and relevance of organizational commitment. Hum Resour Manag Rev. 1998;8(4):387–401.
Mowday RT, Porter LW, Dubin R. Unit performance, situational factors, and employee attitudes in spatially separated work units. Organ Behav Hum Perform. 1974;12(2):231–248.
Mowday RT, Steers RM, Porter LW. The measurement of organizational commitment. J Vocat Behav. 1979;14(2):224–247.
Murphy KR. Honesty in the workplace. Thomson Brooks/Cole Publishing Co; 1993.
Murphy PE, Laczniak GR. Marketing ethics: a review with implications for managers, educators and researchers, in review of marketing. In: Enis B, Roering K, editors. Chicago: American Marketing Association; 1981. pp. 251–266.
O'Reilly CA, Chatman J. Organizational commitment and psychological attachment: the effects of compliance, identification, and internalization on prosocial behavior. J Appl Psychol. 1986;71(3):492–499.
Okpara JO, Wynn P. The impact of ethical climate on job satisfaction, and commitment in Nigeria: Implications for management development. J Manag Dev. 2008;27(9):935–950.
Paine LS. Cases in leadership, ethics, and organizational integrity. Shenyang: Northeast University of Finance Press; 1999.
Peterson DK. The relationship between unethical behavior and the dimensions of the ethical climate questionnaire. J Bus Ethics. 2002;41(4):313–326.
Rest JR. Moral development: advances in research and theory. New York; 1986.
Romer PM. Increasing returns and long-run growth. J Polit Econ. 1986;94(5):1002–1037.
Schneider B. Organizational climate: an essay. Pers Psychol. 2010;28(4):447–479.
Schwepker CH Jr. Understanding salespeople's intention to behave unethically: the effects of perceived competitive intensity, cognitive moral development and moral judgment. J Bus Ethics. 1999;21(4):303–316.
Schwepker CH. Ethical climate's relationship to job satisfaction, organizational commitment, and employment turnover intention in the salesforce. J Bus Res. 2001;54(1):39–52.
Sen A. Collective choice and social welfare. Harvard University Press; 2011. p. 1s.
Sen A. The idea of justice, Belknap Press; 2011.
Shafer WE. Ethical climate, organizational-professional conflict and organizational commitment. Account Audit Account J. 2009;22(7):1087–1110.
Sheldon ME. Investment and involments as mechanisms to the organization. Adm Sci Prod Q. 1971;16:143–149
Simha JS, Ramesh AS. A comparative study of oral acceptors in the three member mission hospitals of Mysore state. J Christ Med Assoc India. 1972;47:513–518.
Simha A, Stanusch AS. The between ethical climate and management success: a study in a polish context. J Bus Ethics. 2013;114(1):55–59.
Sims RL, Keon TL. Ethical work climate as a factor in the development of person-organization fit. J Bus Ethics. 1997;16(11):1095–1105.
Song D, Yue D. Human resource management: an example of a Japanese-funded enterprise in China. Int Econ Coop. 2006;(11):51–54.
Stawiski S, Tindale RS, Dykema-Engblade A. The effects of ethical climate on group and individual level deception in negotiation. Int J Confl Manag. 2009;20(3):287–308.
Steers RE. Antecedents and outcomes of organizational commitment. Adm Sci Q. 1977;22(5):46–56

Stinglhamber F, Vandenberghe C. Organizations and supervisors as sources of support and targets of commitment: a longitudinal study. J Organ Behav. 2003;24(3):251–270.
Swailes S. Organizational commitment: a critique of the construct and measures. Int J Manag Rev. 2002;4(2):155–78.
Tagiuri R, Litwin GH, Barnes LB. Organizational climate: explorations of a concept. Boston, MA: Division of Research, Graduate School of Business Administration, Harvard University; 1968.
Trevino LK. Ethical decision making in organizations: a person-situation interactionist model. Acad Manag Rev. 1986;11(3):601–617.
Valentine S, Lucero GM. Ethical context, organizational commitment, and person-organization fit. J Bus Ethics. 2002;41(4):349–360.
Vardi Y. The effects of organizational and ethical climates on misconduct at work. J Bus Ethics. 2001;29(4):325–337.
Victor B, Cullen JB. A theory and measure of ethical climate in organizations. Res Corp Soc Perform Policy. 1987;9:51–71.
Victor B, Cullen JB. The organizational bases of ethical work climates. Adm Sci Q 1988;101–125.
Vidavercohen D. Moral climate in business firms: a conceptual framework for analysis and change. J Bus Ethics. 1998;17(11):1211–1226.
Wang X. Study on chinese economic ethics. Philosophy 1997;(11).
Wech BA, Mossholder KW, Steel RP, et al. Does work group cohesiveness affect individuals' performance and organizational commitment? A cross-level examination. Small Group Res 1998;29(4):472–494.
Weeks WA, Loe TW, Chonko LB, et al. Cognitive moral development and the impact of perceived organizational ethical climate on the search for sales force excellence: a cross-cultural study. Routledge; 2006.
Wiener Y. Commitment in organizations: a normative view. Acad Manag Rev. 1982;7(7):418–428.
Wimbush JC, Shepard JM. Toward an understanding of ethical climate: Its relationship to ethical behavior and supervisory influence. J Bus Ethics. 1992;13(8):637–647.
Wimbush JC, Shepard JM, Markham SE. An empirical ex Cohen amination of the relationship between ethical climate and ethical behavior from multiple levels of analysis. J Bus Ethics. 1997;16(16):1705–1716.

Chinese References

Chan MH. Job satisfaction and intent to leave. J Soc Psychol. 1997;137(6):677–689.
Changhui Y. Enhance corporate citizenship awareness. Enterp Vitality 2004;7.
Chao G, Xiong Y, Wang L, et al. An empirical study on organizational ethical climate on job satisfaction and employee deviant behavior. Chin J Manag. 2013;10(11):1611.
Chen J, Lin Y, Liu S. Leaders' moderate thinking and organizational performance: study on mechanism of action and situational conditions. Nankai Bus Rev. 2010;13:132–141.
Du J, Ran M, Cao P. Context-contingent effect of Zhongyong on employee innovation behavior. Acta Psychol Sin. 2014;46(1):113–124.
Gai Y. The impact of the hotel's caring ethical climate on employees' organizational commitment. Nankai University; 2013.
Han Y, Liao J, Long L. Model of development and empirical study on employee job performance. J Manag Sci China. 2007;10(5):62–77.
Hou H, Zhang C. The sovereign phenomenon of Japanese operators and the reform of corporate governance structure. Contemp Econ Jpn. 2005;4:51–54.
JIN C. Blocism and the cross-cultural management of Japanese enterprises. JJiangsu Coll Eng Technol. 2011;4:87–90.

Li B. A study on the structure and amendment of organizational ethics climates questionnaire of Chinese enterprises. Shanxi University; 2008.
Li P. Enterprise ethics construction, Japan in the "copy of the road". Chin Foreign Corp Cult. 2003;(3):48–50.
Ling W, Zhang Z, Fang L. A study of the organizational commitment of Chinese employees. Soc Sci China. 2001;2:90–102.
Liu F. The relationship between corporate ethics climate, organizational commitment and organizational citizenship behavior——Wenzhou private enterprises as a practice. J Shenyang Univ Technol. 2010;(4).
Liu J, Shi J. Effects of human resource management practice on employee's organizational commitment. Chin J Ergon. 2005;11(4):21–23.
Liu S, Li Y, Du X. Effects of moral leadership on employee's non-moral behavior: the intermediary effect of organizational ethical climate. J Manag. (Academic Edition) 2013; 09:31–41.
Liu Z. On the embedding business ethics in internal control and promotion of legal effect. J Hunan Univ Sci Technol. (Social Science Edition) 2013;(4).
Liu W. An empirical study on organizational culture affecting employees' anti-production behavior—based on the perspective of organizational ethics. China Soft Sci. 2010;(9):118–129.
Niu J. A study on the lagging factors of localization of Chinese and foreign senior executives—a case study of some Japanese enterprises in Suzhou. Suzhou University; 2008.
Research on cross-cultural human resource management in Japanese enterprises. J Harbin Eng Univ.
Steven JR. Surpass COSO: Strengthen the internal control of corporate governance. In: Fu tao, Lu yuanzhu, editors. Huangcuizhu translation. Beijing: Qinghua university press; 2004.
Sun L. The golden mean thinking in enterprise management. Orient Corp Cult. 2015;23:52.
Tan C, Sun J. Research on the performance structure of middle management personnel in enterprises. Mark Mod. 2009;5:302–304.
Wang C. Discussion on the relationship between ethical climate of care organization and organizational citizenship behavior. Commercial Times. 2014;(3):114–116.
Wang Y, Yu Z. An overview of Innovative climate in foreign organizations. Foreign Econ Manage. 2005;27(8):26–32.
Wang Y, Yu Z. Research progress and forecast of organizational innovative climate. Adv Psychol Sci. 2006;14(3):443–449.
Wang X. Study on Chinese economic ethics. Philosophy. 1997;(11).
Wen Z. Four factor model of job performance. J Capital Normal Univ. 2005;(5):105–111.
Wu H. Study on the ethical climate of western organization. Foreign Econ Manage. 2005;09:32–38.
Wu J, Lin YC. Development of a zhong-yong thinking style scale indigenous. Psychol Res Chinese Soc. 2005;(24):247–300.
Xiao Q. On the basic norms of business ethics. J Lanzhou Jiaotong Univ. 2004;02:1–6.
Xue J, Nishimura H. Localization of Japanese business managers in China. J Jpn J. 2006;01:71–80.
Yanfei W, Yu Z. An overview of innovative climate in foreign organizations. Foreign Econ Manag. 2005;27(8):26–32.
Yanfei W, Yu Z. Research progress and forecast of organizational innovative climate. Adv Psychol Sci. 2006;14(3):443–449.
Yang Z. A case of attempt to combine the Chinese traditional culture with the social science: the social psychological research of Zhongyong. J Renmin Univ China. 2009;3:53–60.
Yin J. Study on human resource development in Shanghai—based enterprises. East China Normal University; 2006.
Yu Z, Zhu Y, Zhang X. Effects of organizational ethics on organizational commitment in hotel. Tour Sci. 2009;(04):50–56.
Zhang J. Research on the performance structure and influencing factors of knowledge workers. China University of Geosciences; 2009.
Zhang S, Li M. Effects of organizational moral climate on organizational citizenship behavior: mediating role of organizational identity. Manag Rev. 2013;25(11):85–94.

Zhang Y. Reflections on the current new humanistic management model—taking Japanese business management experience as a case. Bus Week. 2004;7:42–43.

Zhang H. The transformation and construction of contemporary morality. Guangzhou: Sun Yat-sen University Press; 1999.

Zhang S, Li M. The influence of organizational moral climate on members' behaviors: the mediating effect of organizational identification. Manag Rev. 2013;25(11):85–94.

Zhiyu Z. Assessment of Zhong Yong thinking. Hong Kong J Soc Sci. 2000;18:33–55.

Index

© Science Press and Springer Nature Singapore Pte Ltd. 2020

K. Ryu, *The Impact of Organizational Ethical Climate on Organizational Commitment and Job Performance*, https://doi.org/10.1007/978-981-15-2813-2

The manufacturer's authorised representative in the EU is Springer Nature Customer Service Centre GmbH, Europaplatz 3, 69115 Heidelberg, Germany. If you have any concerns regarding our products, please contact ProductSafety@springernature.com

Printed and bound by CPI Group (UK) Ltd, Croydon, CR0 4YY
30/09/2026
02225251-0002